Democracy vs.
National Security

Democracy vs. National Security

Civil-Military Relations in Latin America

Paul W. Zagorski

Lynne Rienner Publishers · Boulder & London

Published in the United States of America in 1992 by
Lynne Rienner Publishers, Inc.
1800 30th Street, Boulder, Colorado 80301

and in the United Kingdom by
Lynne Rienner Publishers, Inc.
3 Henrietta Street, Covent Garden, London WC2E 8LU

Library of Congress Cataloging-in-Publication Data
Zagorski, Paul W.
  Democracy vs. national security : civil-military relations in
Latin America / Paul W. Zagorski.
      p.   cm.
  Includes bibliographical references and index.
  ISBN 1-55587-300-6 (hc)
  ISBN 1-55587-325-1 (pb)
  1. Civil-military relations—South America. 2. Civil supremacy
over the military—South America. 3. South America—Politics and
government—20th century. I. Title. II. Title: Democracy versus
national security.
JL1856.C58Z34 1992
322'.5'098—cd20   91-26176
                                                        CIP

British Cataloguing in Publication Data
A Cataloguing in Publication record for this book
is available from the British Library.

Printed and bound in the United States of America

The paper used in this publication meets the requirements
of the American National Standard for Permanence of
Paper for Printed Library Materials Z39.48-1984.

For Astrid

Contents ■

Tables ■

Preface ■

Latin America stands at a historical watershed. As the decade of the 1990s began, the last of the military regimes that rose to power in the 1960s and 1970s were replaced by civilian governments. Such transformations, along with similar movements toward democracy in Eastern Europe, Asia, Africa, and even the Middle East, made democratization—or redemocratization—a topic with which even the proverbial man in the street was at least noddingly acquainted. But nodding acquaintance is insufficient for scholars, policymakers, and informed citizens, because the issue of consolidating democracy is one of immediate urgency.

This book explores a significant aspect of that issue in Latin America: civil-military relations. The five countries upon which this study focuses— Argentina, Brazil, Chile, Peru, and Uruguay—provide good instances of the internal dynamics of civil-military relations in the region. Because of their size or remoteness from the United States, their civil-military politics have been influenced primarily by internal factors rather than direct foreign pressure. In toto, the five contain a majority of Latin America's population and account for the lion's share of Latin America's long-duration military governments over the past several decades. In addition, the armed forces of each country have retained significant influence after the transition to democracy.

Comparative and suggestive rather than definitive analyses of any particular country, the chapters in this book are organized around key issues and problems. I have used case studies to illustrate some of the dynamics inherent in the various areas of civil-military conflict. The book cannot provide a detailed road map to Latin America's future, but civil-military relations in Argentina, Brazil, Chile, Peru, and Uruguay constitute a potentially important piece of the practical and theoretical puzzles posed by the imperative of consolidating democracy.

I would like to thank the San Diego State University Press and the *Review of Latin American Studies* for permission to print the case study in Chapter 5, an earlier version of which originally appeared in the *Review*.

Thanks are due also to friends and colleagues who provided useful comments on various drafts of this study, to proofreaders, and especially to my family, for patience and encouragement.

1■

A New Era in Latin American Civil-Military Relations?

In little over a decade, from 1979 to 1991, fourteen Latin American countries replaced military dictatorships or military-dominated regimes with elected governments.[1] Will this dramatic transformation endure? Will democracy be consolidated? Only an unhesitating optimist, or someone unfamiliar with the cyclical nature of Latin American politics, would answer with an unqualified yes. The purpose of this book is to elaborate some qualifications to that yes and explain the importance of the military's place in the political order—civil-military relations—and in the overall process of democratic consolidation.

■ PLACING THE HISTORIC DEVELOPMENTS OF THE 1980s IN THEIR 'PROPER' CONTEXT

It is an old adage that "history doesn't teach; historians do." In other words, the underlying significance of events can only emerge from analysis and evaluation, an undertaking that relies on prior reflection. The case of the democratization process of Latin America in the 1980s is no exception. The facts require analysis and evaluation.

The pertinent facts are clear. On the one hand, the scale of regional democratization has been unprecedented. At no prior time has the region experienced a statistical dominance of elected governments. Also virtually unprecedented has been the economic collapse that accompanied this political change. The lost decade of the 1980s saw living standards decline in countries throughout the region. On the other hand, the democratization that characterized the decade of the 1980s is only the latest in a long series of political cycles within the region. Similar democratic waves swept Latin America in the immediate post–World War II period and, again, in the late 1950s and early 1960s.[2] Moreover, virtually all the region's elected governments have had to contend with a high degree of overt or covert influence exercised by the armed forces.

In almost no case can we declare without reservation that democracy has

1

been consolidated. How, then, should these facts be understood? Is the present era doomed to repeat the past, or has Latin America broken the old pattern of democratic and authoritarian cycles?

□ *Developmentalism and the Case for Democratic Optimism*

One of the most cogent perspectives for evaluating change is modernization or developmental theory. In the words of one text on Latin American politics, "modernization means the introduction or development of viable productive economies, sophisticated dynamic societies, and independent participatory polities. Development is progression from limiting poverty to emancipating wealth, from passive ignorance to creative knowledge, from stagnant personal isolation to constructive social cooperation, and from humiliating authoritarianism to dignifying self-government."[3] Development is a process in which a society moves from a premodern or undeveloped stage to a modern or developed one. Latin America is in the process of transition from the former to the latter stage, and political change in Latin America occurs within this context.

This developmentalist approach, in effect, fuses a number of types of modernization (political and socioeconomic) as different aspects of the same process. Additionally, it relies, explicitly or implicitly, on a standard of modernization derived from Western European and North American experience. For example, in a landmark study, Seymour Martin Lipset found a high correlation between a number of socioeconomic variables (urbanization, literacy, and media participation) and the political variable of political participation.[4] Successful democracies tended to be economically advanced societies with a prosperous, educated electorate. For Latin America, and the Third World generally, the goal has been to induce both sorts of modernization. From the perspective of the policymaker, developmentalism carried the strong implication that political and economic modernization could be—or, possibly, even had to be—pursued simultaneously. Hence, programs such as the Alliance for Progress in the 1960s were supposed to encourage both economic development and democratization.[5]

If developmentalism is correct, unique features of a country or region may have an impact on political development but, in the long run, not a decisive impact. Social and economic requisites allow governments only a limited number of alternatives in forming and reforming political structures and accommodating or suppressing demands. While governments may differ in their approach to development and lack the political will to modernize wholeheartedly, the need to modernize remains. Lack of resources, political as well as economic, eventually will compel governments to borrow at least some practices from the developed, modern West; but modernization, it turns out, is a package deal. Hence, modernization once fully begun cannot be stopped, only retarded. And Latin America has long since passed the point where it can turn its back on Western modernity. From this perspective, democratic consolidation in Latin America is likely to succeed, at least in the long run; and that consolidation will involve the creative adaptation of methods already practiced in the developed world.

The task for policymakers is to transform premodern institutions into modern ones, using at least some established practices and organizations as catalysts for that change. A number of academicians with an interest in this process see the armed forces as one of the keys to development. George Philip divides them into two major groups: the liberals and the neorealists.[6] The liberals, represented by writers such as Edwin Lieuwen, argue that democracy is indeed the wave of the future, despite temporary setbacks, and that both military rule and communism should be opposed. The neorealists, represented by John Johnson, argue that the armed forces can be constructive, and that an expanded role for them would not be dangerous because they cannot afford to deploy much coercive force against civil society. Thus, the armed forces' role is either marginal or benign.

From the developmentalist perspective, the scale of democratization (elections) rather than its depth (the complete modernization or democratization of institutions) becomes the salient fact. The perdurance of democratic governments during the sort of economic crises that in the past heralded their demise further strengthens the argument that Latin America has finally sublimated its antidemocratic impulse.

□ *Praetorianism and Corporatism: Some Grounds for Pause*

The fact that the democratic tide of the late 1950s and early 1960s receded and was followed by an authoritarian countercurrent should give us pause. This reversal gives compelling evidence that Latin America has not followed a First World developmental pattern. Economic and political development have not followed Western patterns, nor have Western institutional forms been readily adopted. There are a number of reasons for this divergence from Western patterns.

Praetorianism: A Symptom of a Developmental Impasse. In contemporary Latin America and the Third World generally, the requisites of economic growth and democratization may be contrary or even antithetical to one another. The historical record of the twentieth century shows that Western patterns of modernization cum democratization have not been duplicated in non-Western contexts. In fact, late modernizers have been drawn to authoritarian rather than democratic solutions.[7] In an explanation drawn directly from the contemporary Third World context, Samuel Huntington argues that instability may arise specifically in situations where political participation outpaces the capacity of political institutions to satisfy demands. Lack of institutional capacity to satisfy demands may, in turn, be largely the result of the limited economic development.

This imbalance can easily lead to confrontational politics and military intervention. Such a society is termed <u>praetorian, not because the</u> <u>armed forces are always in power, but, as in the case of the praetorian guard</u> of ancient Rome, they are frequently the final arbiters of power in a society with, at best, only a weak sense of legitimacy.[8] In praetorian states, "private ambitions are rarely restrained by a sense of public authority or common purpose; [and] the role of power (i.e., wealth and force) is maximized."[9] Politics is not based on consensus; it is based on the principles of war. Power is not limited by a widely shared moral perspective but by countervailing power and the realization that pushing power to the extreme could be self-defeating.[10]

Most Latin American armed forces fit the praetorian mold: They are well established and have long-standing traditions, but they face no immediate threat of a major military conflict. Their primary purpose seems to be as the political arbiter and upholder of public order. As is typical in a praetorian state, the armed forces are not far from the seats of power and quite often occupy them.[11] Thus, while praetorianism is too unnuanced to serve as a complete description of the Latin American political tradition, it delineates a pattern of political behavior that has plagued much of the region. Latin America still faces the danger of praetorianism because of inherent weakness in the political systems in general and a latent military tendency for political intervention in particular.

Corporatism and Latin American Uniqueness. A less jaundiced view of Latin America and the role of its armed forces stresses the fact that there is a consensus (albeit a decidedly undemocratic one) underlying frequent appeals to force. The "corporatist" view sees Latin America as possessing a political tradition and a potential for development that depart, in significant ways, from the developmentalist pattern. History helps account for this difference. While North America and much of Western Europe have a tradition that is Protestant, capitalist, and heavily influenced by the Enlightenment, Latin America and the Iberian Peninsula are Catholic, agrarian, and heavily influenced by medieval thought.

This Iberian tradition is itself capable of curbing the harsher aspects of praetorianism—indeed, the Latin American tradition entails certain moral limits on the use of power—but it is unreasonable to expect Latin America to follow the political patterns of North America and Western Europe. Ideas and practices from North America and Europe have been adapted in Latin America, but with significant practical alterations. Although the revolutionaries and constitutions of the independence struggles in Latin America spoke in the natural rights and egalitarian language of the North American and French revolutions, the substance of the struggle was a contest between governing elites.

If anything, the *criollos*, the locally born Spanish landed elite, were at least as traditional socially and economically as the peninsular governing class from Spain they replaced.[12] The systems they created were personalistic, patronal, hierarchical, and largely closed and were based on the three pillars of the Catholic church, the military, and the landed elite. The privileged groups obtained special legal status, giving them the right to control their own affairs and those of their subordinates. They were corporations: legally recognized entities with special status and rights. As development undermined the established order in the late nineteenth and twentieth centuries, the system changed more by addition than outright transformation. New classes—commercial farmers, entrepreneurs, the middle sectors, and parts of the organized working class—were wholly or partially accommodated, but the system retained many of its primary characteristics.[13] Hence, Latin American institutions are, at least in part, unique.

The proponents of the uniqueness thesis take issue with both the general notion of development as modernization along First World lines and the idea that Latin American armed forces and their activities can be fruitfully compared to those of their First World counterparts. If those who argue for the importance of a unique Latin character are correct, the above-described universalist impulse is overstated at best or bogus at worst. Governments and peoples adopt foreign ideas and practices, but adoption in a new environment frequently alters their original nature and function. In the political realm, elections, constitutions, the law, and the armed forces serve different functions in different regimes. Social pressures can be accommodated or suppressed in various ways. Economic exigencies can be addressed in various ways.

From this perspective, then, the success of democratic consolidation is a completely open question. There is no one right pattern or set of patterns that will work. Possibly none will. And, on another level, the desirability of consolidating democratic institutions patterned on First World models is itself questionable. After all, why should these be considered of paramount importance for societies that have not accepted them unequivocally? Even leaving aside the problem of the moral legitimacy of democracy, the uniqueness position raises unsettling questions about policy and political strategy.

☐ *Some Tentative Conclusions*

Although it is difficult, and probably undesirable, to synthesize the disparate theories described above, together they contribute to a refinement of our understanding of the issues confronting democratic consolidation in Latin America.

Democratic consolidation is part of the uncompleted political agenda of the region. The establishment of *elected* governments, however, is not tantamount to the consolidation of mature democracies. Development (whether seen from a developmentalist or a corporatist perspective) should be understood as a process involving stages. In such a process, habitual adherence to democratic procedures would eventually replace reliance on force, to be replaced, in turn, by sincere commitment to democratic norms on the part of all relevant political participants.[14] Among governmental institutions, the armed forces are in a pivotal position; their acquiescence to democratic procedures or firm adherence to democratic norms is a sine qua non of democratic development. Finally, even though there are deterministic implications in the various theories of development, the determinism involved seems to be sufficiently soft to allow for statesmanship and enlightened political leadership.

It is about the nature of these opportunities that these political theories are most at odds. Will techniques of civilian control of the military that have worked in the First World be beneficial to Latin America? To what extent should their imposition be attempted? What continuing role are the armed forces likely to play in Latin America? An examination of the institutional development of Latin American armed forces is necessary to shed further light on these questions.

■ THE EVOLUTION OF LATIN AMERICA'S ARMED FORCES

The historical development of Latin American armed forces was spurred on by technical and organizational developments outside the region as well as by domestic and international imperatives rooted within the region. The dynamics of this process have created a set of regional institutions with distinctive strengths, weakness, and propensities.

□ *The Legacy of the Independence Struggle and Early Modernization*

The original military establishments of Latin America were traditional rather than modern. The independence struggle and civil wars that ensued gave rise to political leaders whose claims to rule were premised on their personal control of military force. Poorly trained, poorly and often hastily organized, these armies were commanded by *caudillos*, amateur generals from the landed elite, whose claims to command and goals were largely personalistic.

Such armies were hardly capable of meeting the needs of a modernizing state. So, as the nineteenth century wore on, the more-advanced and ambitious states began to develop a more professional force. The late nineteenth century provided a number of technologies that had a direct impact on the art of war: the repeating rifle (and later the machine gun), barbed wire, the telegraph, the steamship, and the railroad. And even before modern technology added to the complexity of commanding and controlling military forces, Europe had already realized, during the Napoleonic period, that a professional, full-time officer corps was essential to the successful conduct of modern warfare. The states of Latin America, though not confronted with the same military exigencies as their European counterparts, still faced the problems of frontier pacification, suppression of local revolts, and the possibility of full-scale war with neighboring states.[15] Thus, a modernization race, if not an arms race, ensued on the continent.

The major countries of the region played host to military missions from Germany, France, and Great Britain. Somewhat later, many of the lesser-developed countries of Central America and the Caribbean were forced to play host to US troops who, among other things, often attempted to establish local militaries with a primarily constabulary function. As a result, most of the countries of Latin America saw the establishment of a professional officer corps, whose character was decidedly different from that which preceded it.

In most countries, by the end of the first several decades of the twentieth century, the new officer corps was no longer drawn primarily from the landed elite. The professional officer corps had managed to secure a significant degree of institutional autonomy for the armed forces. And, unlike its amateur predecessors, it became something of a caste unto itself. The best characterization of this transformed political actor is open to dispute. Did it represent the interests of the emergent middle class from which it, by and large, derived its social origins? Was it simply the armed stratum of the bourgeoisie and hence the guarantor of the capitalist order? Or did the relative isolation of the officer corps from the rest of society and its distinctive ethos render unconvincing the assertion of an automatic affiliation with any other social class? The basic agreement underlying these assessments is more important than their differences.[16] The military emerged as a relatively modern institution, organized along bureaucratic lines, possessing a view of the world and politics that set it apart from other classes and institutions, and, hence, capable of playing a political role that transcended the motives and interests of its individual members.[17]

□ The Evolution of the Political Role of the Armed Forces

The most obvious demonstration of the military's political role has been the coup d'état, although other forms of direct and indirect influence have been even more common. Initially, the military represented a progressive force, many of whose members wanted to replace the conservative, often landed, political elite and construct more modern economic and social structures. What Samuel Huntington terms the "breakthrough coup" to middle-class participation[18] frequently typified the position of the officer corps in the early part of the twentieth century. The military often acted directly to promote change beneficial to the interests of the emergent middle class. Again, whether that position was the result of class origins or a particular view of institutional and national interests need not concern us. The military assumed the role of a modernizing force albeit, in most cases, not a democratizing one once an effective franchise was extended to the middle class.

With further modernization and capitalist development, new social and political actors emerged that the military wanted to contain. The veto coup[19] became a frequently used mechanism for thwarting developments that the military disliked. Socialists, middle-class Radicals, Apristas, and Peronists were removed from power, or prevented from assuming power in the first place, because, in the eyes of the officer corps, they threatened either the military's sectoral interests or the national interest. The armed forces intervened to protect their own autonomy, ensure the enforcement of internal discipline, save the country from anarchy or political deadlock, assure economic stability, and protect the social order against revolutionary change, as well as for a host of other related reasons.

The evolution of the professional military from modernizer to guardian of the status quo illustrates the limits of development within the corporatist system. While new groups can, at times, be accommodated and the character and role of old ones (even the military itself) can be partially transformed, the elitist and conservative nature of the system cannot be successfully challenged. Moreover, transfer of political power by force of arms is as normal (and perhaps legitimate) a process as transfer via elections.[20]

In effect, as a result of the process of technical and organizational modernization, the armed forces became an institutional actor in their own right. Their interests were no longer fused with those of the landed upper class. The military ceased to be the personal instrument of a caudillo. Nevertheless, the military functioned as a praetorian institution, deciding power struggles between other contenders and intervening to defend its own interests. Republican constitutions remained largely a facade behind which contending factions maneuvered for personal advantage.

□ The Armed Forces as Ruler: An Attempt to Transcend the Stalemate of Praetorianism

A significant change in the manner in which the military exercised its political power occurred in 1964 with the Brazilian coup against the Goulart government. As with most watershed events, the coup itself was partially symbolic. It represented, for Brazil specifically and Latin America generally, a partial culmination of less obvious trends. The Brazilian coup is one of Wiarda's "critical coups" because it ushered in a new sort of military government. The military government attempted to rectify the basic problems that made unplanned and sometimes frequent intervention by the armed forces necessary in the first place.

This new objective required a change in the pattern of military governments. Previous coups d'état, of whatever motivation, established military governments that usually were relatively short-lived. Veto coups aimed at reestablishing a slightly modified status quo ante. Military officers occasionally became long-term presidents, sometimes discarding their uniforms for mufti; but military presidents tended to be chary about involving the military, as an institution, in the government. Long-term military representation in typically civilian ministerial posts was limited. Military presidents were careful about subordinating themselves to their military colleagues. Their governments were more *of* than *by* the armed forces. In effect, the military played a moderator or arbitrator function within the political system.[21]

The 1964 coup in Brazil broke this pattern. The Brazilian armed forces intervened and, under the aegis of its doctrine of national security and development, controlled the political system for twenty-one years. The Brazilian military's doctrine was not unique; it had its counterparts in the national security doctrine (to use the more generic term) of the other armed forces of the Southern Cone and, to a lesser extent, the region in general. The national security doctrine focused on the internal enemy—subversives, armed and unarmed—rather than the more traditional threat of aggression by conventional foreign armed forces. Thus, it supplied a rationale for expanding the role of the military. Military intelligence targeted politicians, political parties, students, universities, labor, the church, businesses, or any suspicious individual or institution. Maintaining internal order became the ultimate responsibility of the army rather than the police. Moreover, the national security doctrine attributed political problems to the persistence of significant defects within political, social, and economic systems. Because politicians were unable to address these underlying deficiencies effectively, it thus provided a pretext for long-term military rule.[22]

The national security doctrine was part of an underlying transformation of the military's self-image. By the 1960s, Latin American armed forces had developed their own concept of their status and function within the state. Traditional Western conceptions of military professionalism had stressed subordination to political authority and left coup plotters with only ad hoc justifications or the appeal to past national practices. The new professionalism or integrated professionalism provided a theoretical justification for military intervention. The armed forces were more than impromptu saviors; because of their unique institutional capabilities, they were the agents of change who would promote the development of a better society.[23]

From the perspective of the armed forces, the national security state was desirable because it provided for measured popular participation and protected the society against the danger of subversion. Ultimately, the chief executive as well as the legislature would be civilian and chosen via elections. In most cases, however, timetables for a transfer of power, the role of elections and political parties, and the continuing internal security role of the armed forces remained vague. Eschewing the term *national security state*, military leaders often spoke of democracy but qualified it with such terms as *authoritarian* or *protected*.

Nonetheless, even with their revamped professionalism and systematic approach to change, these new-model military governments were unable to retain their hold on power or to fully prepare the way for a completely acceptable regime headed by civilians.

■ THE RETURN OF ELECTED GOVERNMENTS

Is this just another turn in the historical cycle or is democracy, at last, the wave of the future? It is wise to be skeptical about predictions implying that democracy or anything else is inevitable, yet even taking this caveat into account, real change of a developmentalist or corporatist variety seems to be underway.

□ *New Political Forces*

Since 1980, new parties and leaders have emerged. This phenomenon is far from universal, but given the durability of the Latin American political class, even a partial renewal of the class is noteworthy. Several examples illustrate this change. In Brazil, where the military was in power for twenty-one years, one might expect death or old age alone to renew the field of major presidential contenders. Yet until a year before the two-round process of November–December 1989, the two major contenders were expected to be Ullises Guimarães and Leonel Brizola, politicians well established before the military dictatorship, the latter even borrowing the name of a party of that era. In the first round, however, the top two finishers were men in their forties; in fact, three of the only four finishers to garner more than a negligible percentage of the vote were politicians who emerged since the coup. In the final round, Fernando Collor de Mello narrowly defeated Luiz Inácio da Silva (Lula) the candidate of the Partido dos Trabalhadores (Workers Party, or PT), which emerged during the final phases of the military government.

Indeed, real but unanticipated political development had taken place in Brazil across a wide variety of sectors during the military dictatorship. Although the PT was the only new, mass-based, grassroots party, political mobilization had been widespread, especially since the late 1970s. The church, especially through its affiliated ecclesiastical base communities (CEBs), professional associations, and unions had either been newly organized or had taken on new political relevance by taking part in the struggle against the dictatorship.[24]

In Bolivia, presidential politics in the early 1980s found the country seemingly trapped in a time warp. The first two presidents during the period were Hernan Siles Zuazo (1982–1985) and Víctor Paz Estenssoro (1985–1989), who headed rival political factions they had led since the 1950s. (It was as if voters in the United States were confronted in their 1984 presidential election with a choice between Dwight Eisenhower and Adlai Stevenson!) A third leading figure was Hugo Banzer, the military dictator from the 1970s. Yet by the time of the 1989 election, the picture had changed considerably. Two of the three leading contenders had emerged in the 1970s and 1980s. Besides Banzer, Gonzalo Sánchez de Lozada headed a new conservative movement, and the ultimate winner, Jaime Paz Zamora, a revolutionary turned moderate socialist, headed the Movimiento de la Izquierda Revolucionaria (Movement of the Revolutionary Left, or MIR).

In other countries, it was not so much the emergence of new faces as the appearance of a new realism that gave enhanced credibility to the democratic transition. In the 1980s, the Alianza Popular Revolucionaria Americana (American Popular Revolutionary Alliance, or APRA) became politically acceptable to the generals in Peru. Meanwhile, the Peruvian left split between Marxist fundamentalists and a more accommodationist—and more popular—socialist tendency, whose most popular figure remained Alfonso Barrantes.

In Argentina, the traditional split between the Peronists and the military seems to have been partially mended and is now overshadowed by a still serious, but less sectarian, division between sectors of the armed forces and the political sector as a whole. While it eventually succumbed to its own economic failures, in 1983 the Unión Civica Radical (Radical Civic Union, or UCR) demonstrated that it could win an honest election against the Peronists. Even the supposedly traditionalist Peronist president, elected in 1989, demonstrated that he could temporarily set aside populist rhetoric to undertake politically unpopular economic adjustments.

In Chile, the left and centrist oppositions were finally able to unite their efforts to force an end to the dictatorship. In October 1988, they defeated General Pinochet's bid to extend his term via plebiscite by a 57 percent to 43 percent margin. Then in December 1989, Patricio Aylwin, the opposition's candidate, defeated two rightist opponents by a similar margin for a first-round victory in the presidential vote. The tripartite division of Chilean politics, so critical to the breakdown of democracy in 1973 and the maintenance of the dictatorship thereafter, has been partially eroded.

□ *Human Rights*

There has also been a change in the ideological climate. The corporatist analysis holds that human rights and due process are essentially North American and Western European concepts. The Iberian tradition, incorporated into the Latin American outlook, maintains its own concept of fairness, which certainly should not be confused with anything like the Anglo-American legal tradition.[25] The analysis of North American foreign policy that takes this uniqueness argument into account might declare the human rights policies of the Carter administration and the activism of a variety of private human rights groups to be subversive of Western interests at worst and quixotic at best. According to this realist perspective, it would have been far preferable for Western governments, especially the United States, to take a more modest view of the possibilities of reform and not pressure—and hence destabilize—right-wing dictatorships friendly toward Western interests.[26] But in actuality, this realism has turned out to be shortsighted and paternalistic. Not only has international opinion strongly supported supposedly parochial, Western concepts of human rights, but important human rights organizations have arisen in many Latin American countries.

Chile's Vicariate of Solidarity, sponsored by the Catholic church, is perhaps the most well known and influential of these organizations. The Vicariate's actions have frequently put it at odds with the military government. Members of the Chilean episcopacy and the government have been openly critical of one another. Pinochet's government considered church criticism of its human rights record, lack of social justice, and the possibility of electoral fraud as unwarranted incursions by the church into politics. Consequently, it subjected members of the clergy to harassment including, at one point, the police interrogation of a bishop.[27] Meanwhile, the Vicariate has not only provided succor for those persecuted for their political beliefs, but also helped provide political space for the opposition to organize.[28]

In Argentina, in the late 1970s, the Mothers of the Plaza de Mayo were a voice crying in the wilderness. Fear or indifference ensured that their protest of the fate of nine thousand "disappeared" found little resonance among the general population. In 1983, a human rights lawyer was elected to the presidency and tried, however fitfully, to bring at least some of the human rights violators to justice. No longer complacent about human rights violations, widespread, public protests in October 1989 forced President Menem temporarily to withdraw the proposed second stage of his general amnesty.

In other countries with serious human rights violations—Brazil, Uruguay, Guatemala, and El Salvador—human rights advocates have been outspoken if not markedly effective. Prospects for bringing human rights violators to justice in significant numbers seem remote in every country. Yet, a heightened consciousness about human rights may have a chilling effect on potential violators in the future.

Moreover, the internationalization of the human rights issue provides support for sometimes beleaguered national organizations. But probably the most effective expression of international solidarity to date has been election monitoring, which renders it more difficult for governments to blatantly manipulate the electoral process.[29]

□ *The Travail of the National Security Doctrine*

Policymaking in military regimes represented the triumph of expertise over consensus building. Military presidents eschewed the politicking and compromise, which had limited, as a matter of necessity, their civilian predecessors. The power of the executive was strengthened vis-à-vis the legislature, if the legislature continued to function at all,[30] and the executive branch itself was not staffed by the old politicos but by civilian and military technocrats. Even these civilians, drawn from financial and administrative positions, sometimes lacked meaningful contact and input from civilian sectors of society.[31] One analysis aptly dubbed the technocratic character of policy formulation in these military governments as the "politics of anti-politics."[32] This antipolitical—or at least antipolitician—animus led to charges not only of civilian incompetence but bad faith as well. Witness Augusto Pinochet: "The politicians have never done anything for Chile, because they turned politics into a profitable business. They want to return because, having been out of business for thirteen years, their pockets are empty."[33]

The rejection of traditional politics led to a number of approaches toward the reformation of the political system. In Brazil, the military restructured the system to produce two parties: The Aliança de Renovação Nacional (National Renovating Alliance, or ARENA), meant to be the dominant, progovernment party, and the Movimento Democrático Brasileiro (Brazilian Democratic Movement, or MDB), which was to be the loyal opposition with only limited access to the levers of power. Such a system was to break the dominance of the clientelistic habits of the old political parties. Hence the political system could be transformed without risking the mass mobilization that had apparently been fomenting during the Goulart government.

The Peruvians chose a different tack. General Velasco's government (1968–1975) explicitly tried to mobilize the disenfranchised and so create an inclusionary corporatist system. But, although new groups were given access to the political system, this was definitely *controlled* access, and policymaking remained a top-down process.

In Chile, despite urging from some civilian supporters, Pinochet opted to avoid conventional political methods as much as possible. The regime formed no official party or movement, and, at least officially, the old parties' operations were abrogated by a political recess that lasted until the late 1980s. It relied, instead, on a number of carefully managed plebiscites to provide the aura of popular ratification of governmental decisions.

Military regimes, however, were not markedly successful either in policy formulation or political restructuring. Latin American military governments managed the oil shocks of the 1970s and the debt crisis of the 1980s no better than their civilian counterparts in the region. In fact, borrowing in the 1970s, whether on an ad hoc basis or as part of a systematic plan meant to stimulate economic development and energy independence, was one of the underlying causes of the debt problem and economic stagnation in the 1980s.

In the realm of political restructuring, as well, military self-confidence has been badly shaken. By the mid-1970s, Brazil and Peru were forced to abandon their attempts at wholesale reform of the political system. Velasco was replaced as president by another general, Morales Bermúdez, whose government opted for a gradual return to civilian rule. The Brazilian attempt to build a political support structure for a dominant executive and technocratic rule foundered on the rocks of the increasing popularity of the opposition party. The armed forces were reduced to standbys of the old system: patronage politics and electoral manipulation. Even in Chile, where the military could claim one of the best records of overall economic management, General Pinochet was unable to stand the test of an honestly conducted plebiscite.

The practical experience of military rule has undercut some of the more pretentious implications of the national security doctrine. While dominant sectors of the armed forces may still cling to the notion of subversion and the internal enemy as the greatest danger threatening their countries, the theoretical justification for military rule now lacks credibility. Even traditional pretexts for veto coups have lost their former force, at least temporarily. For example, in Brazil during the December 1989 presidential runoff, when the socialist candidate Luiz Inácio da Silva was poised for a possible come-from-behind victory, the generals, according to Alfred Stepan, "lacked the stomach" to stop him.[34] This was the case despite the fact that Lula raised a number of red flags by attacking many of the vested interests of the armed forces.

While it is certainly too early to assert that military coups are a thing of the past, it appears reasonable to affirm that military intervention has reached a new stage. At least a temporary hallmark of this new phase is an apparent doctrinal vacuum on the issue of military ruler.[35]

□ The Erosion of Old Certainties

Not only have Latin America and its armed forces changed since the mid-1960s, the rest of the world has changed as well. Changes in global alignments and political attitudes show signs of permeating Latin American armed forces.

The Waning of the Cold War. Although the early 1980s saw a revival of Cold War rhetoric and posturing, at least on the part of the United States, the accession to power of Mikhail Gorbachev in the Soviet Union produced a much-improved climate for Soviet-US cooperation. For the first time since the inception of the Cold War, there was a real prospect for serious arms reductions. The internal changes in Eastern Europe and in the USSR further enhanced the possibilities for cooperation between the superpowers and an end to the Cold War. This renders less credible one of the leitmotivs of the national security doctrine: the belief that internal subversion is just one part of a global struggle between international communism and the West. This ideological formulation is certainly not dead,[36] but the disappearance of the ideological struggle between the superpowers promises a number of long-term, salutary effects. It could well presage a more pragmatic US approach to insurgencies in Latin America and help erode Latin American military fundamentalism.[37] The change in the international system also provides a motive for Latin America to reevaluate its own security system.

In the nonmilitary area, the East-West factors were becoming increasingly irrelevant to Latin American foreign policies even before the abating of the Cold War. Latin America needs markets and technology, and, in most cases, ideological considerations have not stood in the way of their development. The hard-line Argentine military government sold grain to the USSR during the US embargo; Brazil became a key target for increasing Soviet regional exports; and by 1988, even the Pinochet government, which had been among the most virulently anti-Soviet governments in the region, had begun to widen contacts with the Eastern Bloc. In 1988, Chile's trade with the Eastern Bloc nearly doubled over the previous year, a Soviet journalist and a Cuban lecturer were allowed into the country, and Chilean aid was sent to victims of the Armenian earthquake.[38] Trade seems destined to remain limited for the foreseeable future, but the pragmatic turn in regional foreign policies is a heartening development.

The waning of the relevance of Cold War postures paralleled the growing significance of North-South issues. East-West alignments play a small, or even nonexistent, role in a number of the major issues troubling the region: the debt problem, the development of an effective formula for securing peace in Central America, regional cooperation, and the management of the inter-American system. From the Latin American perspective, the major antagonist in these areas is not the Soviet Union but the West, particularly the United States.

Perhaps the Falklands/Malvinas War best symbolized the limited significance of the East-West axis of world politics for Latin America as well as the marginality of Latin America in US strategic calculations. After trying to broker a deal to prevent a violent resolution to Argentina's occupation of the islands, the United States provided aid critical to the British victory[39] and ignored Latin American efforts to invoke the Inter-American Treaty of Reciprocal Assistance in the Organization of American States. After that experience, the United States seemed more inclined than previously to go it alone, and Latin American nations even less willing to support it, in interventions in the region. While the US intervention in the Dominican Republic in 1965 had the cover of at least limited regional support, the October 1983 invasion of Grenada was supported by the minimally important Organization of Eastern Caribbean States, and the December 1989

Panamanian invasion was not endorsed by any regional or subregional organization or government, except El Salvador's.

Geopolitical Revisionism. Traditionally, Latin American nations have been good at producing grandiose plans and impressive-looking organizations to promote regional cooperation. But the Latin American Free Trade Association, the Latin American Economic System, the Association for Latin American Integration and Development, the Andean Pact, and the Central American Common Market, to name a few, have all been stillborn or failed to achieve more than modest or temporary benefits for their members. Typically, regionalism has foundered on the rocks of national self-interest. It seemed that Latin American geopolitical thinkers—much more influential in Latin America than their counterparts in North America—were correct: international politics was a matter of conflict over scarce resources, where neighboring states were more likely to be antagonists rather than allies.[40] In a sense, the weaknesses of exclusively Latin American organizations have paralleled the ever more apparent defects in the inter-American system as a whole.

Fortunately, the failure to construct a truly effective, formal system to promote cooperation has been partially counterbalanced by ad hoc cooperative efforts begun in the 1980s. The Contadora and support groups (later called the Group of Eight and then the Rio Group), for example, were formed in response to manifest problems that required immediate action. Pragmatic diplomacy played a greater role than the creation of formal structures. The Rio Group now provides an informal mechanism for coordinating regional diplomacy. The governments of Brazil and Argentina provide another example. They initiated a process of economic integration in response to their national auto industries. Ford (Argentina) and Volkswagen (Brazil) recognized that integration of the automotive sector would benefit them in their respective national markets and enhance their international competitiveness. Although beset by a number of problems, this process may eventually encompass the rest of the Southern Cone.

The hallmarks of these efforts have been a step-by-step approach, a focus on immediate issues and benefits, and a lack of US involvement and, in some cases, US hostility to the efforts. Geopoliticians have begun to provide theoretical support for these trends. This support is more than academic; geopolitical theorists are frequently military officers or closely associated with the military.[41] In effect, cooperation rather than conflict is increasingly seen as the region's manifest destiny.

■ OPPORTUNITIES AND STUMBLING BLOCKS

What does all this mean for the future of civil-military relations in Latin America? Clearly, current trends provide no unequivocal confirmation for either an unnuanced corporatist or developmentalist view. Latin American nations are unlikely to repeat precisely their own or anyone else's history. Historically derived patterns of civil-military relations can serve as guides for analysts and policymakers, but they are models whose applications will necessarily be influenced by the particular set of circumstances confronting decisionmakers in each nation.

More concretely, from either the corporatist or developmentalist perspective, Latin American civil-military relations, and politics in general, have reached a new stage in their evolution. Especially in the more-developed nations of the region, it is unlikely that old-style military coups—either leading to military governments of a moderator or ruler sort—will be repeated. Naiveté about the benefits of either sort of military rule has, by and large, vanished. The establishment of military governments required considerable civilian support or at least apathy in the face of an armed forces' takeover. Yet, experience over the last twenty years has shown that this support was neither broad nor deep enough to give the military the requisite freedom of action to make what it believed were necessary political changes. The military has been able neither to restore the political system nor transform it after its own image. Hence, substantially more serious political and economic crises would be required to induce the military to undertake the risks of new coups. In fact, despite hyperinflation that makes the inflation rate of the 1960s look tame, substantial guerrilla threats in some countries, and the prospect of a Marxist victory at the polls in some others, Latin American militaries intervened in only two countries in the 1980s. These military governments have since been overturned.[42]

□   *The Debt Crisis, Economic Decline,*
    and New Coups

Coups, however, cannot be ruled out completely. Guerrilla insurgencies and a black (illegal) economy based on drugs threaten Peru and Colombia. Guerrillas are a significant force in El Salvador and Guatemala as well. But the most significant threat regionally is economic. A huge debt burden, the flight of domestic capital, and the virtual disappearance of new loans and investments made Latin America an exporter of capital to the developed world throughout most of the 1980s. This, in turn, has led to significant declines in real gross domestic product (GDP) per capita—declines, in some cases, to levels typical of the 1960s and 1970s.[43] Should this situation worsen, popular tolerance and military forbearance may no longer be sustainable. The unprecedented crisis could force the remilitarization of Latin American politics along new paths.

One scenario is the Africanization of Latin American politics: the breakdown of the political order and the economy so serious that an ill-prepared military takes over without any real, systematic conception about what has to be done. Unable to solve underlying problems, the military government relies upon force and may itself be followed by a series of governments, military or civilian, no better equipped to address the problems. Such a scenario entails the decay of public life, policy instability, and increased levels of violence and corruption. While such crises have beset a number of African states over the past decade, Latin American conditions seem to be different. There are few Latin American analogues to the intense tribal and religious conflict, low level of nationalism, and low level of economic development typical of many African states. This scenario seems to apply directly only in the case of Haiti. However, the marginalization of sectors of the working and middle classes and the appearance of spontaneous violence in the face of severe economic hardship may yet raise this specter in other countries as well.

An alternative possibility is the fascification of Latin American politics. Although the epithet *fascist* has frequently been used to describe the military dictatorships in the region, they were not truly fascist or totalitarian in the classic sense of the term.[44] This is more than an academic quibble. Although many Latin American military dictatorships did not blanch at using systematic violence that at times bordered on the mass terror characteristic of totalitarianism and they sometimes attempted to incorporate public life into a constraining, regime-sanctioned structure, they lacked key characteristics of fascism as well. They had no chiliastic ideology, mass-based totalitarian party, or charismatic leader, typical of the most durable totalitarian regimes. In short, while willing to make use of many of the negative instruments typically used by fascists, military governments did not make use of fascist mechanisms to build or retain a political consensus.

In most cases, their attempts at consensus building, by whatever means, were less than effective in the long run. Would future military dictators with a systematic program of social and economic transformation leave politics largely to chance? Would not an even partially open political system be too much of a risk? As with Africanization, there are few direct Latin American analogues to fascism. The Estado Novo in Brazil and Perón's attempt to establish *justicialismo* (a mixture of socialism, nationalism, and corporatism) as the official ideology of Argentina are faint images of what would be required. Efforts to construct a latter-day totalitarianism seem to be out of character for military officers imbued with the antipolitical, technocratic ethos. However, attempts by cashiered Argentine army officers Aldo Rico and Mohammed Alí Seineldín to build a civil-military movement with an ideological base may threaten such a development.

□ *Military Manipulation*

Direct military rule, even in the face of economic decline or insurgent threats, is not the greatest immediate risk. More likely is the continuation and intensification of military efforts to play a preponderant role within a formally civilian political system. These efforts can take many forms, from legally permissible activities, such as lobbying, to outright illegalities, such as mutinies and shows of force against civilian authorities. Cumulatively they constitute a serious challenge to a key democratic principle: civilians ought to exercise ultimate control of the armed forces, even though the apparent significance of individual challenges may not be great.

In short, rather than functioning within a completely democratic context, newly established civilian governments may find themselves operating in the environment of a post–national security state.[45] While full-blown national security states with military presidents, open mass repression of political dissent, and official restrictions on leftist and popular organizations have disappeared from the political scene, successor regimes have retained key elements of the old system. These elements include vestiges of the old national security ideology. For example, in Chile and to a certain degree in Brazil, the old National Security Council (NSC) structure remains. The NSC monitors developments related to internal security and assures that adequate responses are undertaken by the executive branch. Even where such structures have been altered or abolished, the armed forces often retain the potential for an overriding influence in government councils.

Uniformed officers frequently head defense ministries or the ministries of the separate services if no unified defense ministry exists. Military intelligence often undertakes, or aspires to undertake, the function of domestic surveillance. The military frequently exercises de jure or de facto emergency powers, placing in jeopardy due-process guarantees. Human rights abuses in countries such as El Salvador, Guatemala, and Peru continue at significant levels.[46] The armed forces and paramilitary police, meanwhile, have managed to retain a good deal of internal autonomy, thus shielding themselves from civilian supervision by the executive and courts. In short, while yielding political authority to civilians, the armed forces often retain control over a wide range of policy and the prerogative to veto government policies. The current state is neither a true democracy, under the recognized control of the elected, civilian leadership, nor the national security state of a military regime. Civilian leaders must contend with a frequently recalcitrant military power structure much more deeply ensconced in positions of power than is normal for military bureaucrats in a democracy.

Latin American civil-military relations have entered a new era, but it is an era of development and conflict, not one of consensus and firmly established patterns. Praetorianism remains a threat. While civilian governments generally support the full application of democratic principles, the armed forces tend to favor a post–national security state. Statesmanship—and chance—will determine which of these emergent patterns is finally consolidated.

■ **NOTES**

1. The fourteen are Ecuador (1979), Peru (1980), Honduras (1981), Bolivia (1982), Argentina (1983), Uruguay (1984), El Salvador (1984), Guatemala (1985), Brazil (1985), Paraguay (1989), Panama (1989), Chile (1990), Nicaragua (1990), and Haiti (1991).

2. For a contemporaneous, optimistic reaction to events in the latter period, see Szulc.

3. Williams and Wright, p. 5.

4. Lipset, p. 42. Lipset's work first appeared as "Some Social Requisites of Democracy: Economic Development and Political Legitimacy," *American Political Science Review* 53 (1959):69–105.

5. For a discussion of some of the leading contributions to developmentalism, see Huntington and Dominguez, pp. 5–10.

6. Philip, pp. 3–6.

7. Moore. See especially pp. 417–418.

8. Huntington, 1968, pp. 32–59, 196–197. A similar view, based specifically on Latin American experience, is expressed by O'Donnell. O'Donnell's famous bureaucratic-authoritarian thesis states that democratic political development and equitable distribution of income eventually fly in the face of the need for capital accumulation and technological modernization. Thus, countries such as Brazil and Argentina are frequently induced to establish authoritarian regimes with the hope of furthering the modernization process.

9. Rapaport, p. 72.

10. For a discussion of the paradoxes of power in authoritarian societies (and strategy in general), see Luttwak, pp. 62–65, and pp. 1–64 *passim*.

11. Rapaport, pp. 72–74.

12. While the trajectory of development in Brazil was slightly different from that of most of Spanish America, Brazil possessed the essential attributes of the corporatist system. Neither the Portuguese heritage nor the fact that Brazil did not fight a war for independence contributed to the formation of a more liberal society. If anything, the large African population and the persistence of the institution of slavery until 1889 reinforced the maintenance of the corporatist tradition.

13. For a discussion of the durability of corporatism, see Wiarda, 1981; Pike and Stritch.

14. Compare Rustow, pp. 353–361.

15. See Philip, pp. 85–92.

16. For a discussion of middle-class influence in the officer corps, see José Nun, "The Middle-Class Coup Revisited," in Lowenthal and Fitch, pp. 59–95. For a review of Nun's argument and that of his critics, see Philip, pp. 15–20.

17. For a discussion of the military mind, the outlook into which members of the officer corps are socialized and which sets them apart as a corporate group, see Huntington, 1964, pp. 59–79, and Abrahamsson, pp. 75–79.

18. Huntington, 1968, pp. 198–205.

19. Ibid., pp. 219–227.

20. Howard Wiarda develops the analogy one step further by arguing that coups are not only normal but often mirror the underlying realignment of social and political forces. By doing this they function much the same as critical elections in established democracies. Howard J. Wiarda, "Critical Coups and Critical Elections: The Process of Sociopolitical Realignment in Latin America," in *The Continuing Struggle for Democracy in Latin America* (Boulder, Colorado: Westview Press, 1980).

21. Stepan, 1971, pp. 74–75; Perlmutter, p. 143.

22. For a general analysis of the national security doctrine in Latin America, see Comblin; Alfred Stepan, "The New Professionalism of Internal Warfare and Military Role Expansion," in Lowenthal and Fitch, pp. 134–150.

23. Stepan, "The New Professionalism of Internal Warfare"; Potash, p. 8.

24. Moreira Alves, pp. 219–220.

25. Wiarda, 1981, pp. 127–133.

26. Kirkpatrick, 1979, pp. 34–45; Kirkpatrick, 1981, pp. 29–41.

27. Foreign Broadcast Information Service (FBIS), "Bishop's Interrogation Displeases Catholic Church," AFP, January 22, 1987, FBIS-LAM-87-019, January 29, 1987, p. E2.

28. "Bishops Are Taking a Hard Line," *Latin American Regional Reports: Southern Cone Report*, December 25, 1986, p. 3.

29. The 1988 Chilean plebiscite and the Panamanian election of 1989 are two examples of the inhibiting effect of international observers. While the Chilean armed forces respected the results, the Panamanian government refused to recognize an opposition victory, but not without cost. Even the Panamanian electoral commission was unwilling to claim a victory for the progovernment coalition and voided the results instead.

30. For a discussion of Brazil, where except for two forced recesses, the congress continued to carry out its functions, at least nominally, see Dillon Soares, pp. 104–126.

31. María Susana Ricci and J. Samuel Fitch, "Ending Military Regimes in Argentina: 1966–73 and 1976–83," in Goodman et al., pp. 60–63.

32. Loveman and Davies.

33. FBIS, "International Pressure 'Inhibits' Pinochet," Santiago, Radio Chilena, July 30, 1986, FBIS-LAM-86-148, August 1, 1986, p. E1.

34. James Brooke, "Brazil Will Vote with Eye on Army," *New York Times*, December 15, 1989, p. 7.

35. In the case of Brazil, Stepan, 1988, pp. 48–54, argues that the modification of the armed forces' national security doctrine allowed for the incorporation of the key concepts of opposition, participation, nongovernmental parties and elections into the doctrine. Nonetheless, the Brazilian military was doctrinally and practically incapable of moving from liberalization to real democratization. Events, in any case, overtook them. Moreover, in regionwide terms, an examination of public statements of senior military officers after the transition to democracy reveals a virtually unanimous, formal acceptance of the democratic regime.

36. The linkage of the internal and international threats was one of the key themes of the Conference of American Armies in December 1987. Clovis Rossi, "Pact Between 'Armies of America' Leaked," *Folha de São Paulo*, September 25, 1988, in FBIS, FBIS-LAT-88-187, September 27, 1988, pp. 1–2.

37. *Fundamentalism*, in this context, refers to the position of military hardliners supporting the national security doctrine in its harshest aspects. This position is extremely conservative and often links Western civilization with extreme, right-wing Catholic values.

38. "Opening Up Trade to the Eastern Bloc," *Latin American Weekly Report*, February 23, 1989, p. 8.

39. "America and the Falklands: Case Study in the Behavior of an Ally," *Economist*, November 12, 1983, pp. 31–42.

40. Child, pp. 89–111.

41. Jack Child, "Geopolitical Thinking," in Goodman et al., p. 155.

42. The two are Haiti and Panama. In many ways both are special cases more typical of a bygone era of personalistic military institutions. In neither case was military intervention motivated by fear of Marxism or economic collapse. In both cases, the personal interests of the commanders in chief of the armed forces better explain the coups.

43. For example, by 1987, Mexico and Uruguay had fallen to the level of GDP per capita they had attained in 1979; Peru hit 1974 levels; Chile 1971 levels; and Argentina 1969 levels. IBRD, April/May, 1989, p. 3.

44. For an exposition of the characteristics of totalitarianism, see Friedrick and Brzezinski, p. 126; Arendt, pp. 389–479.

45. The notion of post–national security state involves a loose adaptation of the sort of analysis underlying the concept of the post-totalitarian state found in Linz, pp. 336–350.

46. For example, Amnesty International reports the disappearance of three thousand prisoners while in government custody during the last seven years. Thousands more have been killed in mass executions with no significant improvement in sight. "Rights Group's Report on Peru Shows Rising Tide of Abuse," *New York Times*, August 24, 1989, p. 6. Three hundred of these disappearances took place in 1989. Amnesty International, *Report 1989*, p. 144.

2■

The Incomplete
Democratic Transition

The nature of the transition to civilian rule has decisively shaped civil-military politics under the newly established civilian governments. The five transfers of power in South America upon which we are focusing (in Peru, Argentina, Brazil, Uruguay, and Chile) have all been forced transitions. They were neither revolutions nor procedures executed under complete military tutelage. The armed forces had a major influence over the shape of the transition process, but they could not control the exact shape of the final outcome.

■ THE CRISIS OF MILITARY AUTHORITARIANISM

The transfer of power to civilians was necessitated by the failure of the armed forces to consolidate the regimes they established or, more accurately, to prepare the way for a transfer of power to acceptable successors. This failure was underlined by their legitimacy crises. The creation of a sense of legitimacy is never an easy matter. Policies that are crafted to enhance legitimacy attack long-established institutions and habits, and, if they are to succeed, the new policies require systematic application over a considerable period of time. Consider Max Weber's remarks:

> An order which is adhered to from motives of pure expedience is generally much less stable than one upheld on a purely customary basis. . . . But even this type of order is in turn much less stable than an order which enjoys the prestige of being considered binding, or, as it may be expressed, of "legitimacy." The transitions between orientation to an order from motives of tradition or of expedience on the one hand to the case where on the other a belief in its legitimacy is involved, are naturally empirically gradual.[1]

Even though they exercised a significant degree of repression, military governments were unable to convert day-to-day political power into legitimate power. National security doctrines were unable to provide any convincing alternative to democratic ideology. Military rhetoric about protected or authoritarian democracy—favored in contradistinction to naive (liberal) democracy—illustrates the ideological vacuum of present-day authoritarians.[2]

The lack of legitimacy made short-term policy success even more critical than it otherwise would have been. Juan Linz has pointed out the connection between effectiveness (the ability to execute policy), efficacy (the ability to address society's perceived needs), stability and performance, and legitimacy. Efficacy and effectiveness contribute to regime stability and performance; moreover, the feedback effects of enhanced efficacy, effectiveness, and performance reinforce a regime's legitimacy. Legitimacy has an indirect effect on the other three factors.[3] In other words, the four factors are mutually reinforcing or, in a situation of breakdown, mutually debilitating. A regime that is supported by a strong sense of legitimacy can choose efficacious policies to address basic problems and implement these policies effectively. As a result, it will perform well and be stable. This overall success, in turn, will enhance that regime's legitimacy and its ability to perform effectively in the future, while the inverse is also true.

Pushed one step further, Linz's analysis yields an interesting implication: If a regime is underpinned by only a weak sense of legitimacy, its stability depends almost entirely on success in the policy area. In effect, regimes with weak legitimacy are subject to the same sort of withdrawal of political support that governments (administrations) suffer from in societies where the form of government (the regime) is nevertheless considered legitimate. Societies that possess a consensus about the form of government may suffer from governmental instability (incumbent administrations unable to win reelection or forced from office because of no-confidence votes); such societies do not suffer from regime instability. Conversely, societies with no such consensus are prone to regime instability; loss of public confidence in a particular set of officials and their policies is likely to entail loss of support for the form of government responsible for those policies. Hence, military regimes in the late 1970s and early 1980s were unable to retain power, while their civilian successors, no more successful overall, have not as yet witnessed a popular withdrawal of support for democracy as such.

The lack of political legitimacy held military governments hostage to short-term policy success. Faced with policy failures, they were unable to replace the old praetorianism with new-model institutions.

■ OUTLINES OF FIVE TRANSITIONS

Despite their differences, these five transfers of power shared a number of common characteristics. First, in most cases they were provoked by a crisis, usually economic, but often included other important elements as well.

Regardless of the nature of the crisis, it became apparent to the military government that it had failed to achieve at least some of its important goals. Second, as the transition process accelerated, it was often accompanied by mass mobilizations that the military regime had not foreseen and was ill equipped to handle. Finally, the process made apparent the factionalism within the armed forces themselves. This factionalism was often based on different approaches to the issue of the transfer of power to civilians. So-called hard-liners opposed the transfer, or at least aimed at a more constrained process culminating in a new regime that retained strongly authoritarian features. Soft-liners were in favor of a more rapid opening resulting in the establishment of a more liberal regime. Neither of these groups wished to accommodate fully the demands of the civilian opposition or implement full democracy.[4] Often, interservice or interbranch rivalries reinforced the above splits or provided crosscutting fissures.

□   *Peru (1975–1980)*

Prior to the period of military rule initiated in 1968, the pattern of civil-military relations had followed the praetorian pattern outlined in Chapter 1. While the armed forces had been modernized to the degree that they ceased to function as a mere vehicle for caudillos from the landed elite, they nonetheless exercised considerable direct and indirect influence over the political system. By the 1930s, the primary antagonist of the armed forces was the American Popular Revolutionary Alliance (APRA)—an eclectic, radical party inspired by both European and Latin American ideas—whose program threatened the landed elite. In 1931, the military intervened to prevent the Apristas, victorious in the election, from assuming office. Further interventions and sometimes violent Aprista reactions followed.

By the 1960s, a leading faction within the armed forces realized that Peru's praetorian pattern had to be altered. Consequently, for a limited period of time, Peru's military government became the most coherent and systematic in its approach to national transformation of all the military regimes in South America. Under the government of General Juan Velasco Alvarado (1968–1975), the armed forces undertook drastic political and economic reforms to preempt a revolution.

One of the intellectual progenitors of the reforms was the armed forces' war college, the Centro de Altos Estudios Militares (Center for Superior Military Studies, or CAEM). The school, founded in the early 1950s, transcended its initial mission of preparation for conventional conflict with its neighbors—most notably Ecuador—and developed a more encompassing focus of national security and development. CAEM developed an ideological perspective similar to the popular North American developmentalist thesis that economic backwardness was the ultimate source of political and social violence.[5] A second and possibly even more influential source of military ideas was Army Intelligence, some of whose members were making detailed and sweeping analyses of Peru's developmental problems.[6] In short, before the Velasco coup, the army had reached a limited consensus on the need for reforms in a number of key areas such as land reform and the nationalization of foreign oil holdings.[7] It was on this basis that the military government under General Velasco could undertake a revolution from above.

The Velasco government undertook a bewildering series of reforms, difficult to categorize, that eventually tested the underlying military consensus about reform initiatives. The government's program, Plan Inca, entailed the nationalization of significant foreign and domestic holdings, including an extensive program of land reform, and called for the state to be the exclusive owner of basic industries. Social mobilization was encouraged, but the whole process entailed co-optation and control. Organizations heretofore independent were to become part of a new state-controlled structure: Sistema Nacional de Apoyo a la Movilización Social (National System for the Support of Social Mobilization, or SINAMOS). Newly organized labor sectors and the defense of workers' rights, generally, were also placed under the overall rubric of SINAMOS. In the judgment of one critic,

> there is little doubt that this initial program was intended to be the beginning of a much broader project aimed at implanting military values in civil society in order to militarize it and instill discipline, so that once the country was "united"—which is to say without political parties—it would be possible to manipulate it like a military regiment.[8]

The domestic program was associated with foreign policy and defense initiatives that enhanced the visibility of Peru on the regional and global scenes. The government attempted to build trade relations with Eastern Bloc states hoping to diversify its markets and capitalize on what was perceived to be a growing commodity shortage.[9] Peru also led the fight that broke the Organization of American States (OAS) trade embargo on Cuba and established both diplomatic and trade relations with that communist government.[10]

By 1974, the government's development plans had gone awry. Rates of economic growth had leveled off and begun to decline (see Table 2.1). Anticipated new oil revenues had failed to materialize. The regime had undertaken an ambitious program of social and economic reconstruction without the financial and administrative resources to carry it through to completion. Popular-sector organizations, initially supportive of the regime's leftist-sounding program, had begun to rankle at the restraints imposed by the government's corporatist methods of control. Even within the military, the government was losing substantial support. General Velasco attempted to play off military factions against one another as he reshuffled his cabinet. In February 1975, he appointed General Francisco Morales Bermúdez prime

Table 2.1 Peru's Annual Growth (GDP per capita, percentage)

1967	1968	1969	1970	1971	1972	1973	1974	1975	1976	1977
1.2	0.0	1.3	4.9	2.3	3.4	3.2	3.2	0.0	1.0	−4.2

Source: IBRD

minister. With Velasco in failing health, the armed forces turned the presidency over to Morales Bermúdez in August 1975.

The selection of the new president marked a staged retreat from the ambitious goals of the original revolutionary government. In January 1976, Morales Bermúdez announced Plan Inca II or the Plan Tupac Amarú. This proved too radical for right-wing elements in the military and the president was compelled to issue a revised plan in February 1977. Meanwhile, the economic crisis continued to deepen, and labor unrest eventually culminated in three nationwide general strikes, one of which lasted for three days. An institutional crisis paralleled the worsening situation in the economy as charges of corruption and contraband trading and other crimes became rife. The military was compelled to leave power to save itself as a viable institution.[11]

The chosen path was a constituent assembly, elected in 1978 and scheduled to return power to an elected civilian government by 1980. The armed forces prohibited the assembly from acting as a provisional government, retaining the power to run the government until the formal transfer of power. It thus secured a breathing space and proceeded to pressure for a constitution and successor government to its liking.

The final stages of the drama involved a number of important political actors: the left, revitalized by the mass mobilizations of 1977; the center (composed of the Acción Popular [Popular Action, or AP] and APRA); and the armed forces. While popular pressure from the left strengthened the hands of centrists vis-à-vis the armed forces, it was in the interest of the center to seek the patronage of the armed forces, which hoped to play off the major centrist aspirants against one another. During the final stages of the constituent assembly, the armed forces suppressed a teachers strike to demonstrate its commitment to fulfill an agreement with the International Monetary Fund (IMF), as well as to break the capacity of popular sectors to interfere with the orthodox economic policy of the Morales Bermúdez government.[12]

In an odd historical reversal, Fernando Belaúnde Terry, the president ousted by the military coup of 1968, returned as president in mid-1980. The return of civilians to power, however, was premised on a number of guarantees to the military. They were guaranteed institutional autonomy for the armed forces, the right to intervene to secure public order, and veto power over measures that might compromise national security.[13]

□ Brazil (1980–1985)

Prior to the 1964 coup, civil-military relations fell within a praetorian pattern, but one that relied predominantly on indirect control and manipulation of the political system. The armed forces were instrumental in overthrowing existing regimes in 1889, 1930, and 1945 and in provoking a presidential resignation in 1954. The influence of the armed forces was widely accepted, especially by more-conservative sectors. They became, by law, the guardians of the constitution. This provided a ready pretext for intervention.

As noted earlier, the coup of 1964 was symbolic of the new style of military rule. The Brazilian military government, which lasted from 1964 to 1985, was the most long-lived and one of the most complex in its internal dynamics. There was persistent tension between hard-liners and soft-liners; the latter were initially associated with systematic reform and advocated a certain degree of openness in the military government. The partial alternation of the presidency between the two factions often made the regime's handling of policy seem less than sure-handed. Nonetheless, the Brazilian case represents the best example of long-term military rule based on a coherent conception of the need for and direction of substantial reform.

The intellectual force behind the model of military government was the Escola Superior de Guerra (Superior War College, or ESG). It provided an important coterie of plotters against the Goulart government in 1964[14] as well as leading figures in successive military governments. While the first military president, Humberto Castello Branco, and his chief mentor, General Golbery, wished to return power to civilians eventually, the transfer of power would require a number of political changes. Thus, the government introduced measures aimed at correcting what it perceived to be the old system's underlying faults. The executive branch was strengthened vis-à-vis the legislature. The aim was to make the legislative process more efficient and less subject to partisan roadblocks and logrolling. A second aim of the program was to undercut the left. The government removed opposition figures from office and forced the retirement of others in the civil service and education.[15]

To secure an acceptable party system that would provide political support for the military government and could eventually ease the way to civilian rule, the regime created two new parties in 1965. The National Renovating Alliance (ARENA) was a grouping of proregime politicians susceptible to military direction. Its counterpart, the Brazilian Democratic Movement (MDB), included opposition politicians not in exile or banned from active politics. Other parties were disbanded, and the regime instituted a system of indirect elections for president and state governors. The government retained the right to ban members of the opposition and censor the media. Certain elective posts, such as mayors of state capitals, were made appointive. This artificial arrangement never took firm root. Differences between hard-liners (who favored the use of repression) and soft-liners (who favored liberalization) prevented the armed forces from reaching an enduring consensus.

In the economic and social field, the government pursued a state capitalist policy, organizing the economy along capitalist lines but providing a large role for the state in several areas. The state provided investment in key areas required for industrial modernization—filling the void created by insufficient private investment in economic infrastructure and industry. The state also provided a host of subsidies and protective mechanisms to stimulate the development of key industries—such as computers, steel, and chemicals—and to promote the export of their products. The state provided a legal framework to suppress labor demands and keep working-class organizations under control. An alliance among domestic capital, the state, and multinational corporations supported the system. The regime became the prototype of O'Donnell's bureaucratic-authoritarian state.[16]

By the 1970s, the system was under political pressure from within and without. ARENA was hardly an acceptable vehicle for conservative politicians because it placed them in the position of supporting the executive's initiatives but did not ensure executive support for initiatives of ARENA members. Bills from ARENA legislators had no more chance of ultimate enactment than bills submitted by the MDB legislators. In congress, by the mid-1970s, the MDB took the lead in presenting bills and delivering speeches.[17] In the broader society, the repeal of some of the more repressive measures allowed a wide range of groups to begin mobilizing opposition to the regime. The Catholic church, the bar and press associations, neighborhood associations, and labor became increasingly active and outspoken about the need to reestablish democratic rights.[18] It became apparent that the regime was even loosing its hold on the elite sectors of society, whose interests it was supposed to guarantee.

By the 1974 election, the political fortunes of the MDB, which had languished in the political wilderness for almost ten years, began to change. While in 1970 it held only 7 of 63 seats in the senate and 87 of 310 seats in the Chamber of Deputies, in 1974 it added 13 seats to its total in the senate and strengthened its contingent of deputies by 78.

For the armed forces, liberalization had gone too far. The response was repression and electoral manipulation. Before the 1976 municipal elections, the government imposed the Falção Law (named for the justice minister who drafted it). The law severely restricted the use of television for electoral propaganda. Moreover, contrary to the constitution the military itself had imposed, the government announced that governors would continue to be elected by indirect vote. In protest, the MDB withdrew from one-third of the races, resulting in an ARENA victory. The next year, to recoup ARENA's flagging congressional strength, the Geisel government enacted the April Package, after first suspending the legislature.

The package allowed for the passage of constitutional amendments by a simple congressional majority (to protect the freedom of action of ARENA's diminished majority) and extended the Falção Law to national elections. One-third of the senate would be appointed by state legislatures in the hands of ARENA. Other measures were introduced to aid the government party by increasing the political weight of small, rural states, which tended to vote for ARENA. The scheme of proportional representation was modified by doubling the minimum number of seats for each state to enhance the strength of smaller states. The scheme of representation was further altered so that representation was based on total population rather than registered voters. The government hoped to further strengthen its legislative support by counting illiterates in rural ARENA strongholds without enfranchising them. In part, the reform backfired because it failed to take into new account the mass migration of people into pro-opposition urban areas.

By 1979, the military's attempt to renew the party system by eradicating traditional personalistic factions had been played out. In November of that year, the government enacted the Law of Party Reform to undercut the MDB by playing on its factionalism. The ten-year suspension of political rights imposed on numerous opposition politicians had expired, and the 1979 political reform allowed their return to active politics. Politics as usual was reemerging and so were many of the old politicians. The new rules eased the restrictions on the formation of political parties, providing the opportunity for opposition politicians to escape the MDB umbrella and give their personalistic or ideological factions party standing. Furthermore, the reform also required that parties have "party" as part of their official title; this, it seemed, would force the MDB to abandon its old designation rendering even the rump organization hard to identify. Hence, the opposition was expected to dissolve into a gaggle of new parties from which the government party might be able to choose moderate, working partners.

The process did not proceed quite according to plan. While ARENA reemerged as the Partido Democrático Social (Social Democratic Party, or PDS), the MDB changed its name to the Partido do Movimento Democrático Brasileiro (Party of the Brazilian Democratic Movement, or PMDB), thus retaining its old identification. On the whole, the new party system preserved more cohesion for the opposition than the regime desired. The PMDB was composed of a number of ideological tendencies and figures who believed that a large, diverse party was the best vehicle for challenging the military government. A breakaway faction, the Partido Popular (Popular Party, or PP), continued for two years but then reintegrated into the PMDB. Several other new/old parties and leaders reemerged. Ivete Vargas, niece of the former president and original founder of the Partido Trabalhista Brasileiro (Brazilian Labor Party, or PTB), joined with former president Janio Quadros to establish another edition of the PTB. Leonel Brizola, brother-in-law and protégé of the deposed president, João Goulart, formed the Partido Democrático Trabalhista (Democratic Labor Party, or PDT). And a new party, which had grown from the grassroots, the Workers Party (PT), was led by Luiz Inácio da Silva, a new figure who had emerged since the coup.

By the time of João Batista Figueirdo's presidency (1980–1985), the *abertura* (political opening) had opened to the point where it would have been difficult to reverse without the risk of a serious upheaval. Furthermore, by means of a 1979 amnesty, the armed forces had seen to it that there would be no trials of military officers for human rights abuses. Even though the hard-liners, most closely associated with the Serviço Nacional de Informaçoēs (National Intelligence Service, or SNI), continued to try to disrupt the process, even their ex-chief, the new president, was committed to carrying it through.[19] By 1981, Brazil's economic growth (measured in terms of GDP per capita) was negative, and the cumulative decline from 1981 to 1984 was −8.9 percent (see Table 2.2). This gave added impetus to the middle-sector opposition as this group, once the beneficiary of the economic growth during the military government, saw itself falling again into the lower class.

Table 2.2 Rates of Economic Growth (GDP per capita)

Country	Year of Transition	1980	1981	1982	1983	1984	1981–1984 Accumulated
Argentina	1983	−0.9	−7.7	−6.6	1.4	−0.9	−11.8
Brazil	1985	4.8	−3.8	−1.3	−5.3	1.3	−8.9
Chile	1990	6.2	4.1	−15.7	−2.4	3.6	−11.2
Uruguay	1985	5.3	1.2	−10.3	−5.3	−3.5	−16.2

Source: Economic Commission for Latin America and the Caribbean

The ultimate state of electoral manipulation came during the preparation for the 1982 elections. According to the 1979 electoral law, the members of congress and six members from each state assembly were to serve as an electoral college for the president, who would assume office in 1985. To assure a PDS majority, the government added 59 new seats to the Chamber of Deputies in districts of PDS strength. More tellingly, the government introduced measures making it very difficult for opposition parties to compete effectively. Straight party voting was required for all six offices on the ballot, and the ballots were blank, containing only the spaces where the voter was required to write the name or identification number of candidates. Any mistake would void the entire ballot. The better-organized, patronage-supported PDS was strategically positioned to field candidates for all offices, gain support on local issues, and marshal its voters to run the gauntlet of confusing ballot procedures, while the opposition was poorly equipped to do the same. In addition, the media law, which had been put into effect before the 1978 election, limited campaigning during the last two months before the election. The president, however, continued to make liberal use of prime-time television. The electoral result, as expected, favored the PDS, but not overwhelmingly. Nonetheless, with 41 percent of the valid votes (less than the PMDB), the PDS seemed to be in comfortable control of the electoral college. But the prospect of victory proved an illusion.

The transition plan ran into two stumbling blocks: the growing popular distaste for the military government and the factionalism within the government party itself. Given the 1982 election results, the choice of the next president seemed to be an intra-PDS affair; hence, the real locus of decisionmaking was expected to be the 1984 PDS convention, which would select the party's nominee. The convention, which had hitherto restricted its role to ratifying the military's choice, showed promise of independence. It was that independence upon which Paulo Salim Maluf, a former governor of São Paulo State, intended to rely in his bid to secure his nomination in place of a nominee handpicked by the generals. With neither a popular following nor the support of the armed forces, he used a strategy he had employed to win the governorship in 1978. In early 1983, Maluf began to work on members in PDS local organizations likely to be influential at the convention, almost two years away. Although two other leading contenders eventually emerged, neither was able to gain the united backing of the military establishment or overcome Maluf's headstart.

The intraparty struggle was played out against the backdrop of growing popular discontent that made defections from the PDS and formation of new alliances more attractive. The opposition's initial thrust was to call for a change in the electoral system to allow for direct popular election of the president in 1984. Blocked in congress, their strategy was to put popular pressure behind the call. Rallies were held throughout the nation in early 1984, including a demonstration of 200,000 to 400,000 in São Paulo in January and a rally of up to one million in Rio de Janeiro in April.

The government held firm, hinting at a limited compromise—direct elections after 1985 or a consensus candidate—but it refused to concede on the fundamental point: open, direct elections in 1984. The government was forced to declare a state of siege to block demonstrations in Brasília, while congress was considering the government's own amendment on the question.

Nonetheless, one thousand protesters occupied congress on April 24. The government's amendment failed. Dissident members of the PDS accused Maluf of trying to buy the election and bolted the party in July, forming the Frente Liberal (Liberal Front, or FL) and issuing their own election manifesto.

These developments set the stage for the government's final attempt to finesse the election for the PDS. As 1984 progressed, it became increasingly evident that Maluf's nomination by the party would not secure him the presidency; defections from the PDS and popular pressure on members of the electoral college made it increasingly possible, finally almost inevitable, that the opposition coalition, united behind the candidacy of Tancredo Neves, would prevail. The carefully crafted system of manipulative machine politics had broken down, but the government had one last ploy; it attempted to force PDS members to vote for the party's nominee on the basis of party discipline, threatening them with loss of mandate for failure to support the nominee. The attempt was rebuffed by the supreme court. Tancredo Neves secured 480 votes to Maluf's 180 in the electoral college balloting on January 15, 1985. Neves was unable to assume the presidency, however, dying before he could be inaugurated. His running mate, José Sarney of the FL, assumed office instead. Sarney had been a long-time associate of the military and a former PDS member. In effect, after a series of tactical retreats, the armed forces had managed to salvage a strategic stalemate.

□ *Argentina (1982–1983)*

For much of the twentieth century, Argentina seemed to be the quintessential praetorian state in South America. For better than half a century, no elected civilian president transferred power peacefully to an elected successor. Although the primary antagonist of the armed forces in the 1930s was the Radical Civic Union (UCR), in the late 1940s a new political actor emerged: the Peronistas, or Partido Justicialista (PJ). Juan Domingo Perón, the eponymous founder of the movement, rose from the position of army colonel, heading a minor ministry of the military government, to president of the nation.

In political terms, the country was slipping into sclerosis. Since 1930, military and civilian governments had followed one another into office without either being able to consolidate a democratic or authoritarian regime. The closest approach to such consolidation occurred during the early 1950s, when Perón attempted to solidify his party's and his own hold on power by institutionalizing justicialismo as the nation's official ideology. The attempt foundered and Perón was replaced in a military coup in 1955, but Perón left his legacy: a labor movement and Peronist party that exercised a de facto veto over attempts by other civilian and military governments to consolidate an alternative system. By their strength at the polls when they were actually allowed to compete openly, or their ability to mobilize popular protests when they were not, they undermined the claims of non-Peronist governments to a credible mandate.

While Perón tried to cultivate the armed forces as well as the labor movement, his effort to Peronize the military backfired. It was regarded as a political attempt to deprive the armed forces of their professional status and their legitimate institutional prerogatives. Thus, Perón's legacy was also one of enduring antipathy between the armed forces and the somewhat nebulous Peronista movement (largely based on an internally divided labor movement). Although deposed in 1955, Perón returned to power in 1973, near the end of his life. He was seen by most Argentine factions as the only possible savior in a desperate national situation. Even the armed forces, who were at the end of their political and economic rope after another one of their periodic attempts at direct rule, acquiesced to his return. Perón survived only a year in the presidency, and upon his death, he was succeeded by his wife, the vice president.

The military government of the Proceso (officially, El Proceso de Reconstrución Nacional, or The Process of National Reconstruction) came to power in 1976 in a coup that removed Isabel Perón from the presidency. Under the Proceso, the military once again attempted to solve political and economic problems that had plagued Argentina for decades—and to solve them once and for all.

These problems were manifested in a number of persistent symptoms. In the decades of the 1960s and 1970s, Argentina's rate of per capita GDP growth was a sluggish 2.4 percent per annum,[20] while other countries in the region were experiencing dynamic growth. Argentina had failed to retain the position of economic dominance it had in the region in the 1950s, when a smaller but wealthier and more modern Argentina could well discount the economic and political weight of its larger but more backward neighbor, Brazil.

The economic and political problems that beset Argentina seemed to call for drastic action. In the words of a news publication, the country was "a first world country with third world management."[21] In 1976, the armed forces believed they were just the ones to take action.

The new regime tried to avoid some of the pitfalls of the Onganía military government of 1966–1970. Onganía had ruled over the armed forces as well as over society. He had not felt compelled to follow the advice or wishes of other senior military leaders. This isolation eventually led to his ouster by the armed forces themselves. The new military government of 1976 was collegial, structured with a military president (separate from the commanders in chief of the three armed services) and a junta, composed of these same chiefs. Presidential succession was to be regularized, with the president serving a fixed term. Such a structure seemed to assure adequate control for the armed forces as an institution. The policies of government ministers thus required the support of the military as an institution. If the armed forces were to bear the responsibility for the government under the Proceso, they wanted to have an effective influence over its councils as well.

The military undertook a number of policies that were ultimately its undoing. In the face of violence, much of which was perpetrated by groups formerly associated with the Peronist movement, it intensified repression begun under Isabel Perón's administration. The dirty war, as it was named, eventually caused the disappearance and presumed death of at least 8,960 people.[22] The systematic nature of the campaign required the involvement of a broad stratum of the officer corps. While the public was largely silent initially, justice for human rights violators eventually became a cause célèbre and a basis for popular mobilization against the regime.

The government undertook a policy of economic transformation, turning economic policy over to a team of civilian technocrats under the direction of José Antonio Martínez de Hoz. The thrust of its program was the opening of the economy, the control of inflation, and the overall rationalization of the structure of Argentine production, including limiting labor demands and privatizing the state sector. A restrictive monetary policy was established and interest rates were freed.

In December 1978, the team decided to control inflation by allowing the rate of revaluation of the peso to lag behind inflation, thus artificially lowering the price of imports. This was meant to have a shock effect on the inefficient industrial sector and inflationary expectations rampant in the economy. In a sense, the policy worked all too well: It first produced a consumer boom, made possible by the availability of relatively low-cost consumer goods, then the policy boomeranged. Unable to compete with imports, many Argentine firms went bankrupt. At the same time, the exchange rate policy exacerbated the country's balance-of-payments situation. By 1981, Martínez de Hoz was out. But the new team was unable to stimulate real growth. While GDP per capita fell significantly in 1980–1981, it was again strongly negative in 1982 and only recovered moderately in 1983–1984 (see Table 2.2).

The year 1981 also marked the transfer of power to a new military president, but it ended up producing a partial rupture of the regime's succession agreement. The general designated to assume the presidency, Roberto Viola, was eventually outmaneuvered by the new army commander, Leopoldo Galtieri, who obtained the office for himself. Contrary to the regime's initial terms of succession, General Galtieri retained his post as army commander in chief. Disagreement over economic policy and the succession helped widened the fissures in the regime; meanwhile, the social and political sectors reacted. The *multipartidaría* (multiparty group), composed of the old political parties, pressured for democratization, and the Madres (Mothers) de la Plaza de Mayo agitated persistently for an accounting of the disappeared.

The regime had one last recourse: nationalism. Argentine claims to the

Falkland/Malvinas Islands had gone unvindicated since the British seizure of the islands a century and a half before. By the 1960s, the United Kingdom seemed to be losing interest in the islands. British military presence diminished to a platoon of Royal Marines, the islands became more and more economically dependent on Argentina, only 400 miles away, and the British opened desultory negotiations with Argentina over the islands' eventual status. The Conservative Thatcher government, however, was unwilling to accede to a transfer of sovereignty and required that the wishes of the islanders, roughly fifteen hundred people of strongly pro-British sentiment, be respected. Argentina pledged to respect the interests of the islands' inhabitants but argued that the Malvinas, as Argentina called them, were rightly part of Argentina on the basis of historical claims and their geographic location on the continental shelf.

It was there that the matter rested when the military junta decided to activate plans to invade the islands in the early months of 1982. Initially, the attack appeared to be a master stroke. Argentina occupied the Malvinas, as well as other islands in the South Atlantic claimed by both nations. This was accomplished without a single British fatality and was meant to present the British government with a fait accompli. But the calculation of British acquiescence proved badly wrong. The British mounted an invasion to retake the islands. Neither the United States, with whom Argentine relations had improved under the Reagan administration, nor the Soviet Union, apparently anxious to weaken Western influence, provided meaningful diplomatic support for the Argentine cause. Instead, the United States, after posturing as an honest broker in the conflict, provided critical assistance to the UK, while the USSR dithered and provided little meaningful help in the United Nations Security Council.

The Argentine military badly mishandled its campaign to defend the islands. Forces that were too numerous and too poorly trained were sent to the islands; by and large, they and their commander remained passively in garrison as British forces landed and eventually reoccupied the islands. The only bright spot in the military record was the valiant attempt by the air force and naval aviation to repulse the British fleet, otherwise unchallenged by any naval combatants. The military commander was eventually court-martialed for dereliction of duty.

The fall of the islands sent a shock wave through Argentine politics. All the members of the junta, including the president, were forced to resign, and a caretaker military government was eventually installed. The armed forces attempted to negotiate an orderly transition and a guarantee of amnesty for military human rights violators. Failing to achieve the latter, a self-amnesty was proclaimed that had little chance of being respected by the successor civilian government.

Argentina represents the most precipitous return to elected government of the five cases. Even so, from the crisis provoked by the Malvinas debacle in June 1982 to accession of the civilian administration of Raúl Alfonsín in December 1983, there transpired a period of a year and a half. The military retreat from power was disorderly, but it was not a revolution. The military, its prestige and self-confidence badly battered, remained a force to be reckoned with even after it lost formal power.

□ Uruguay (1980–1985)

The establishment of a military regime in Uruguay in the 1970s represented a dramatic political reversal in a country that apparently had a strongly democratic political culture. For decades, Uruguay, with its prosperous agro-export economy, had supported a democratic political system and an extensive social welfare system as well. It seemed to be the Switzerland of South America, surrounded by more-backward or more-turbulent neighbors. Small in numbers and primarily European in origin, the population enjoyed the benefits of political tolerance and a military unused to political interventions. Uruguay seemed not to be a praetorian society at all, and the armed forces seemed obedient to Western norms of professionalism and political neutrality.

But the economic basis for democratic stability and Western-style civil-military relations had been undermined by developments going back to the 1950s. While in the 1944–1951 period economic growth averaged 5.4 percent per year, the end of the commodities boom thereafter caused stagnation in the agricultural sector. Although the economy as a whole continued to grow at a credible rate (averaging 3.0 percent) until the mid-1950s, this growth was based on a policy of import substitution implemented through multiple exchange rates, quotas, and tariffs designed to encourage local manufacture and discourage imports. From 1956 to 1967, the economy suffered periods of trade deficits, inflation, and widening budget deficits. The policy of inward-looking import substitution seemed to have reached its limits.[23]

Meanwhile, the political system seemed ill equipped to deal with the problem. From 1953 to 1968, Uruguay operated under a plural executive that was modeled after the Swiss multiple presidency. This constitutional arrangement weakened the ability of the executive to provide leadership in the face of declining circumstances. Even after the introduction of a strong executive, parties continued to be organized around factions that were able to preserve their identities even in presidential elections, thanks to an unusual ballot system. The ballot allowed for what amounted to a simultaneous party presidential primary and general election. Voters cast their votes for one of the candidates nominated by legally recognized factions within the parties. The winner was the candidate with the most votes from the party that received the most votes. Such a system promoted factional leaders at the expense of party unity and, in the 1971 elections, produced a president who received far fewer votes than the strongest vote-getter overall.

Decentralized party politics went hand in hand with a patronage system that controlled jobs in the extensive public sector.[24] Although in a time of diminished resources systemic change was needed, the political structure seemed better crafted for dividing up the spoils. Furthermore, as the economic situation continued to worsen and the political system stagnated, a substantial portion of the country's youth were radicalized. The Tupamaro movement emerged with revolutionary objectives and an urban guerrilla strategy.

The military followed the situation with growing distaste. Initially, it was divided along various lines. Hard-liners, distrustful of the politicians, favored a Brazilian solution; populists, also committed to a firm response by the armed forces, favored a Peruvian solution; while legalists were committed to maintaining Uruguay's traditional democratic system. In a short time, the legalists virtually disappeared.[25] The police, operating under temporary emergency measures adopted in the late 1960s, proved unable to stem the tide of violence, and in February 1973, the military presented an ultimatum to President Bordaberry.

The establishment of the military regime was a gradual process. In its ultimatum, the armed forces leadership demanded the elimination of corruption, the addressing of rural problems, and the establishment of the Consejo de Seguridad Nacional (National Security Council, or COSENA). The council was the instrument of the military commanders and was designed to advise the president on matters of national security. Later that year, COSENA advised and the president carried out an *autogolpe*—a coup by the executive against the democratic system. The president dissolved congress and ruled by decree. By 1976, Bordaberry himself was forced to resign, and the military imposed its own civilian candidate.[26] In 1976, fifteen thousand former politicians were banned, and the military retained a firm hold on the civil administration. Although they did not cultivate a new party or attempt to co-opt existing party patronage networks,[27] the armed forces continued to appoint civilians to the presidency until finally, in 1981, General Gregorio Alvarez, a leading figure throughout the militarization process, assumed the presidency.

The armed forces took over the battle against the Tupamaros from the police and brutally crushed the guerrillas. One hundred and sixty-four people disappeared—a relatively small number compared to Argentina's dirty war— and as many as fifty thousand people were, at one time or another, swept up into the repressive network. These victims suffered detention, imprisonment, and other forms of sanctions.[28]

A neoliberal economic program implemented under military tutelage began opening the Uruguay economy to global influences and removing many subsidies and controls. This stabilization program produced growth rates of 5 percent per annum from 1974 through 1980, providing legitimacy to a regime that had apparently solved deep-seated problems in the economy.

By 1981, however, the growth rate slowed considerably, and by the next year, the economy was in a steep decline (see Table 2.2). The second (1979) oil shock, the ending of the Argentine tourist boom, and the removal of subsidies from nontraditional exports had combined to send the economy into a tailspin. With these economic failures the regime lost its legitimacy. One sector after another was alienated from the government as it continued to pursue a hard-line neoliberal policy and refused to rescue failing enterprises or entire sectors of the economy.[29]

Contemporaneously with the regime's initial economic difficulties, the plan of the armed forces to regularize their role in government foundered. In the 1980 referendum, a military-drafted constitution failed to win popular support. The proconstitution forces were able to garner only 42.7 percent of the vote, even though they controlled most of the media and provided very little opportunity for the opposition to organize. The proposal called for the retention of the National Security Council, provided for an executive power to declare states of emergency without legislative approval, and required that the president be chosen by a single-candidate ballot after the nominee had been approved by both the traditional parties and the National Security Council.[30]

After the failed referendum, a protracted series of maneuvers and negotiations ensued. This process brought to light divisions within the military and the civilian opposition. The two traditional parties, the Colorados and Blancos, and the Frente Amplio (Broad Front, or FA) were unable to maintain a unified negotiating stance. Nevertheless, military moderates were able to secure the transition to a civilian government against hard-line opposition. Popular mobilizations also put pressure on the military to negotiate an acceptable transition. A key point in the transition was reached with the informal Naval Club Pact, supported by the military, the Colorados, and the Broad Front. It provided for:

- Presidential appointment of the service commanders from a list of nominees, three for the army and two for the navy and air force;
- The survival of the National Security Council as an advisory body—meeting at the request of the president—with a majority of government ministers;
- Legislative authority to vote a state of insurrection suspending guarantees of individual rights;
- A new mechanism to allow individuals to appeal government decisions to the courts;
- Trial by military courts for those arrested during a state of insurrection;
- A National Assembly elected in 1984 to act as a constituent assembly; and

- Submission to the people of any amendments in a plebiscite in November 1985.[31]

The elections of November 1984 resulted in a divided vote: Colorados—41 percent, Blancos—35 percent, and Broad Front—21 percent. The leading Blanco politician, Wilson Ferreira Aldunate, was still under the military-imposed ban and not allowed to stand for election. Authoritarian and neoliberal supporters of the military government did poorly. The leading Colorado politician, Julio Sanguinetti, assumed the presidency on March 1, 1985.

□ Chile (1983–1990)

Until the coup in 1973, Chile, like Uruguay, was a country in which democracy seemed to have taken firm root and the military seemed adverse to undertaking traditional Latin American interventions. By 1973, the military had tolerated a socialist-communist coalition government for three years. However, the country was becoming increasingly polarized by shortages, popular mobilizations, demonstrations and strikes, seizures of private property, and the formation of left-wing militias. The political right and center were ready to welcome a military coup. It came on September 11, 1973, and established a regime that many of the politicians who had originally welcomed the coup—especially those of the centrist Partido Democrático Cristiano (Christian Democratic Party, or PDC)—were not willing to accept.

In Chile, the armed forces assumed the ruler role with a vengeance. The military declared a political recess and within several years had developed an elaborate official presentation of the political transformation it wished to effect. During that same period, General Augusto Pinochet established himself as unquestioned leader and later president of the nation. Although the general professed his desire to return Chile to regular democratic rule, he made clear that this democracy would not be the sort that Chile had before. Pinochet's authoritarian democracy provided very little scope for political parties. Parties were not to serve as instruments of mass mobilization or interest articulation; rather, they were to represent political currents influential only in proportion to the propriety of their judgment.[32] Government would stand above party. Authoritarian democracy would avoid the naive pluralism that characterized liberal democracy; some political currents would be peremptorily excluded.

The "democratic" element in this system was decidedly plebiscitary in character. In 1978, the government used a referendum to inoculate itself against international criticism and provide a degree of legitimacy. In the face of widespread international condemnation of its human rights record, including four condemnations by the United Nations General Assembly, the government called for a vote of popular support. Voters were required to vote yes or no on the following proposition:

> In light of the international aggression unloosed against the government of our *patria*, I support President Pinochet in his defense of the dignity of Chile, and I reaffirm the legitimacy of the government of the Republic to lead sovereignly the process of institutionalization of the country.

To make the choice even clearer, the Chilean national flag headed the yes block on the ballot and the black anarchist flag headed the no block.[33] A similar maneuver was used in the 1980 referendum when the government called an election only one month before the actual balloting and allowed little opposition campaigning. Under such a system, the government had little trouble winning both votes.

The 1980 constitution was meant to be the capstone of the new institutionalization process. It provided for an extended transition period extending to 1989–1990, in which the powers of Pinochet as president and the military junta, composed of the four service commanders, as legislature were unchecked in any meaningful way. The final stage would be initiated by a plebiscite on the junta's nominee for president (presumably Pinochet). If the junta's candidate lost, a contested presidential election would follow. Under the new system, Marxist parties (or any parties advocating class struggle) were proscribed, the president was given a dominant position over the legislature, approximately one-third of the senate was appointed, the National Security Council was constitutionally recognized, and the service chiefs were not removable by the president for the first term. In addition, it was relatively easy for the president to suspend guarantees of individual rights under a number of various emergency provisions.

The regime's nemesis was not so much its political highhandedness as it was an economic crisis that galvanized the opposition into meaningful action. After an initial period of hesitation, the government had undertaken an extreme, neoliberal economic program: opening up the economy to foreign imports, attempting to place stringent controls on monetary emissions, wholesale privatization, and severe restrictions on organized labor. After a period of economic stabilization in the mid-1970s—the need for which could be attributed to the quadruple-digit inflation and growing economic chaos that characterized the end of the Allende period—Chile's GDP grew at an average annual rate of about 8 percent from 1979–1981. In 1982, however, the financial and import-induced prosperity burst; GDP declined by a precipitous 15.7 percent (see Table 2.2). Pinochet responded with a number of shake-ups in the economic team that resulted in the abandonment of Chile's scheme of fixed exchange rates and a partial abandonment of the low-tariff policy. Unemployment reached an official 20 percent; the inclusion of underemployment would have pushed the figure higher.

The regime had managed to maintain its political balance by developing an economic policy that brought prosperity to the upper and some of the middle sectors, by raising the twin specters of anarchy and communism should the opposition undermine it, and by dividing the opposition. While the regime could count on the passive support of much of the right, the center and left constituted a potential threat to its permanence. Under the precoup balance of political power, each of these divisions could garner about a third of the electorate's votes. Thus, unity between the center and left constituted a potential threat to the durability of the military regime. Divisions between the center and left were deep, however, especially after the PDC, the dominant centrist party, had supported a military coup against Allende, believing the PDC would be the beneficiary of a prompt return to civilian rule. After the coup, the government treated different sectors of the opposition differently. The PDC was accorded a certain amount of political space, despite the political recess, and had a limited degree of access to the public through party publications and occasionally the broadcast media. Member parties of the Allende coalition, Unidad Popular (Popular Unity, or UP), were singled out for the most intense repression. It was from their ranks that most of the detentions, disappearances, and exiles came.

The catalyst for mass opposition came not from the old political parties but from younger members of the labor movement; notable among these was Rodolfo Seguel of the copper miners' union. By early 1983, protests had spilled over into the broader society and a national day of protest was called for May 11, 1983. The protest movement produced a marked shift in the PDC position. Less than a year before the protest, the party president, Gabriel Valdes, ruled out a broadly based, multiparty coalition to pressure the government;[34] but after the initiation of protests, the PDC became a core member in the Alianza Democrática (Democratic Alliance, or AD), formed to pressure the government for reforms.

Protests were widespread and protesters used a variety of means. Three more national days of protest followed in the succeeding three months, and the government appeared to be buckling under the pressure applied by parties, unions, and a wide range of interest associations, including even some military officers. But there were cracks in the opposition's facade of unity. Labor's demands were directed at the replacement of the government by a democratic one, while such groups as the powerful truckers' association were content to negotiate with the existing government. Such divisions become apparent by June. These and other divisions among politicians could be exploited by the government.

Pinochet's appointment of a new interior minister, Sergio Onofre Jarpa, sent a signal that the government might be willing to begin early liberalization. Jarpa, an old-line Nationalist politician, was a figure well suited to open a dialogue with the opposition. His negotiating strategy seemed twofold: to divide the bulk of the politicians from the mass of the protesters and to exploit divisions among the politicians themselves. The possibility of dialogue enticed some members of the Alliance to call for the abandonment of the fifth national day of protest, scheduled for September. The left, especially the Socialists, was unwilling to call off the protests because it feared being cut off from its base of support in the *poblaciones* (the urban slums). While the Alliance dithered, Jarpa began discussions with leader of PRODEN, a slightly older, center-right group of opposition politicians. The Partido Comunista de Chile (Chilean Communist Party, or PCCh) and the Socialists formed a separate alliance, dubbed the Movimiento Democrático Popular (Popular Democratic Movement, or MDP), premised on hard-line opposition toward the government. Additionally, elements of the military, especially the air force, undertook discussions with the church and other elements of the opposition.

Little was accomplished. The Alliance broke off its tentative dialogue with the government while the government continued to adhere to the principle that democratization would have to follow the schedule in the 1980 constitution. The protests continued, but at a diminished tempo. Jockeying continued for the remainder of 1983 and 1984. Proregime soft-liners formed or refurbished a number of groups in general support of the regime's long-term objectives but supporting liberalization as the method for maintaining the regime. According to one local observer, they sought to map a "Brazilian road to democracy,"[35] perhaps an unfortunate reference given the later, more precipitous moves to democracy in Brazil. In late 1984 and 1985, however, the proregime hard-liners gained the upper hand in the government's councils in the face of mounting pressure from the poblaciones, unions, and students. A state of siege was declared and repression escalated. In February 1985, Jarpa resigned and was replaced by Ricardo García Rodríguez, a lawyer without previous political experience. Although the opposition continued to try to advance the timetable for elections and speed up the liberalization process, the government held firm to its position that the 1980 constitution had to be respected.

The 1988 presidential plebiscite found the government in a favorable economic position as rates of growth had largely recovered from the 1982–1983 collapse. The proregime politicians, however, were in a state of disarray. Pinochet's antipolitical attitudes prevented him from cultivating a new party on the right or making the old Nationalist Party the regime's political vehicle. Instead, he allowed various sectors of the right to go their own ways, refusing to endorse the efforts of one of them in preference to the others. Hence, the right divided into precoup conservatives, essentially pragmatic in their orientation, and a more ideological new right that supported neoliberal economics and a latter-day variety of corporatism.

Meanwhile, the opposition parties formed a new united front, the Concertación, aimed at defeating the regime at its own electoral game; but the Marxist left remained outside the organization. Cooperation with the right was essential because voter registration was costly for the poor and a communist-socialist call to boycott the process, though it might have helped delegitimize the results, would have assured an easy progovernment victory. The center would thus have been trapped between the left's demands for overthrow of the government and the regime's claim, however flawed, of legality. Cooperation between the Concertación and left-wing opposition parties outside it, however, set the stage for defeating the military regime at its own game.

Thanks to the vigilance of the opposition and international observers, the plebiscite on a new, eight-year term for Pinochet (as expected he was the regime's candidate) was conducted honestly. The general lost by a 54 to 43 percent margin. There had apparently been a government plan to add one million votes to the yes tally if the results were unfavorable. The plan was reportedly opposed by the police, air force, and some progovernment politicians.[36] Any possibility of stealing the election probably vanished when the air force commander admitted that the opposition had won. The rest of the junta could do nothing.[37] The depth of the divisions in the military over the election can be gauged by rumors that 40 percent of the *caribineros* (the militarized national police) voted against the government.[38]

Fresh from its victory, the Concertación wanted to speed the pace of what it hoped would be democratization and not just a liberalization of an authoritarian regime that would retain its central character. Some movement in the direction of a real change in the system was necessary to keep the left and center together. Democratization involved changing a number of terms of the 1980 constitution: the ban on Marxist parties; the structure and authority of the National Security Council; the powers of the president; the number of nonelected members of the senate; and the continued tenure of service commanders despite the wishes of the newly elected president.

In December 1988, prospects for constitutional change in Chile improved with the announcement by the Renovación Nacional (National Renovation Party, or RN), headed by Sergio Onofre Jarpa, that it favored constitutional reform that coincided in several areas with the amendments proposed by the left-center coalition. The RN and PDC also indicated that they favored the continuation of the current economic model with increased wages and basic social services.[39] Contradicting previous assertions that he would never permit the modification of the 1980 constitution, Pinochet allowed his interior minister, Carlos Cáceres, to meet with the opposition to discuss constitutional reform. Even before the March 14 meeting, Pinochet hinted at ending the ban on Marxist parties, shortening the presidential term to four years, and abolishing the president's power to exile opponents and close congress. He also indicated he might loosen the armed forces' grip on the National Security Council, which was empowered to overrule the president on national security issues.[40]

On April 28, Cáceres called a plebiscite for nineteen proposed reforms to the constitution. The most important were:

- Article 8 (banning Marxism and class struggle) was to apply to acts, not ideas;
- The controller-general was included in the membership of the National Security Council, equalizing civilian and military representation;
- The council's powers were toned down to "making known" to the president, congress, and the constitutional tribunal its opinion regarding threats to national security;
- The presidential term was reduced to four years with only one re-election; and
- Presidential power to dissolve the Chamber of Deputies was eliminated.

Not included were reforms reducing the number of appointed senators and limiting the length of time commanders in chief could hold their positions.[41] Nor did the list include other changes originally agreed to by the PDC and RN: virtual removal of all nonelected members of the senate; expansion of the membership of both legislative chambers; and easier mechanisms for constitutional reform. The reforms were approved by an overwhelming margin.

The plebiscite on constitutional reform set the stage for presidential elections in December. The Concertación managed to hold together and nominate a single presidential candidate, a conservative Christian Democrat, Patricio Aylwin, as well as a single slate of nominees for the legislature. The right, however, nominated two candidates; the leading one was Hernán Büchi, the government's economics minister. The right was also unable to unify its legislative slates. The election produced a 55 percent vote for Aylwin, assuring him victory on the first round. Aylwin, however, faces a senate in which the right may be able to block the passage of measures critical to the government. Moreover, Pinochet has expressed his intention to remain as commander in chief of the army and has taken a hard line against any human rights trials.

■ THE ARMED FORCES AFTER THE TRANSITION

In each case, the capacity of the armed forces to protect their interests and influence national policy has been influenced by particular developments in each country. Some of the different factors affecting this capacity are listed in Table 2.3. The last four columns of the table are an indication of the military's prestige and capacity to control events.

Table 2.3 Characteristics of Military Regimes

Country	Duration of Regime	Economic and Social Policy	Result of Policy	Duration of Transition	Transition Pact	Military Timetable
Argentina	1976–83 (7 years)	Neoliberal	Failure	18 months	No	No
Brazil	1964–85 (21 years)	State Capitalist	Qualified success	5 years	Informal	No
Chile	1973–90 (17 years)	Neoliberal	Qualified success	7 years	No	Yes
Peru	1968–80 (12 years)	Leftist Corporatist	Failure	6 years	Informal	Yes
Uruguay	1973–85 (12 years)	Neoliberal	Failure	5 years	Yes	(No)

The worst-case scenario from the perspective of the military is one in which it is compelled to leave power precipitously in the face of its own regime's policy failures and where it exercises little control over the transition timetable or the prerogatives of the incoming civilian government. Even the Argentine case, the worst of the five from the military's point of view, is not quite worst case. The best-case scenario for the military is a staged transition, the timing and outcome of which are controlled by the armed forces. Such a transition would amount to the completion of the military's original project. Two of our cases come close. Had the Chilean junta nominated a proregime civilian in place of Pinochet in 1988, and had the candidate been able to win a fair election, the armed forces would have been in a stronger position to stymie attempts to modify the 1980 constitution. The process might have lead to the true authoritarian democracy that Pinochet had claimed to be his goal. The Brazilian case also comes close to the military's most desirable. But for the internal disarray of the PDS and the manner in which José Sarney assumed office, the transition process went as well as the armed forces could have expected.

The existence of an amnesty law prior to the transfer of power to civilians is not a critical feature in the transition process if the law is not supported by a formal or informal agreement between the armed forces and civilian politicians or if military prestige is low. Where such an informal pact existed, as in the case of Brazil, or where the armed forces retained a significant degree of influence, as in Chile, civilian regimes face significant difficulties in reopening the human rights issue. On the other hand, the Argentine military regime's self-amnesty was easily swept aside by the incoming civilian administration because the military lacked the political capacity to sustain it.

The results of the transition process are critical for the ensuing process of democratic consolidation. In accordance with the dictum of Thomas Hobbes that "the reputation of power is power," the success or failure of the armed forces in controlling the transition process will have a significant effect on their ability to influence events immediately thereafter. Hence, the military's impact on the transition can serve as a rough measure of their initial prestige—their reputation of power.[42] For our five cases, military prestige ranges from low in Argentina to moderate-high in Brazil and Chile. In the Argentine case, the armed forces had the ability to retard the pace of events but lacked the capacity to form a civil-military pact or otherwise restrict the policy of the incoming civilian administration. In the latter two instances, the armed forces controlled the pace and nature of the transition process but were unable to secure succession for their civilian protégés. (A country-by-country distribution is found in Table 2.4.)

With variations in each country, then, the transfer of power from military to civilian governments placed at least a limited amount of initiative in civilian hands. However, the initial balance between civilians and the armed forces is likely to be temporary, and the commitment of the armed forces to civilian rule is likely to be tactical or provisional. Thus, the transfer of power merely sets the stage for the struggle to consolidate democracy.

Table 2.4 Prestige of the Armed Forces

Country	Rating
Argentina	Low
Peru	Moderate
Uruguay	Moderate
Brazil	Moderate-High
Chile	Moderate-High

■ NOTES

1. Weber, p. 125.

2. Alain Rouquié, "Demilitarization and the Institutionalization of Military-Dominated Polities in Latin America," in Guillermo O'Donnell et al., vol. 3, *Comparative Perspectives*, pp. 110–112.

3. Linz, 1978, pp. 18–23, defines efficacy as "the capacity of a regime to find solutions to the basic problems facing any political system," while effectiveness is "the capacity to implement policies formulated, with the desired results." His definition of legitimacy is somewhat different from mine. For him, legitimate government is the least evil of available alternatives.

4. For a discussion of the distinction between liberalization (providing more political freedom within a structure still dominated by the armed forces) and democratization (the establishment of elected, civilian government with full authority to deal with all social and economic issues), see Guillermo O'Donnell and Philippe C. Schmitter, "Defining Some Concepts," in O'Donnell et al., vol. 4, *Tentative Conclusions About Uncertain Democracies*, pp. 7–8; Stepan, 1988, p. 6; and George A. Lopez and Michael Stohl, "Liberalization and Redemocratization in Latin America: The Search for Models and Meanings," in Lopez and Stohl, p. 3.

5. Pion-Berlin, 1989b, p. 424.

6. Stepan, 1978, pp. 146–147.

7. Ibid., pp. 136–137.

8. Víctor Villanueva, "Peru's 'New' Military Professionalism: The Failure of the Technocratic Approach," in Gorman, p. 162.

9. Robert H. Swansbrough, "Peru's Diplomatic Offensive," in Hellman and Rosenbaum, p. 122.

10. Grayson, p. 62.

11. Villanueva, op. cit., pp. 165–166.

12. Pion-Berlin, 1989b, pp. 154–155.

13. Julio Colter, "Military Interventions and 'Transfer of Power to Civilians' in Peru," in O'Donnell et al., vol. 2, *Latin America*, p. 153.

14. Stepan, 1971, p. 184.

15. Dillon Soares, pp. 114–115.

16. O'Donnell.

17. Dillon Soares, pp. 119–120.

18. Moreira Alves, pp. 153–166, 191–210.

19. For a discussion of the dynamic between the hard-liners and the soft-liners, see Stepan, 1988, pp. 35–44.

20. International Bank for Reconstruction and Development, *World Development Report*, 1981.

21. "Don't Cry for Me, Weimar," *Economist*, April 29, 1989, pp. 71–72.

22. Argentine National Commission on the Disappeared, p. 284. Other estimates range up to 30,000.

23. Hanson and de Melo, pp. 478–480.

24. Charles G. Gillespie, "Uruguay's Transition from Collegial Military-Technocratic Rule," in O'Donnell et al., vol. 2, *Latin America*, pp. 174–176.

25. Ronald H. MacDonald, "The Struggle for Normalcy in Uruguay," *Current History*, February 1982, pp. 69–70.

26. Ronald H. MacDonald, "Redemocratization in Uruguay," in Lopez and Stohl, pp. 178–180.

27. Gillespie, op. cit., p. 179.

28. "Uruguay Human Rights Amnesty Shows Fragility of Civilian Rule," *Christian Science Monitor*, December 30, 1986, p. 10.

29. Gillespie, op. cit., pp. 179–180.

30. Ibid., p. 181.

31. Ibid., pp. 189–190.

32. Pinochet, p. 8.

33. Thomas G. Sanders, "The 1980 Constitution and Political Institutionalization in Chile," in Handelman and Sanders, p. 68.

34. *Latin American Weekly Report*, June 25, 1982, p. 4.

35. *Latin American Regional Reports: Southern Cone Report*, May 25, 1984.

36. FBIS, "Post-Plebiscite Meetings, Statements Detailed," *Que Pasa*, October 20, 1988, FBIS-LAT-88-232, December 2, 1988, pp. 41–45.

37. Clara Germani, "Chile's Remarkable Triumph," *Christian Science Monitor*, October 7, 1988, p. 1.

38. "That Was Nice, Now the Hard Bit," *Economist*, October 15, 1988, pp. 50–51.

39. Tim Frasca, "Prospects Brighten for Negotiations in Chile," *Christian Science Monitor*, December 15, 1989, p. 9.

40. "Did I Say That?" *Economist*, March 18, 1989, p. 41.

41. "Cáceres Gets His Way on Reform," *Latin American Weekly Report*, May 11, 1989, p. 5; FBIS, "Cáceres Proposes Constitutional Amendments," Santiago Domestic Service, April 19, 1989, FBIS-LAT-89-082, May 1, 1989, pp. 43–46.

42. This concept of prestige obviously relies on qualitative judgments rather than quantitative measures, such as public opinion poll data. However, I believe the qualitative judgment is better for a number of reasons. First, it attempts to assess ability to influence rather than popularity. While both are fleeting, the latter is more so. Second, survey data taken under conditions where repression is a possible threat is of questionable utility. For example, in a 1987 Chilean poll, 86 percent of respondents told survey-takers that it was unwise to reveal your political opinions to strangers. "Opposition Gives Regime High Odds," *Latin American Weekly Report*, October 1, 1987, p. 3.

3■
Democracy Versus the Post–National Security State

The civilian governments newly established in Latin America during the 1980s face the challenge of consolidating democracy. They have inherited from their military predecessors the task of establishing stable regimes in the face of long-standing traditions of praetorian politics.

■ TASKS OF DEMOCRATIC CONSOLIDATION

A stable democracy must meet a number of requisites, the achievement of which challenges the traditional pattern of Latin American civil-military relations in a number of basic ways. In a democracy, the society must first control the state, and then the state, in turn, must regulate the diverse interests within society. The position of the state in the middle of this formula highlights its critical role: The state must be properly organized both to respond to the popular will and to regulate divergent interests.[1]

□ *Institutionalizing Legitimacy*

Democracy means popular sovereignty. Democratic governments must achieve the general and enduring acceptance, by all significant sectors of a society, that the democratic *form* of government is the morally proper one for the society (they must achieve legitimacy). These sectors must accept the principle that society, as a whole, ought to control the state for the general interest. As an essential concomitant of this, these governments must help create structures that adequately embody this principle of popular sovereignty (they must achieve *effective* legitimacy).

Democratic demands can be forwarded by mass mobilizations. To a degree, the transitions to elected governments were made possible because pressure from society at large reinforced the politicians' demands for the transfer of power from the military to an elected government. Yet, it is impossible to sustain a high level of popular mobilization indefinitely.

Thus, a mobilized populace cannot serve as the primary linkage between society and the state.[2] The maintenance of democracy requires the strengthening of other more systematic links between the political leadership and the members of civil society.

A sketch of the full range of activities involved in institutionalizing such linkages is beyond the scope of this book. We do, however, consider at least one issue most salient to civil-military relations: the ability of the armed forces to interpose themselves between civilian political leaders and the society at large. The nature of military governments, and the transition process itself, involve such interpositions. Under military governments, the armed forces substitute their will for that of the majority as expressed through the electoral process. In the transition process, the negotiations that typically occur represent interpositions of a more limited kind. They limit the freedom of action of the new civilian governments. Democratic consolidation requires emancipation from these restrictions.

In brief, the structures of democratic political life—constitutions, interest groups, and parties—have existed in Latin America, hand in hand with a nondemocratic ethos. In the past, key sectors, including the armed forces, have been willing to abandon democratic forms when they believed their interests were at stake. Thus, the present adherence to democratic procedures may prove to be only temporary. The new democracies face the problem of transforming this current widespread acquiescence to democratic norms into an enduring belief in the legitimacy of democracy. To do this they must build functioning democratic institutions.

□ *Developing Effectiveness*

For democracy to be stable, democratic governments must be effective. Yet democratic governments in Latin America frequently have a reputation for ineffectiveness that is, almost as frequently, well deserved. Although military regimes lacked legitimacy, the armed forces often retained a reputation for competence that outlived their policy failures when compared to their democratic successor. For example, according to a São Paulo survey taken in early 1989, although 70 percent of respondents expressed support for democracy and only 20 percent desired a return to military rule, 58 percent thought life in Brazil had indeed been better under the military.[3] In December 1989, grafitti proclaiming "Viva Pinochet!" appeared in Buenos Aires as the Argentine government failed to master the economy's slide into hyperinflation.[4]

Furthermore, a reputation for incompetence has damaged the parties of presidential incumbents. In Peru's presidential elections in both 1985 and 1990, the political party of the presidential incumbent ran a poor third with 16 percent of the vote. Argentina's Radical Civic Union (UCR) president had to transfer power to his Peronist successor five months early because of a lack of popular confidence caused by the serious mid-1989 financial crisis. In addition, the 1989 elections in Brazil represented a solid rejection of the Sarney administration when the parties of the governing coalition became virtual footnotes in the presidential election statistics.

This lack of effectiveness has disturbing implications for the long-term process of consolidating democratic legitimacy. Yet, when governments attempt to reform ineffective state procedures, they often face powerful opposition from private interests, entrenched civilian bureaucrats, and the armed forces.

□ Assuring Equality Before the Law

Democracy means that all citizens are equal before the law. While the government is supposed to respond to the popular will in crafting general policies, the administration of those policies ought to be done in a neutral and unbiased manner. This neutrality of the state vis-à-vis individuals never reaches the Rousseauian ideal, which states that interests ought to have no impact on either the enactment or implementation of policy. As a practical matter, the state is not and cannot be completely neutral.

Latin American practice, however, intensifies the problem of lack of neutrality. Latin American practice ignores democratic norms by privatizing the state—creating a system of formal and informal privilege. In accordance with the corporatist tradition, the Latin American state often treats different groups differently—and blatantly so—without even the appearance of nominal state neutrality. Social programs are frequently tailored and administered for the benefit of specific sectors. For instance, even when urban labor obtained the right to organize, that right was not immediately extended to the rural population. Access to benefits, supposedly guaranteed by law, often requires political connections. The beneficiaries often are not members of the general public but readily identifiable employees, suppliers, and buyers of the subsidized products of the state sector.[5] Furthermore, the extensive role of the state as employer and producer in such countries as Brazil tends to negate the formulation that the state sector acts for public purposes. The armed forces compound this problem both by defending certain privileged sectors and by being a privileged sector itself.

□ Establishing Civilian Control of the Armed Forces

The armed forces should not and cannot be excluded from the discussion of public policy in which they have a reasonable claim to expertise; however, the range and character of military discourse must be altered. Democracy requires that the armed forces, as well as other nonelected sectors of the executive branch, be subordinated to and governed by elected officials. Modern democratic theory provides a formula for establishing such control over the military and other recalcitrant sectors of the executive branch: a single, elected chief executive who controls a civil service that in turn is governed by legal and bureaucratic norms. The chief executive is supposed to make policy, while the bureaucracy—civil and military—is supposed to execute or administer that policy. The bureaucracy itself is organized and recruited on the basis of technical competence within narrowly defined administrative fields. In other words, such a system subjects the military to civilian oversight and the rule of law.

However, the application of this politics-versus-administration distinction in Latin American civil-military relations encounters two problems. First, as in any environment, the distinction is clearer in theory than practice. Second, the conception of the armed forces as a bureaucratic entity applies only imperfectly in the Latin American context. By tradition, the Latin American military is a corporate entity with roots going back to medieval Iberian practice. It is a holder of power, a guarantor of the established order; it is emphatically not an anonymous cog in an impersonal bureaucratic machine. It possesses a certain status and has privileges that it believes must be respected. This status is buttressed by long-standing practices and legal codes that often render military officers exempt from the system of civilian justice.

The advent of the national security doctrine has only served to increase the military's privileged corporate status. The armed forces have often secured hyper-representation of their interests within state councils. The creation of national security councils with dominant military participation, the frequent continuance of separate ministries for each armed service, the staffing of ministerial and secretarial posts with military officers, the control of state and parastatal entities by the armed forces or their administration by uniformed officers, and the establishment of military-dominated domestic intelligence services place the armed forces in a strong bureaucratic position. The military frequently has the mission of suppressing strikes or public disturbances, fighting insurgents or terrorists, and providing a modicum of law and order in outlying regions. The existence of such missions provides the military with the opportunity to operate with a high degree of autonomy regardless of the intentions of the law or the chief executive's desires.

In such situations, the armed forces' perspective of what constitutes proper economic policy and good social order, or who is the internal enemy, can lead them to favor capital over labor, large landholders over campesinos and indigenous peoples, or conservative interests over public-sector interests. Thus, democratic consolidation requires that the role of the armed forces be defined in such a way as to minimize the possibility of such abuse of power. Furthermore, democratic consolidation requires civilian oversight via mechanisms legally and technically competent to assure that the armed forces function as a loyal and subordinate element of the state.

■ **THE SOURCES OF
MILITARY INTRANSIGENCE**

The requisites just described conflict in many ways with the corporatist tradition in Latin America. The establishment of fully democratic procedures would undercut the traditional political role of the armed forces. Hence, policies based on such dictates are inherently controversial and risky. Students and practitioners of Latin American politics may not wish to see them enacted, or may wish to see them enacted only with considerable restrictions.

Moreover, regardless of the attitude of the public or politicians, the armed forces are likely to see efforts toward establishing a complete democracy in a different light from that of most civilians. They are likely to defend the prerogatives of what I have termed post–national security states. Hence, efforts to consolidate democracy, subordinate the armed forces to constitutional authority, and define their role in a narrow manner will often threaten or appear to threaten military interests.[6] While the armed forces may be unable or unwilling to push back the clock and reestablish military governments, they retain interests at variance with the dictates of democratic consolidation.

□ *Institutional Integrity*

The demand for self-governance is characteristic of professionalized military institutions in Western Europe and North America as well as in Latin America. The most critical institutional interest for the military is the integrity of the military institution itself. The norm of professionalism requires that the armed forces should be largely self-governing in matters pertinent to their particular expertise. Huntington lists them as follows: first, in the organizing, equipping, and training of the armed forces; second, in the planning of military activities; and, third, in directing military operations in and out of combat.[7] This listing of professional military concerns is somewhat ambiguous since professionalism is compatible with civilian oversight of major policies affecting the military. Hence, the civilian leadership can determine the level of armament although military professionals provide advice.

A similar relationship applies in determining the organization and operation of the armed forces. It is normal for civilian governments to appoint the top echelons of the high command or to ratify military recommendations in this regard. From a professional perspective, however, the political role ought to be strictly limited or it constitutes the politicization of the armed forces by substituting political for technical criteria. Moreover, from the standpoint of many members of the officer corps, the expansion of civilian oversight, within limits normal by international standards, may seem to be politicization if it exceeds traditional national practices.

Although the interpretation of the precise dividing line between legitimate civilian oversight and politicization does differ from country to country and sector to sector, it is worth noting there are certain actions that have typically provoked military intervention. The armed forces have overturned governments for actions that, in part, threatened military discipline (Brazil in 1964 and Chile in 1973); they have intervened, in part, because the government made senior military appointments without reference to seniority and militarily defined merit (Brazil in 1964 and Argentina in 1930); and they have threatened the civilian government when reorganization threatened their interests (Peru in 1987).

□ Military Caste Privileges

Latin American armed forces have retained privileges not generally recognized as a necessary part of professionalism. These privileges are, more than anything else, remnants of the medieval Iberian tradition.[8] Among these privileges is the exemption of military officers from trial by civilian courts even when charged with civilian crimes. While this military privilege may have significant effects in inhibiting civilian oversight of the military, even more serious today is the protection it provides to members of the armed forces and the institution as a whole against prosecutions for serious human rights violations. The number of these violations, many of which are attributable to the armed forces, is significant.[9]

The military has also secured other privileges and career opportunities. Officership includes certain perquisites, among which are housing, orderlies, servants, and access to special stores. In many countries, the armed forces have also played a significant role in the management of the arms industry, shipping, and transportation as well as ports and communications. While these activities are hardly an essential part of the military's role as understood in the First World, they constitute important career opportunities for officers and a means for the armed forces as an institution to influence or control civilian policy.

□ The Military Budget

The military budget is another area of critical interest to the armed forces. Adequate budgetary resources are required for an adequate national defense, the maintenance of military pay and perquisites, and the continuance of prestige projects. However, adequacy is partly a matter of perception. Although budgetary stringency would threaten the survival of the armed forces only in the most extreme cases, relatively low budgets affect morale and the military's ability to execute its missions.

By and large, the overall size of the defense budget is beyond the direct control of the armed forces in civilian regimes. Even the military ownership of firms doing a substantial amount of business in the civilian sector cannot guarantee a method of funding the military budget completely independent of civilian oversight. For example, in Argentina, such firms account for a considerable percentage of the state's budget deficit.[10] It is possible, however, to finance domestic intelligence operations and other special projects without direct legislative review. This can be done by a variety of means ranging from hidden ownership of supposedly private companies to siphoning money from the civilian to the military budget.[11] Yet, as these undertakings become more visible and costly, they may be impossible to hide from general public scrutiny.

□ Military Control of the Civilian Population

The exercise of military control over the civilian population involves a multitude of different aspects. The most obvious and direct aspect of military control exists in emergency zones in countries facing persistent guerrilla problems, where very frequently the armed forces assume general police powers. There are a variety of states of emergency provided for in Latin American constitutions and statutes. Under them, the military's powers can include: the establishment and military enforcement of curfews; searches, seizures, and detentions (sometimes without cause); trial of civilians by courts-martial; the creation and military direction of model villages to control peasants in guerrilla areas; and the development of military-directed civil defense patrols. In a recent instance in Colombia, the military received the legal power to act as public prosecutor and judicial police where such judicial officials were not available.[12] Faced with insurgencies, civilian governments may find it difficult to deny the military significant police powers and yet provide little civilian judicial scrutiny.

The military may also exercise functions under the rubric of civic action that are only military in scope if one defines nation building and winning psychological support for the military/government as a proper military mission. Perhaps an extreme instance of such an expansion of the military role is the Salvadoran army's assumption of the task of coordinating and distributing earthquake aid.[13] Although the armed forces may not be the most appropriate institution organizationally for executing nation-building tasks, this role expansion not only is commensurate with typical bureaucratic propensities but also provides a means of political influence and control.

The internal defense mission and the national security doctrine have provided a rationale for military intelligence services to assume functions quite different from those associated with external defense. The intelligence services have gone far beyond surveillance and the compilation of information; at times, they have infiltrated businesses, universities, labor unions, and political parties.

□ *Special Programs*

In a number of countries, most notably Brazil and Argentina, the armed forces have undertaken a number of autonomous projects of unusual importance. Nuclear programs provide the most dramatic examples. While denying their intent to build an atomic bomb, both the Argentine and Brazilian armed forces have undertaken costly programs of nuclear research leading to the mastery of the fuel cycle (the production of enriched uranium necessary for building reactors or weapons) and, in the case of Brazil, the preparation of a nuclear detonation test site. Regardless of the concerns expressed by the Sarney administration in Brazil and the Alfonsín administration in Argentina, neither country has ratified global or regional nonproliferation treaties or bilateral treaties guaranteeing the nondevelopment of nuclear weapons. The rationalizations given for these programs seem disingenuous. For example, spokesmen for Brazilian nuclear programs have been adamant that their programs are primarily for peaceful purposes and label international attempts to limit proliferation as disguised attempts by the nuclear club to limit the commercial opportunities of others.

□ *Evaluation*

The motivations and interests behind the resistance of the armed forces to change are various. First, the armed forces want to preserve their institutional integrity. This means they need to maintain internal discipline and control within the armed forces themselves; they need to secure governmental adherence to the principle of promotion by merit and seniority; and they need to assure civilian respect for the professional judgment of the armed forces. These are typical requisites for preserving military professionalism as such. Second, as bureaucratic entities the armed forces want salaries and official perquisites, military appointments to governmental posts not requiring uniformed officers, and a substantial military budget. Third, the armed forces want to continue internal security and counterinsurgency missions—the new professionalism. Proponents of the new professionalism believe it is essential for the national interest that the armed forces have authority to perform certain functions: surveillance of civilians, administrative and judicial control of the civilian populations when a serious threat of internal subversion exists, and military involvement in a broad range of other policy decisions.

■ RESOURCES OF MILITARY INTRANSIGENTS

The coup d'état is the most striking form of military intervention against civilian governments, but it far from the only or even the most normal method.[14] The armed forces, or sectors within them, can use a host of methods to influence or control policy. These range from the legal, using routine administrative channels, to the violent and illegal, of which the coup is the extreme example. Each method has certain advantages and entails certain risks for those who employ it.

□ *The Coup d'État—Golpe de Estado*

The direct replacement of a civilian government by force of arms—the classic coup d'état—is both the most effective means for changing policy in the direction favored by the armed forces as well as the riskiest method for effecting that change. In the short term, coup plotters face problems typical of any conspiracy. The need for secrecy conflicts with the need to make their intentions known to potential collaborators. The need for careful planning, lest plans misfire, runs counter to the need for immediate action, lest the government discover the plot. In addition, there is the overarching fear that the established order has the resources to beat off attempts to establish something new.[15] Failure could lead to the severest professional and legal sanctions.

It is not surprising, then, that successful coups normally occur only when certain preconditions have been met that minimize short-term risks. Basically, the coup leaders must have relative assurance that the civilian government will be unable to defend itself. This, in turn, means the plotters must be assured that the armed forces as a whole will support or at least accede to the coup, and that the coup will be supported by some civilian sectors and acquiesced to by a majority of society. A common scenario is a civilian-military precoup coalition where civilians take the initiative in calling for a coup.

The seizure of power itself is conducted as rapidly as possible and primarily involves the use of ground units stationed near the capital and other important governmental and economic centers. The mission of these troops is to seize government officials and offices as well as communication and transportation centers. The rapidity of the coup is meant to confront potential civilian and military opponents with a fait accompli. The effectiveness of this typical coup strategy means that, in many cases, successful coups are anticipated long before they actually occur. Potential plotters wait until the political situation guarantees adequate civilian support before seeking out possible collaborators. Not all coups follow this pattern. For example, the slow-moving coup against the civilian government in Uruguay that led to the closing of congress in 1973 and the removal of the president in 1976 looked more like a palace revolt than a classic military coup. In effect, the military exercised an informal vote of no confidence and implicitly threatened to use force without ever having to use it.

The long-term risks of a coup include the nonlegitimation or early delegitimation of the government newly installed by the armed forces and strains within the military itself. These risks are not as easily assessed or minimized, but they become a key consideration when the military intends to assume a long-term ruler role. Various tactics have been tried to mitigate these risks: installing a civilian government or figurehead (Uruguay in 1973–1981 and Argentina in 1961–1963); minimizing direct involvement by the armed forces in the government (Argentina in 1968–1970); assuring the collegial participation of the armed forces in the government (Argentina in 1976–1983 and Uruguay in 1973–1985); cultivating a new mass movement or party (Peru in 1968–1975); or co-opting existing political forces (Brazil in 1965–1985). None of these tactics has been markedly successful. They have bought time but have not immunized the new regime against eventual collapse. Thus, the long-term risks have had a chilling effect on military coups.

□ Barracks Revolts

If a coup d'état is a direct strike against the government with some reasonable hope of immediate success, a barracks revolt represents an attempt to change the government or policy by armed forces members not so well positioned as typical coup leaders. While a coup often has the connivance of senior military leaders, a barracks revolt is often led by garrison commanders or their subordinates. While a classic coup involves heavily armed ground forces near the capital, a barracks revolt may only involve provincial units or units of limited combat potential. If the revolt is directed toward the replacement of the government, it is a true revolt. If it is directed against specific government policies that are supported by the high command, it is really a mutiny.

Barracks revolts are a symptom of military unrest. While they seldom succeed in their immediate objective, like general strikes in the civilian society, they put the government on record that its policies have produced significant dissatisfaction. In fact, this dissatisfaction has to be great enough to induce some officers to risk their careers and face potential legal sanctions. From the point of view of the high command, the barracks revolt is a double-edged sword. Even when senior commanders are sympathetic to the goals of the rebels and may welcome pressure on the civilian government to accede to them, such rebellion strikes at the core of the military ethos. It is an act of insubordination, it undermines discipline, and it constitutes an explicit or implicit criticism of the high command itself. While none of the five countries we are focusing on had a coup or serious coup threat in the 1980s, Argentina suffered from three barracks revolts.

□ Acts of Indiscipline

Acts of military indiscipline, as we will use the term here, are a kind of odd, mirror image of civil disobedience by individuals or groups in civil society. In both cases, established legal or social norms are openly violated to induce lawful authorities to change their policies. But there the similarity ends. The practitioners of civil disobedience accept the legal consequences of illegal action and seek to appeal to the moral principles generally accepted by society and the government. Civil disobedience is an act of persuasion. Military indiscipline, on the other hand, is an attempt to pressure or embarrass the government into supporting military interests (whether these interests are common to the entire military or not). Its practitioners attempt to avoid the legal consequences of their actions and, in fact, make a narrow sectoral appeal. Members of the officer corps from service commanders to junior officers have engaged in this tactic. Instances can be readily found in four of our five countries that returned to civilian government in the 1980s: Argentina—display of Nazi regalia at military ceremonies and failure to take the oath to support the constitution; Brazil—seizure of a town hall by an army captain and troops to demand better pay; Peru—buzzing of the presidential palace by air force planes in protest over the creation of a unified defense department; and Uruguay—order by the minister of defense to armed forces members not to testify in human rights trials in civilian courts.

The high command may countenance acts of indiscipline carried out by subordinates, and the perpetrators, if known, may receive little or no punishment if the military hierarchy is sympathetic to their demands. However, public statements by active or retired officers in disagreement with the views of the high command are often treated as serious breaches of military discipline. These outspoken officers may face serious sanctions, even when their actions would be permissible under Western European or North American norms.

Acts of indiscipline may involve little immediate risk or cost to the military as an institution. They may, however, have a long-term cumulative effect by undermining the prestige and internal discipline of the institution.

□ *Transition Pacts, Laws, and Constitutions*

The armed forces have made use of a number of legalistic devices to maintain their status under civilian successors. Regardless of its own use of force against legally constituted governments, the military has a tendency to appeal to legality to protect its interests.

Although they are not binding legal agreements, political pacts between the armed forces and civilian political sectors are a frequent means of guaranteeing an acceptable transition. They morally bind the dominant political sectors to respect certain key military interests by prohibiting the exercise of certain legal powers theoretically in the hands of the civilian government. Immunity for human rights violators is usually a key element of explicit or implicit transition pacts. Other agreements deal with military missions and the preservation of the national security council and its prerogatives. The enforcement of such pacts depends on the good faith of civilian politicians and the capacity of the armed forces to intimidate successor civilian governments.

Constitutions also play a significant symbolic role in the political balance between the armed forces and civilian authorities. Military interventions—even coups d'état—are often justified by ambiguous constitutional provisions making the armed forces the guarantor of law and order.[16] Military-crafted constitutions can also be used to control the transition process and limit the power of the civilian government. Chile is the only one of our five cases where the armed forces were actually able to oversee the writing of a new constitution while they were not under significant pressure to transfer power quickly. That 1980 document, perhaps the quintessential description of a post–national security state, has been used to support the military's political objectives. The regime's spokesmen repeatedly argued that the constitution must be respected.

Statutes passed by military governments play a similar role to that of constitutions in securing military interests. Here again, amnesty is often the central concern. The military governments of Brazil, Argentina, and Chile passed self-amnesties prior to the transfer of power to civilian authorities. In Brazil, the amnesty held, while the new Argentine government abrogated it. The durability of such statutes depends upon the political strength of the military in the immediate post-transition period. In Chile, the armed forces have attempted to take the process of legally securing their positions several steps further. A package of statutes not only would have secured the size of future military budget and virtually insulated the armed forces against meaningful civilian oversight, but additional measures were also crafted to reorganize the state copper mining company and the central bank. The military provisions, chiefly backed by the army, were passed by the junta (the military government's legislature) after only the central bank reform managed to receive opposition backing.[17]

□ Threats and Blackmail

The armed forces stand in a unique position to use two common, if unscrupulous, methods for attaining political objectives: threats and blackmail. The armed forces can threaten the use of force or other dire repercussions if the government does not conform to military opinion. They are in a better position to be taken seriously in making these threats than any other political actors. The Brazilian military has turned the delivery of threats almost into an art form. Civilians listen attentively to the casual remarks of military ministers to interpret their import. Such "vetoes" of public policy proposals receive wide currency. The chief drawback to threats is that one may eventually have to be carried out. In the interim, the Brazilian armed forces seem well positioned to play this game of political chicken.

While generalized threats of illegal resistance are blackmail in a certain sense of the term, blackmail in the narrower sense of revealing embarrassing information is also available to political operators in the armed forces. The military intelligence services have been weaned imperfectly, if at all, from the role of domestic political surveillance; thus, they possess a significant capacity to gather compromising information about government officials and party leaders. This information is an asset that can be used against potential victims to defend military interests.[18] For such threats and blackmail to be effective, there must be some assurance that their habitual exercise will not cause a backlash in civil society.

□ Bureaucratic Opaqueness and Inertia

The armed forces can also defend their interests on the intrastate level with the same sort of weapons available to other bureaucratic organizations. The military is directed by professionals—technical experts—whose full-time responsibilities are the management of their own technical areas. To challenge an expert in a narrow area of specialization, a challenger must possess similar expertise or be outclassed by the military expert's mastery of detail. In Latin America, there are few research institutes, scholars, legislators, or civilian governmental officials specializing in defense and strategic matters, unlike Western Europe and North America. In part because of this deficiency, the inner workings of the armed forces establishment are inaccessible even when they are not officially secret. In such an environment, reformers can often open a political but not a technical dialogue.

This opaqueness of the military bureaucracy enhances its other capacity for resistance: bureaucratic inertia. Plans take time to generate and implement; reforms require the reallocation of resources and adequate planning; results take time; the most well intentioned individuals and organizations may not be competent. Faced with these kinds of problems, reformers may be good at generating proposals and plans but poor at carrying them out. Successful reform requires political capital and time; the bureaucratic opposition often needs only to wait. Bureaucratic obstructionism is not usually illegal, though it often constitutes a sign of bad faith.

□ Lobbying

Sometimes something more than bureaucratic obstruction is required. Here, another mode of bureaucratic resistance comes into play—lobbying. Even though there are few civilian experts in military affairs in Latin America, in many cases political connections between senior military officers and certain politicians are strong. In such instances, the armed forces can protect themselves within the executive branch, or against the executive branch, by appealing to allies in the legislature. Possibly the most extensive use of formal lobbying took place during the Brazilian constituent assembly, 1987–1988, when the armed forces fielded a team of thirty lobbyists and produced a booklet defending the position of the armed forces. While it can be used as a method of resistance, lobbying is legal and normal, and indicates a certain degree of acceptance of the existing political process.

□ *Some Hypotheses*

Although the military can be expected to defend its interests, all such interests are not created equal and are not likely to be defended with the same intensity or tolerance of risks. Thus:

Hypothesis 1: The armed forces will vigorously defend their fundamental interest—the armed forces' survival as an institution. The armed forces will defend other interests only to the degree that they are necessary for survival or the maintenance of core interests. In the 1980s, there were no substantial challenges to the military that would call into question its survival, such as the creation of a parallel armed institution, the systematic undermining of international discipline, or the systematic politicization of officer appointments as had been the case in previous precoup environments.[19] But the military's self-image has been challenged and a substantial number of military officers have come under threat of legal prosecution because of human rights violations. Other interests affected during the period include the military budget and military pay. Although important, these would be less fundamental. Under this hypothesis, no distinction is made between those interests derived from the armed forces as a bureaucratic entity or derived from Western professionalism, on the one hand, and those interests derived from the new professionalism and the national security doctrine. Any far-reaching change in any area is likely to meet with resistance from the armed forces.

Hypothesis 2: The more fundamental the interest, the greater the likelihood of the high command's involvement in or tolerance of potentially risky or costly means of resistance. Coups d'état and barracks revolts are inherently risky to their participants and potentially costly to the prestige of the armed forces. So too are lesser acts of indiscipline that have the potential of undermining the internal discipline of the armed forces. It is unlikely the high command will participate in or tolerate such behavior unless they view the provocation as substantial. On the other hand, lobbying, threats, bureaucratic obstructionism, and failure to follow orders may involve substantial publicity and substantially less risk. These would seem to be the preferred methods of supporting military interests.

Hypothesis 3: The more uniform the interest across the various sectors of the armed forces, the more likely the success of the armed forces' action in defense of this interest. There are diverging interests within the military. Leaving ideological interests and personalistic factions aside, these are based primarily on the functional differences between the sectors of the armed forces. First, every service or branch can be expected to play some role in policy orientation of members of its own officer corps; this is a well-established pattern in military and bureaucratic organizations in other parts of the world. Second, an officer's involvement in internal security functions typical of the new professionalism can induce interests different from those of an officer involved in more conventional military functions.[20]

Interests largely restricted to one sector of the armed forces and to which other sectors may be indifferent or hostile are potentially vulnerable. Hence, it would seem that civilian government might well be able to undertake military restructuring and the alteration of military missions, provided they are not seen by the armed forces as an attack on the institution itself. (For a summary of some of the major implications of these first three hypotheses, see Table 3.1.)

Hypothesis 4: The lower the prestige of the armed forces and the higher the prestige of the civilian government, the more likely the success of the civilian authorities' efforts to reform the military. Reform, and the resistance to reform, is a complex process. In situations short of outright war, political

Table 3.1 Military Interests

Activity	Motivation	Anticipated Importance
Internal discipline	Professionalism	Core interest
Promotions and assignments	Professionalism, bureaucratic self-interest	Core interest, but certain high-level appointments are normally made or ratified by civilian authorities
Salaries and perquisites	Bureacratic self-interest	Peripheral interest except if status and prestige are seriously threatened
Military budget	Bureaucratic self-interest	Core interest only when the overall mission of the armed forces or their prestige is seriously threatened
Military direction	Bureaucratic self-interest	Peripheral interest except for selected sectors
Civic action and nation-building activities	New professionalism	Core interest when instability is seen as a serious threat to the state or the military itself
Control of civilian population, domestic surveillance	New professionalism	Core interest when instability is seen as a serious threat to the state or the military itself

power comes not out of the barrel of a gun but is largely a matter of perception. Institutions, parties, and individuals who have the look of success—in short, prestige—are likely to succeed. Those who look like losers are likely to live up to, or down to, their appearances. While prestige may be fleeting and intangible, it is real and shapes real events. Thus, we might expect that the character of the transition to a civilian regime will affect the success of the first civilian government. The more forced the transition, the less prestige and resultant political power of the armed forces.

■ THE CONTINUING PROBLEM

Post–national security regimes are neither democracies, where the civilians clearly control the military, nor national security states, where the armed forces make all important policy decisions. Each regime has its position somewhere on the continuum between the two. Moreover, in the 1980s, none of our five countries has had time to fall into a settled pattern of civil-military relations as in Western Europe, North America, and even Latin American countries such as Mexico, Costa Rica, and Venezuela. While national and Latin American peculiarities will play a substantial role in influencing the evolution of civil-military relations, outcomes are likely to depend as well on the statesmanlike adaptation of already understood patterns.

■ NOTES

1. Rousseau, bk. 3, chap. 1, pp. 272–274.
2. Here, other liberal democratic theorists departed from Rousseau. Rousseau held that consistent and intense popular involvement in political affairs was necessary to have a democracy at all. Liberal thinkers substituted a multitude of interest groups (compare James Madison's *Federalist* 10 and Dahl) in place of the totally involved, virtuous republican citizenry. Besides being more realistic in terms of popular psychology, the substitution also made a large democratic state intellectually defensible. Rousseau's prescriptions preclude such a state.
3. "Soldiers Celebrate 1964 Coup," *Latin American Weekly Report*, April 20, 1989, pp. 4–5.
4. Shirley Christian, "Argentina's Military Chiefs Warn of Anarchy," *New York Times*, January 2, 1990, p. 3.
5. Fernando Henrique Cardoso, "Associated-Dependent Development and Democratic Theory," in Stepan, 1989, p. 308.
6. The basic categories discussed below largely follow those of Nordlinger, pp. 66–78. For an alternate listing, see Stepan, 1988, pp. 94–97.
7. Huntington, 1964, p. 11.
8. In the Iberian tradition, rights were not associated with individuals but with the social group to which they belonged. In effect, society is a complex of special privileges (*fueros*) belonging to groups. The functions of these groups were ascribed to them; they were related horizontally and vertically to other groups within the society. For a brief account, see Wiarda, 1981, pp. 34–47.
9. As of 1986, a West German agency published the following estimates of

the number of unaccounted-for disappearances: Argentina—30,000, Bolivia—156, Brazil—125, Colombia—620, Ecuador—407, Guatemala—587, Honduras—164, and Mexico—536. FBIS, "Latin American Missing Person Situation Summed Up," April 14, 1987, FBIS-LAM-87-077, April 22, 1987, pp. A1–A4.

10. For example, one of the leading military-industrial groups in Argentina lost $700 million in the 1983–1989 period while seeing its own technological base deteriorate. Colonel Ernest Bonta, "End of the Military Enterprises Seen Near," Buenos Aires, *Ambito Financiero*, July 17, 1989, FBIS-LAT-89-169, September 1, 1989, pp. 42–43.

11. For example, it was possible under the Brazilian military regime to keep the exact nature of the country's military nuclear program secret. According to *Veja*, in an article published after the return of civilians to power, for almost a decade the military nuclear program had involved considerable resources as well as secret efforts to obtain or buy nuclear secrets via espionage. Reportedly, three thousand people worked for the program. Bank officials revealed that the program had quick access to $200–300 million in foreign bank accounts. The working of the program has not changed much under Sarney. One scientist estimated that two uranium enrichment projects will cost $1.4 and $2 billion, respectively. Four years ago, Navy researchers were able to produce a small amount of plutonium in a facility at the University of São Paulo. The article further reported that it was discovered in 1986 that the Cachimbo Air Base in southern Para State has all the characteristics of a site for testing a nuclear bomb. FBIS, "Newspaper Comments on Parallel Nuclear Program," São Paulo, *Veja*, April 22, 1987, FBIS-LAM-87-090, May 11, 1987, pp. D1–D6.

In Argentina, reports surfaced that President Alfonsín signed a secret decree (no. 1774/85) upholding questionable privileges enjoyed by army intelligence. The decree supported three secret decrees signed by previous military presidents authorizing security forces to carry out covert money-making activities without having to report their sources to state auditors. However, army sources said that such activities covered just .24 percent of intelligence spending, which in 1983 totaled $30.6 million. The department involved in the money-making activities claimed to employ 250 people and handle forty contacts a month. However, one informant suggested the total was much greater than the amount stated by the army. FBIS, "Alfonsín Signs Secret Decree; Army Benefits," *Buenos Aires Herald*, July 7, 1988, FBIS-LAT-88-131, July 8, 1988, pp. 19–20.

12. "Postscript," *Latin American Weekly Report*, March 5, 1987, p. 12.

13. Peter Ford, "El Salvador Staggered by Cost of Quake Relief," *Christian Science Monitor*, October 10, 1986, p. 15.

14. For an alternate discussion of modes of military intervention, see Finer, pp. 127–149.

15. The classic presentation of the problems facing conspirators is in Machiavelli, 1950, bk. 3, chap. 6, pp. 416–417, 425–427. An exhaustive analysis of the contemporary literature on coups can be found in O'Kane.

16. The most striking example of this is Brazil. Stepan, 1971, pp. 75–76. The issue of the formulation of the military's role was also an important matter of contention in the 1980 constitution.

17. "Don't Touch 'My' Men, Says Pinochet," *Latin American Weekly Report*, October 26, 1989, p. 3.

18. Almost by definition, successful blackmail attempts involve the nonrevelation of the blackmail threat as well as the victim's fulfillment of the blackmailer's demands. Sometimes, however, reports of such attempts create substantial notoriety. In Uruguay, for instance, the military was reportedly able to pressure civilian politicians by threatening to reveal information about

extensive civilian corruption. "Uruguay Human Rights Amnesty Shows Fragility of Civilian Rule," *Christian Science Monitor*, December 30, 1986, p. 10.

19. For example, Argentina in 1930—politicization; Brazil in 1964—politicization and the undermining of discipline; and Chile in 1973—undermining of discipline and the creation of a parallel armed force.

20. For example, Brazilian hard-liners were typically associated with the intelligence services. Stepan, 1988, p. 28.

4■

Patterns and Strategies
of Civil-Military Relations

We have been analyzing the problem of the military and democracy essentially on a grand scale: political traditions, the task of democratic consolidation, and the military's general position vis-à-vis elected authority. It is appropriate now to focus on the methods civilian governments can employ to effect civilian control over the armed forces as an institution, and to focus on the role the armed forces play in regard to their (real or nominal) civilian superiors. Although the term is a contemporary one, civil-military relations have been an issue for virtually every modern and premodern regime and a topic of modern political theorists since the time of Machiavelli.

■ PATTERNS OF CIVIL-MILITARY RELATIONS

This ongoing theoretical discussion provides an interesting variety of perspectives on civil-military relations as well as a variety of diagnoses of and prescriptions for praetorianism. By and large, any given pattern of civil-military relations grows out of particular social conditions. A pattern may persist over time and survive a change in regime, but the relationship is not one of simple determinism. Systematic policies aimed at changing civil-military relations can, in turn, alter social conditions.

□ Praetorianism 1: Caudillismo

The theme of praetorianism and the task of controlling military leaders entered modern political thought with the writings of Nicolò Machiavelli. Machiavelli's analysis of the problems faced by the republics in Renaissance Italy has a clear resonance with the traditional, nineteenth-century pattern of civil-military relations in Latin America. In both cases, military and civilian authority was often indistinguishable, and leadership was based on personal loyalties. The chief executive gained and maintained authority chiefly by force of arms.

In Latin America, the caudillos—soldier-presidents and their rivals—were amateur officers; they achieved their rank on the basis of their social position, not formal, professional training. Republicanism and constitutionalism had a largely formal existence; thus, those in power often ignored constitutional and legal limitations. Power relations were personal rather than institutional. In Machiavelli's Italy the central figure was the *condottiere*, a professional soldier and often a foreigner. The condottiere was either an incompetent, adverse to taking risks and thus unable to defend the state, or an internal threat to the state because he was motivated only by personal ambitions.[1]

Contemporary writers, echoing Machiavellian themes, developed the concept of the praetorian military as the archetype that describes the problems faced by Latin American as well as other societies. The praetorian military stands above the political system and dominates it. It is occasionally subject to manipulation but never systematic control. The armed forces are a center for intrigue, and they are courted by those in and out of power. The officer corps "invariably attracts two distinct political types—the political adventurer willing to gamble all in a dangerous stroke and the petty bureaucrat anxious to hold his rank in successive regimes, and therefore reluctant to proceed vigorously against a rebel group."[2]

Praetorianism, and the praetorian military, is not inevitable. Machiavelli's classic prescription for escaping it is what is known contemporarily as the nation-in-arms.

□   *The Classic Alternative: The Nation-in-Arms*

The nation-in-arms prescription rests on a diagnosis of the underlying cause of praetorianism as the isolation of the armed forces from both the society and the government. In Machiavelli's time, the officers who presented the greatest danger were often foreigners, either mercenaries or commanders of allied military forces. In the context of historic Latin American praetorianism, the separation was social rather than national in origin. The caudillos came from within their own countries but were often socially and culturally removed from the masses of the population.

Even contemporary Latin American officer corps maintain a social separation, although the causes are different. Though drawn largely from the middle class, prospective military officers are socialized intensely during extended periods in preparatory schools and the military academies. Afterwards, a military career may entail postings to remote parts of the country and limited contact with other professional sectors. In both the Renaissance and modern cases, the government, unless headed by the military, has often had little competence in or control over military affairs. This military isolation within a generally unconsolidated democratic context is a recipe for disaster.

The nation-in-arms solution is to arm the citizenry and make military matters an important concern of the government.[3] This is not an insignificant policy change; it amounts to a social revolution.[4] Arming the citizenry requires the establishment of a large and efficient reserve system that places heavy demands on its part-time soldiers. Only a strong sense of patriotism and belief in the propriety of national policy can sustain such demands. In the best case, a military spirit infuses the nation, and a popular spirit infuses the armed forces. The professional officer corps, a rather small group, interacts on a continuing basis with long-term reservists who are not simply recruits to be trained but associates whose technical competence and professionalism are necessary for accomplishing the mission.

Nations-in-arms have existed from the time of the polis in ancient Greece. Modern examples include Sweden, Switzerland, and Israel.[5] Commonly, they exist in situations where war or the threat of war is real and persistent. They presume a degree of social democracy and public-spiritedness that may be hard to sustain. No Latin American government currently follows this pattern, although Paraguay had such a system over a century ago. Moreover, there are few serious proposals for such a transformation.[6]

The virtual absence of the nation-in-arms model either as an existing pattern of civil-military relations or as the basis for reform is not hard to account for. Such a system entails not simply a different approach to civil-military relations but reconstruction of the armed forces itself, a project likely to be resisted by well-established institutions. Moreover, Latin America seems to lack the social basis and international environment that would make such an alternative military policy sufficiently attractive to the government and society to warrant its high economic and social costs.

□ Western Professionalism and the Cadre Army

A less demanding alternative to the nation-in-arms is the cadre army based on an officer corps suffused with the ethic of Western professionalism. Such an army normally exists when there is a persistent threat of war and when significant resources may ultimately have to be brought to bear to wage war if war should actually occur. The permanent professional armed forces, while possibly quite large in absolute terms, are modest in size when compared to the forces that could ultimately be mobilized or to the size of the much more rapidly mobilized nation-in-arms. The purpose of a cadre army is to counter threats requiring less than a major national effort and to serve as a base upon which to build a much more extensive force should full national mobilization be required. A national policy relying on cadre armed forces places modest direct burdens on most citizens; most are not compelled to serve in the armed forces, except in wartime, and instead pay taxes to support the national military establishment. The relationship between the career soldier and the erstwhile civilian member of the armed forces is primarily that of professional to recruit.

Although a cadre army would seem to bear a close similarity to praetorian forces, a number of factors distinguish them in practice.

Historically, countries of a more or less democratic political culture developed cadre armies in the nineteenth century.[7] Hence, cadre armies operate within a different social and political context. The institutional isolation of the officer corps is less than in the typical praetorian force. Moreover, the distinctiveness of the military as an institution seems to be breaking down in First World states that have followed a cadre armed forces policy. While the armed forces still manifest many institutional characteristics—esprit de corps, exclusivity, and nontransferability—they are undermined by trends toward interchangeability of civilian and military expertise and the tendency of many officers to regard the armed forces as another career option rather than a way of life.[8]

Civil-military relations within the Western professional context place ultimate control over military affairs in the hands of civilian authorities. Military officers are largely restricted to narrowly technical spheres of competence. The military is not the final judge of policies with security implications. The armed forces must lobby their civilian superiors, who themselves are responsible for weighing military advice against other administrative and political considerations. Thus, the armed forces generally develop an apolitical character.

☐ *Praetorianism 2: The New Professionalism*

Latin America began to adapt the professional cadre army during the latter part of the nineteenth century with the introduction of modern weaponry and organization and the establishment of military academies and schools, mainly under the auspices of foreign military advisers. Thus began the extended process of creating a professional military, where promotion is based on technical competence, formal training, and seniority. The creation of a professional military, however, did not solve the problems created by a praetorian military; it merely reshaped them.

While in North America and Western Europe professionalism went hand in hand with the promotion of civilian control of the armed force, it developed differently in the Latin American setting. This disparity can be attributed to a number of factors. First, as Nun points out,[9] the professionalization of Latin American armies took place at a different time and in a different context than the professionalization of European armies; in short, the Latin American middle class did not have the same degree of independence and cohesion as the European bourgeoisie and hence was never able to subordinate the state and the military to its class interests. Second, professionalism as a method of control requires a strong, stable polity where civilian politicians do not require explicit military support.[10] Such a situation did not obtain in most of Latin America.

Third, the Latin American officer often felt torn by a tension that resulted from competing dictates of professionalism. A professional military is defined in terms of its technical role within the state, is granted a significant degree of autonomy within its specific sphere of activity (technicism), and exists for the good of the nation (nationalism). Within the context typical of most developed Western nations, technicism does not usually conflict with nationalism. Normally, a high degree of regime legitimacy and widespread consent to governmental policy allows the armed forces to assume an apolitical posture. Obedience to the government of the day is not in conflict with the military's duty to the nation. Hence, analysts such as Huntington can list the attribute of being apolitical as an essential element of professionalism.[11]

But the normal Western context is not that of Latin America. In Latin America, lack of consensus, regime illegitimacy, and the undermobilization or hypermobilization of various sectors of society are more frequently the norm. Thus, the late nineteenth- and twentieth-century professionalization of the armed forces produced a different effect and led to the potential for conflict between technicism and nationalism in the minds of the officer corps. While technicism produces a bias toward an apolitical stance, nationalism impels the armed forces to political intervention when the national welfare appears to be seriously threatened by the action or inaction of the government of the day.

This tension between nationalism and technicism does not appear as an outright contradiction in military thinking. An excellent illustration of what to Western democrats are contradictory attitudes appears in the address Argentine army commander in chief General (later President) Onganía gave to the 1964 Conference of American Armies.

[The armed forces are bound] by positive norms established in the constitutions of the republics of America, which fix unequivocally the role of the armed forces in a representative democracy. . . . Custodians of the national sovereignty [in the wars of liberation], they took up arms only to gain a continent for the cause of liberty. . . . [It is] a necessary consequence of the republican order and the system of representative government [that] the nature of the armed forces of the Americas is to be *apolitical, nondeliberative and essentially subordinate to legitimately constituted authority*, respecting the constitution and the laws the respect for which is above every other obligation. . . . [But] in emergencies this disposition of the armed institutions for the service of the constitution certainly ought not to permit them to remain impassive, under the pretext of a blind submission to the established power, so that they would convert themselves into instruments of an illegitimate authority.[12]

It is not surprising that Onganía was an advocate of limiting the political involvement of the armed forces in the late 1950s and a leader of a military coup a decade later. The above statement can justify either course of action. To a significant degree, military intervention in politics represented a natural organizational response to a particular social, economic, and institutional environment. Yet, adherence to Western-style professional norms coupled with occasional political interventions to meet particular crises was essentially a dead end. Such interventions left the underlying social and political environment basically unaltered, and the tension between technicism and nationalism remained a recurring problem.

The new professionalism was an attempt to resolve that tension by addressing underlying causes. For example, the failure of prior interventions became an object lesson about what was required in the future. Under the new professionalism, the basic dictates of professionalism remained the same, but it assumed new missions and functions. Expanding the definition of the military's competence to include these new missions and functions presented the prospect of decisively resolving the tension between nationalism and technicism. A professionally competent military would engage in a wide-ranging process of nation building and ferreting out subversion. In this way, interventions could be justified in professional terms, and when they were successful, the armed forces could return to a more limited role.

Hence, the concept of professionalism accepted by Latin American armies underwent a role expansion in the mid- to late twentieth century. This expansion of the professional role of the military was also induced by US concern over the vulnerability of its Third World allies to guerrilla warfare and internal subversion—two vulnerabilities of Latin American praetorian societies. Thus, as Stepan argues,[13] the version of professionalism that stresses defense against external threats was not fully appropriate to Latin America, where a new professionalism—what Potash terms "integrated professionalism"[14]—focused on internal problems that required intervention by the military as an institution in the general policymaking sphere. This intervention has, in fact, culminated in the displacement of civilian authorities at the highest levels and their replacement by military personnel or the development of new institutions or policies crafted by the military.[15] From the point of view of constructing democratic pluralism, the new professionalism became part of the problem rather than its solution.

The pattern of civil-military relations typical of the new professionalism was described earlier as the national security state and post–national security state. Whether in or out of power, the armed forces attempt to control certain elements of policy normally under the control of civilians and to veto civilian actions that in the military's judgment threaten national security. Thus, the new professionalism entails the military penetration of the rest of the state and society.

To recapitulate, apoliticalness is not a primary characteristic of professionalism but one derived from political and social relationships in which professional military institutions operate. If these relationships are at least roughly correct, it means that something more than establishing technical criteria for the recruitment and management of the armed forces is necessary to reproduce an apolitical military ethos in the Latin American context.

It is tempting to believe that the problem can be addressed directly by abolishing the armed forces. After all, Latin American countries have not faced the obvious security problems of First and Second World states. Although the state probably cannot exist without organized instruments of force subject to its control, their size and mission can be modified. The patterns of civil-military relations previously discussed assumed that defense against a major attack by a foreign state was the raison d'être of the armed forces. Even if they undertook other missions, as armed forces that followed these models often did, their overall size and level of armament were justified on the basis of conquest or defense against foreign attack. Foreign war, while not always likely, was the most serious business of the armed forces.

The constabulary model turns this principle on its head. It begins with the assumption that the possibility of a major international conflict involving the state is negligible. The military must be structured and armed to control frontiers against smugglers and bandits and to provide law and order in parts of the country where there are no municipal police forces. While this model may seem to imply the virtual abolition of the armed forces themselves, it does not solve the problem of military intervention. Although constabulary forces are small compared to forces with a more conventional mission, size alone is not much of a determinant to military intervention; in fact, small forces may be more likely to intervene.[16]

The important tactical advantage the military has in interventions against civilian opponents is not the result of its absolute size or its size vis-à-vis foreign military establishments. Its advantage stems from its near monopoly over the means of violence within its own society. The Somoza dictatorship in Nicaragua and, more recently, the Panamanian Defense Forces that dominate the Panamanian political system arose from military institutions built on the constabulary model. Meanwhile, the constabulary character of the Costa Rican armed forces may enhance the effectiveness of other means of civilian control. Reduction of the size and mission of the armed forces provides no instant solution.

■   TECHNIQUES OF CIVILIAN CONTROL

There are a number of basic techniques for effecting civilian control that have been employed in a variety of social and political environments. In his analysis of Western militarism, Huntington argues that there are two basic methods of civilian control: the subjective and objective.[17] Subjective control has a number of forms. Control by governmental institution is one form whereby the military is loyal to and recognizes the legitimacy and direction of a particular institution within the civilian government, for example, the British Parliament, the US Congress, or the president. A second form of subjective control is control by social class. Huntington illustrates this with the example of the eighteenth-century European bourgeoisie, which used the slogan "civilian control" in an attempt to link the military to its own rather than aristocratic interests. A third form of subjective civilian control associates control with constitutional form. In this case, civilian control of the military is legitimized by the form of the regime, and military obedience to the government is held to be obligatory because of the ideological principle upon which that government is based—be it democratic, national socialist, or communist. In the case of the latter two, civilian control can also be enforced by separate party military forces, political commissars, or state terror. The second major type of civilian control, objective control, provides for military autonomy under the rubric of professionalism: The military controls matters within its own proper sphere but does not challenge the supremacy or overall direction of civilian institutions.

Nordlinger uses a slightly different schema to develop a threefold division of control: the traditional model (corresponding to the aristocratic version of Huntington's control by social class), the liberal model (roughly corresponding to a combination of what Huntington describes as objective civilian control and control by constitutional form), and the penetration model (corresponding to the totalitarian version of Huntington's control by constitutional form).[18] McKinlay lists three methods of control relevant here.[19] His control via specialization is similar to Huntington's professionalism. Control via insulation is seemingly another aspect of professionalism but stresses the relative unimportance of the military vis-à-vis the civilian government (this is also highlighted in Nordlinger's liberal model). Finally, McKinlay's control by infiltration stresses the overlap of personnel in the top leadership; this bond between civilians and military officers is frequently consolidated by a common class or ideological base. Hence, this method is similar to Huntington's control by social class and Nordlinger's penetration model. In attempting to summarize the literature, Stepan lists the forms of civilian control as: the aristocratic (Nordlinger's traditional model), the communist (Huntington's totalitarian version of control by constitutional form, Nordlinger's penetration model, and a variant of McKinlay's infiltration), the liberal (Huntington's control by constitutional form, Nordlinger's liberal model, and McKinlay's infiltration), and the professional (Huntington's professionalism, Nordlinger's liberal model, and McKinlay's insulation).[20]

Limiting our consideration to patterns that have functioned or potentially might function successfully in modern democracies, we might regroup the forms described above as follows. First, professionalism: All the above theorists recognize professionalism as a method of control compatible with modern democracies. Second, democratic ideology: All also recognize a form of democratic control based on the armed forces' loyalty to democratic principles. And third, bourgeois penetration: All recognize that civilian control of the military is possible when the bourgeoisie have a predominant position in both the government and the military. It should also be noted that these methods of control are not mutually exclusive but serve to reinforce one another. One feature of modern democratic civil-military relations is especially noteworthy: the virtual ubiquity professionalism enjoys as a method of control in modern democracies.

■ STRATEGIES OF CIVILIAN CONTROL OR SURVIVAL

How can these techniques of civilian control be applied to promote the emergence of a stable pattern of civil-military relations in which civilian authorities retain a predominant position? A number of strategies emerged from twentieth-century experience. These strategies can be understood in light of the categories of civilian control discussed above and range from the civilian government's refusal directly to confront the problem of an interventionist military to the government's attempt to impose radically new patterns of civil-military relations. The present analysis focuses on the strategy choices, explicit or implicit, made by the civilian government.[21] The choices, however, must be understood as the result of a complex dynamic of forces: the political strength of the civilian government, its policy goals, the characteristics of the armed forces at the time (their morale, unity, doctrine, and political outlook), and forces operating in the broader society. These strategy choices, in effect, represent points on a continuum rather than discrete and contradictory strategies. Moreover, it is possible to combine certain methods appropriate to different strategies, and actual governments have sometimes done so.

□ Wholesale Restructuring

The most dramatic option for asserting civilian control is that of wholesale restructuring: the complete abolition of the old military institution and its replacement with a new one. Under such a process, personnel, symbols, doctrine, organization, equipment, and the relation of the military to civilian authority would all be transformed. Under a restructuring strategy, the government attempts to establish civilian control of the armed forces by addressing each of the three basic tasks in establishing the legitimacy of democratic institutions: establishing civilian oversight, enforcing the rule of law, and redefining the basic role of the armed forces. Restructuring is a contemporary phenomenon, distinct from the professionalization of the military in the nineteenth and twentieth centuries. Institutional restructuring implies the prior existence of a professional and bureaucratic military with the institutional means of resisting change. Such a transformation rarely occurs outside of a revolutionary context or a situation of complete defeat after a major war where the military's capacity to resist fundamental change is negligible.[22]

Although this sort of transformation may be desirable, there is little likelihood that current civilian governments in our five countries could take such drastic measures. A policy aimed at transforming a cadre army either to a constabulary force or the nucleus of a nation-in-arms would require truly wrenching changes in the military establishment involving manpower, budgets, and day-to-day operations. Even the thorough renovation of a cadre army would involve almost as many costs and risks. Instances in Latin American history where this strategy was employed—Costa Rica in the late 1940s and Cuba after 1958—bear little resemblance to the current situation in the five countries we are considering. They involved a balance of power in which the civilian government far outweighed the influence of the old military institutions.

□ *Politicization of the Military*

Another less ambitious method of attempting to assert civilian control is through the piecemeal method of politicizing the armed forces. Instead of rebuilding the military from the ground up, civilian authorities attempt to make certain decisions for the armed forces—decisions that the dictates of professionalism reserve for the armed forces themselves. This civilian intervention in military affairs is aimed at promoting the political reliability of the armed services in the eyes of the chief executive. Hence, I use *politicization* here as a strategy of establishing subjective civilian control by attempting to create a military establishment *personally* loyal to a particular leader, party, or government rather than to the regime. Politicization attempts to establish the detailed oversight of the military and to attain the armed forces' support for the government; it does not necessarily address the issue of the role of the military.

In effect, if pushed very far, this strategy runs the risk of conflict with bureaucratic and democratic norms. The politicization strategy uses such means as promotion, retirement, reassignment, and reinstatement in the officer corps, as well as changed criteria for earning commissions.[23] These personnel procedures are normally recognized as being legitimately under civilian control, and budgetary as well as other considerations may lead to their alteration. Changes in personnel procedures do not necessarily constitute politicization. Changes become political when they are made more for the personal advantage of the incumbent government than for strengthening the constitutional system, or when they egregiously interfere with the professional criteria of advancement by merit and seniority.

This strategy may seem to have the virtue of directness. In seizing the bull by the horns, as it were, the civilian politicians would appear to have the opportunity of solving once and for all the problem of military intervention; and there are relatively modern Latin American precedents where this technique has been applied. In Mexico, the armed forces were essentially co-opted by the civilian authorities. Over a number of administrations, beginning in the 1940s, the impulse of generals to dominate the political system was curtailed through the extension of benefits to the military and the incorporation of the armed forces into the hierarchy of the ruling party. The military no longer dominates the system; it is part of it.[24] In Costa Rica, the regime has avoided the creation of a professionalized military force by making officer appointments in the civil and rural guard a matter of political patronage.[25] In Venezuela as well, patronage becomes a factor in the promotion of officers. Promotions have to be approved by the legislature, and though only about 5 percent receive close scrutiny, officers feel compelled to associate with one of the two major parties in order to avoid potential vetoes of promotion to senior levels. In addition, since the establishment of democracy in 1958, the president has been assured of a close personal connection with the armed forces.[26]

However, such precedents may be deceptive. Mexican politicization took place in a postrevolutionary context and involved a military not based on modern concepts of professionalism. In effect it was partial depoliticization (or repoliticization) coupled with professionalization and not outright politicization of a professional force. The Costa Rican example shares some peculiarities with Mexico. There too a new government came into power after defeating the old government's military forces. Plus, the military's status was never high in Costa Rica to begin with.[27] The Venezuelan instance is hardly more compelling. The politicization that does exist plays a rather minor—and maybe even a negative—role in securing civilian control.[28]

Moreover, such a strategy is fraught with problems, especially when the military considers itself to be a professional force. While politicization bears superficial resemblance to the establishment of bourgeois-class control, it does not really correspond to that mechanism. In Latin America today, few if any parties can claim to be the sole legitimate spokesman of the middle class or some similar class; and the lack of a powerful, cohesive middle class (as noted above) renders an appeal by their legitimate representative of dubious political value. In addition, few other actions are as likely to cause even a faction-ridden military to coalesce against the government as an overt attempt to subvert the professionalism of the force. Actions that threatened to politicize the armed forces were important contributing factors to coups in Argentina (1930), Brazil (1964), and Chile (1973). At the same time, blatant efforts to gain partisan advantage provoke other political and social sectors into open opposition in defense of the principle of constitutionalism. In short, there does not seem to be a viable contemporary variant of democratic, bourgeois control in the Latin American context, or any direct, short-range method of establishing it.

The strategies of wholesale restructuring and politicization assume civil-military politics to be a zero-sum game. The success of such strategies demands preponderant power, at least temporarily, in the hands of political authorities. Restructuring and politicization, then, become the means of rendering that power balance permanent. As already noted, the power balance in contemporary Latin America is inadequate for such civilian strategies.

□   *Civilian Government as Client or Hostage*[29]

When a civilian government finds itself in a position of weakness vis-à-vis the military or other nonmilitary sectors, that government is apt to become a client or hostage of the armed forces. This has been the position of such Central American governments as Guatemala and El Salvador in the 1980s. In effect, the government eschews the task of attempting to establish control over the military. The civilian government can be seen as a client when it is in essential agreement with the military or its dominant faction(s) on general matters of governmental policy. One would more properly denominate the government a hostage when it is forced to adhere to military policy preferences even when its own predilections would lead it in another direction.

Such a strategy—or more properly a choice made by default—allows the government to remain in power only by catering to military preferences and interests. The civilians cannot govern without explicit support from the armed forces and must permit the intrusion of the military into the policymaking sphere, which is normally the exclusive domain of the civilian government. This approach does allow the government minimal freedom of action. Although the military intrudes into the civilian sphere, the civilians retain at least nominal control overall and the freedom to initiate policies the military supports or to which it is indifferent. Civilian governments, caught in this situation, assume an essentially caretaker role.

Again, the zero-sum game presumption holds: Civil-military politics is the struggle for power between competing bureaucratic or political structures. While the armed forces may believe they need a civilianized front, they believe they are the best judge of the national interest and are unwilling to accord civilians much policy discretion. The aim of civilians is to retain formal power and assure formal adherence to constitutional norms in the hope that formal adherence to democratic norms will eventually become more substantive. In effect, they address the task of establishing the regime's legitimacy indirectly, but they allow the continuation of violations of democratic norms. This strategy is a temporizing policy that assumes time is on the side of the civilian government and constitutionalism. In theory, the longer the military refrains from direct intervention, the less likely it is to intervene in the future, and the greater the legitimacy of civilian institutions.

□   *Civil-Military Coexistence*

A slightly more ambitious strategy for asserting control entails the partial emancipation of the government from military tutelage. In effect, the government assumes that the norms of military professionalism of the older sort will be largely obeyed. In such an instance, the civilian government feels secure enough to embark on a course of action independent of specific endorsement for its policies from the military establishment. But in a post–national security state context, thorough obedience to the civilian interpretation of military professionalism cannot be assumed. Hence, the government is forced to recognize that it must observe certain key limits on its actions. These limits include respect for an exaggerated degree of autonomy for the armed forces and acquiescence to the armed forces' far-ranging views on national security.

When the military is divided by internal factions based on personal, interservice, or ideological rivalries, or when the government appears to have a significant degree of support from society at large, coexistence can be an attractive strategy with relatively few risks. Coexistence assumes civilians have more ability to take the initiative in areas of marginal interest to the armed forces. It offers the prospect of consolidating civilian rule, while at the same time placating the military and forestalling renewed military intervention. Nonetheless, it entails zero-sum assumptions, since little effort is made to alter the new professionalism of the armed forces. At best, this strategy addresses the tasks of democratic consolidation only indirectly and ignores difficult issues that some governments must ultimately face.

□   *Establishing Control via Doctrinal Change*

The strategies discussed so far fit onto the following continuum:

Weak Government <——————————————————> Weak Armed Forces

Client/	Coexistence		Politicization	Wholesale
Hostage				Restructuring

The central position on this continuum has been left vacant intentionally. We now need to explore that middle-range strategy most appropriate to the balance-of-power situations in which new democratic governments in Latin America find themselves.

This alternative strategy of securing civilian control aims at the reformulation of the armed forces' mission, organization, strategy and tactics, and legal status—in short, its doctrine—so that the reformed institution adheres to democratic norms. If politicization, changing personnel within the armed forces, alters the military's matter, a systematic change in military doctrine can be viewed as altering its form. While it is highly unlikely that doctrinal changes will be unconnected to significant changes of personnel, a civilian strategy that aims at establishing control of the military by means of systematic reorganization avoids some of the dangers inherent in a simple politicization strategy. In effect, by dealing with the military as an institution and not with selected military officers as individuals, the civilian leadership preserves the norm of professionalism, while at the same time changing the content of that professionalism. Changes in doctrine would, most assuredly, affect certain military sectors adversely, but such changes would benefit other military sectors and preserve the integrity of the institution as a whole. Hence, they are less likely to arouse the type of internal opposition that is provoked by a politicization strategy.

This strategy is, above all, a process that should be pursued consistently over an extended period of time. Doctrinal reform is the endpoint that will be reached if this process of instituting incremental but principled changes is successfully completed. Doctrinal change assumes that civil-military politics is not a zero-sum game and presupposes a dialogue between the military and civilians about national security and the armed forces' role in attaining it. It is not easy to implement. A civilian government that attempts to change basic elements of the military institution faces the same sorts of checks involved in the attempt to alter any long-established bureaucracy. The government requires a durable base of popular support and at least tacit recognition from significant elements of the armed forces that some type of fundamental change is necessary. Doctrinal change represents a long-term means of effecting a long-term solution to the problem of military intervention; it attempts to establish the Western version of professionalism and loyalty to democratic institutions. Moreover, it assumes civilian participants in the dialogue have a competence in military affairs that allows them to speak as technical equals with their military interlocutors.

Dialogue in this sense is more than formal discussions between political and military elites; it is a range of interactions that are quantitatively and qualitatively different from those typical of the other strategies. Components of this strategy include the redefinition of the armed forces' sphere of competence and the establishment of constitutionalism and the rule of law as norms for both society and the armed forces. These components have a number of steps ranging from the pro forma to the substantial. In effect, doctrinal change induces the armed forces to alter both their technical and nationalistic conceptions. Reform is premised on the fact that the military, in part, already holds to principles that stress its apolitical character and loyalty to democratic institutions. Reform seeks to make these orientations paramount and not subject to the overriding provisos of Onganía's West Point speech.

Reformers must promote a view of nationalism that links loyalty to the nation with loyalty to the democratic regime and respect for the authority of the executive, legislative, and judicial branches of government. At least, the armed forces should express in an authoritative manner their support for these institutions. Statements of support, however, are only a first step—indeed, a step often compatible with a client or coexistence strategy. Besides this, an oath to obey the constitution rather than follow the flag, a reform in the code of military justice making officers responsible for abuses of power, strengthening the authority of civilian courts, and the punishment of previous abuses of power are appropriate additional steps. Each one is more difficult to undertake as one advances down the list since they increasingly threaten military interests and challenge military perceptions in a more substantial manner.

To be successful, reforms should engage the armed forces in a process of reformulating their role as executors of state policy. That is to say, their sphere of competence must be modified to bring it more in line with conceptions of Western professionalism. This reformulation is an interactive process that involves both military and civilian authority at various levels of policymaking and execution. The state's grand strategy—its conception of its primary enemies and threats and whether to respond with military or other action—should be formulated by civilians with military advice. The resulting grand strategic conceptions should be credible in military eyes. Strategy—the manner in which wars are to be fought—should be developed by the armed forces with the general direction and approval of civilian authorities. Tactics—how weapons and organizations are to be used to win battles— should be almost totally under military direction. Military policy—the provision for manpower, materiel and other military resources, and the general principles of organizing the military system—should be almost totally under civilian control. These components of national policy should fit together into a coherent whole.[30] These dicta, while important in any national context, are doubly important when civilian authorities want to promote the military's redefinition of its own role. In short, credible conventional missions must be found to distance the armed forces from civilian areas of responsibility.

■ STRATEGIES FOR ESTABLISHING CIVILIAN CONTROL IN FIVE COUNTRIES

The choice of civilian strategies for establishing control over the armed forces is likely to be the result of a number of factors. Two of these are the political strength of the elected government and the political strength of the armed forces as they emerge from the political transition. These factors limit what measures it would be reasonable to pursue. A third factor is also critical, if more subjective—the judgment and political skill of the civilian government.

Given that our five cases were chosen because they manifested a significant degree of similarity, we might expect that their strategies would come from a range considerably smaller than the whole continuum developed above. That expectation is borne out by the facts. Nonetheless, there are significant differences between countries.

□ *Peru: Coexistence and Hesitant Doctrinal Change*

The post-transition experience of Peru is divisible into two periods corresponding to the two presidential administrations since 1980: Fernando Belaúnde Terry (1980–1985) and Alán García (1985–1990).

The conservative Belaúnde had been overthrown by the military in 1968 and in 1980 faced armed forces that had to retreat from political power but had been forceful in defending their prerogatives during the denouement of the military regime. Internal divisions within the armed forces between radicals and moderates remained but were manageable. However, support for the armed forces from society in general appeared to be minimal. General Morales Bermúdez, who ran as a presidential candidate in 1985, managed to garner only a derisory 1 percent of the vote.

Belaúnde was initially popular, but the president suffered from a number of handicaps. His Popular Action Party (AP) lacked a mass base, and his economic program attempted to overturn some of the popular gains made during the preceding military regime. Moreover, the early 1980s was a period of economic disaster for Peru. The country's economy faltered in the first half of the decade. In 1983, the worst year, GNP per capita plummeted a remarkable 14.1 percent. And with it went the credibility of the Belaúnde government. During these same years, the Sendero Luminoso (Shining Path) insurgency began in the southern Andean departments, putting further strain on the government.

Belaúnde's approach can be characterized as a coexistence strategy. He began by taking the unprecedented step of appointing retired officers (who had opposed the 1968 coup) as his military ministers.[31] While the military had little direct impact on foreign and economic policies, the armed forces' influence was notable in spheres more directly related to their immediate interests. The defense budget increased, even during a period of increasing economic exigency. It had a significantly higher economic impact during the first portion of Belaúnde's administration than during the last part of the former military government (see Table 4.1). The armed forces were given a more or less free hand in fighting the Sendero insurgents. This freedom of action resulted in numerous human rights abuses.[32] The government survived its term of office, but the military continued to exercise many prerogatives typical of the national security state.

The Alan García administration began much more auspiciously. In office with a first-round victory in the presidential election, García was backed by the strongest mass party in the region, the American Popular Revolutionary Alliance (APRA). A youthful figure, he won control of APRA after the death of the party's founder and longtime leader, Victor Raúl Haya de la Torre. García's image of youthful dynamism was enhanced by a political program

Table 4.1 Military and Civilian Defense Budgets

Country	Year of Transition	Military Expenditure (% of GDP)	
		Last 3 Pre-Transition Years	First 3 Post-Transition Years
Argentina	1984	5.9	3.5
Brazil	1985	0.8	0.7
Peru	1980	5.6	8.7
Uruguay	1985	3.3	2.2

Source: Stockholm International Peace Research Institute

that sought to solve simultaneously a host of problems facing the country. A cap, equal to 10 percent of export earnings, was placed on the repayment of Peru's debt. The government began an expansionary economic program to reactivate an economy buffeted by natural and policy disasters. The administration took a combative line toward drug traffickers. Internationally, Peru took a combative stance toward the United States and the IMF.

In regard to the military, García took steps that seemed to herald a policy of doctrinal change. He acted aggressively on a number of issues left festering by his predecessor. While not a full-fledged policy of doctrinal change, García's initiatives challenged a number of important military prerogatives. The government reduced an air force purchase of Mirage 2000 jet aircraft[33] and announced the reorganization of the troublesome paramilitary Republican Guard.[34] The president challenged the armed forces over its counterinsurgency methods and human rights violations by appointing a new commander in the emergency zone.[35] He forced the resignation of the chief of the armed forces joint staff and put in place a successor who pledged to bring rights violators to justice.[36] Organizationally, the government cut the number of general officers,[37] and the armed forces were placed under a single ministry.[38]

Although these initiatives were significant, the political momentum behind them could not be sustained. After several years of renewed prosperity under APRA, economic and political crises emerged when the president announced plans to nationalize the banks in July 1987. Per capita GDP growth, which averaged better than 5 percent annually in 1986–1987, plunged in 1988 by nearly 11 percent. Many other nagging problems continued to fester or grow dramatically worse. The Sendero's strength increased, and as efforts were made to crack down in their Ayacucho heartland, Sendero simply expanded into other areas. Drugs became an even more serious problem, rendering government control of a number of areas of the country impossible.

Even before the government began its political free-fall, efforts to bring the armed forces under control were beginning to flag. Faced with prison riots by Sendero inmates in 1986, the government, like its predecessor, waffled. Then it attempted to cover up the murder of over one hundred inmates after they had surrendered.[39] Although two officers eventually received sentences for exceeding orders in regard to the action,[40] they were the only rights violators from the military to be sentenced during the struggle against Sendero. By the end of García's administration, human rights standards were no better respected than during Belaúnde's.[41] The establishment of a unified defense ministry provided little appreciable benefit for civilian control as an army general was eventually appointed defense minister. The García government seemed to lack both the durable political popularity as well as the persistence and expertise in military affairs to undertake a consistent policy of doctrinal change.

□ *Argentina: Doctrinal Change Miscarried*

The Radical Party government of Argentina assumed power in December 1983 with a very strong position vis-à-vis the military, which allowed President Alfonsín to pursue a strategy of doctrinal reform. The military had presided over economic stagnation and a national debacle in the Falklands/Malvinas War and had eventually aroused strong public reaction because of numerous human rights violations during the dirty war against subversion during the late 1970s. These factors provided the opportunity for President Alfonsín to address directly the lack of respect for democracy among civilian and military sectors:

> The coups have always been civilian-military in character. The undoubted military responsibility for their operational aspects should not make us forget the heavy responsibility of civilians who plotted them and gave them ideological basis. The coups always reflected the loss of the sense of legality inherent in society, not just the loss of the sense of legality in the military.[42]

To restore the sense of legality in society and the military, the Alfonsín government undertook steps to establish the traditional conception of professionalism as the basis of the Argentine military ethic. A new national defense law was promulgated to prohibit the military from assuming emergency powers to maintain law and order.[43] The military code was modified to expand the jurisdiction of civilian courts over military personnel.[44] The military intelligence services were placed under a civilian head.[45] Military industries were scheduled for privatization or civilian control within the defense ministry. Most significantly, certain high-ranking officers were brought to trial for human rights violations, and others are scheduled for trial in the future. The government also undertook ambitious schemes of privatization, labor reform, and transfer of the national capital. During this process, the military budget has shrunk, along with the purchasing power of officers' salaries.

Perhaps the limits of the ability of the government to democratize and reprofessionalize the military along Western lines were most dramatically revealed in the April 1987 revolt, when a number of army garrisons mutinied in support of a middle-ranking officer's refusal to report to a civilian court on human rights charges. The incident led to a mass outpouring of support for the government and democratic control of the military. The mutineers, however, came away far from empty-handed, even though the leaders of the mutiny were cashiered and nine of the ten senior generals from the army high command were retired. Most critically, the government introduced a due-obedience bill, which, as modified, provided an amnesty to all personnel at the rank of brigadier general or below who were not responsible for *planning* human rights violations, who did not commit particularly heinous crimes, and who did not exceed their orders in executing the plan of repression.[46] Of over four hundred officers slated for trial, only fifty (including fourteen generals) were expected to stand trial.[47] The government also hastened to announce its intention to amend the military code to eliminate a provision that practically affirmed the principle of blind obedience to superiors.[48] The government's troubles did not end there. Two more mutinies followed, and Alfonsín was forced to abandon all trials except those for the highest-ranking officers.

The deflation of the Alfonsín administration's capacity to deal with the armed forces went hand in hand with other political and economic failures. Labor reform, revision of the constitution, the building of a new capital to shift the country's political center of balance, and an economic stabilization policy were all either stillborn or badly miscarried. The capacity of the government to induce the armed forces to accept new missions and abandon its domestic role was badly undercut by a deepening economic crisis. Without financial resources, the government could offer few incentives. Moreover, while depriving the armed forces of their internal security missions, the government provided no credible conventional ones.[49]

□ *Brazil: Coexistence*

Brazil represents an instance of coexistence strategy that, by the end of the Sarney administration, had suffered considerable decay. In large measure because of his vice presidential position on the ticket and weak personal support, the executive was dependent on military support and in turn supported military interests. The political authority of the president was further undermined by the factionalism of the coalition that elected the Neves-Sarney ticket and controlled congress. Nonetheless, during the first part of his administration, the president possessed the ability to take independent initiatives. Moreover, there were internal efforts in the executive branch to demilitarize some aspects of the state. There was, in effect, a rough balance between the military and civilian elements in the administration. This balance can be seen, in part, in remarks made by President Sarney in his 1986 annual message to congress:

> In 1985 the Armed Forces General Staff (EMFA) [Estado Major das Forças Armadas] continued to carry out studies regarding the military policy, strategy, and doctrine, and to elaborate and coordinate plans and programs related to joint activities of the Armed Forces. Among the most important aspects . . . are . . . [p]reserving the Armed Forces' basic functions, reducing *as much as possible* their participation in regions or activities in which the civilian sectors of society can act.[50]

In effect, while civil control was to increase, it would be at a pace determined by and under the guidance of the armed forces themselves. Yet, the attitude of the executive branch was only one element of the equation. The progovernment coalition that had been responsible for Sarney's election had a firm hold on both houses of congress, and elements of that coalition pushed for a more intensive demilitarization.

While the military wanted to guide the process, it could only lobby, influence, and threaten, not command. Armed forces spokesmen were anxious to support rather than pressure the executive. Since President Sarney's personal political base was weak and he had worked closely with the military in the past, there existed a natural coincidence of interest between the armed forces and the civilian government. However, Sarney took a populist line on such issues as economic policy and land reform.[51]

The military, for its part, attempted to portray itself as democratic and modified some of its functions: the number of operatives in the military intelligence community was reportedly decreased and the armed forces enhanced external defense and border security missions. But a naval building program and expansion of the ground forces were planned even before the advent of the civilian government. Furthermore, the military remained heavily involved in the design and production of military equipment, which is becoming a major Brazilian export industry. A host of new initiatives, including a nuclear-powered submarine and medium-range missile, were also well underway before the transfer of power.[52] In effect, the Brazilian military had a fallback position should it be forced to abandon its internal security role.

During the Sarney administration, the position of the civilian government vis-à-vis the military declined because of a number of factors. The most telling was the loss of popularity by the president. This was largely the result of an economic policy that was immensely popular, initially, but was ultimately an economic and political disaster. The economically heterodox Cruzado Plan (introduced in February 1986) first boosted the president's popularity to new heights only to plunge him to a 65 percent negative rating after its collapse.[53] This negative evaluation was not restricted to the popular sectors. A poll taken of businesspeople virtually duplicated the results from polls of the general public.[54]

The second factor was Sarney's decision to press for a six-year term for himself from the constituent assembly that met from early 1987 to late 1988. Unable to rely on popularity, Sarney chose tried and tested methods of patronage politics (awarding federal money and lucrative television licenses) to win support for an extension beyond the promised four years.[55] Such maneuvers, while they yielded an extended term of five years, did little to raise his political capital. On the contrary, Sarney was more and more forced to rely on the armed forces for explicit and implicit support, at times threatening an *autogolpe*, whereby the military would intervene to retain him in power despite the wishes of the majority of the political community.

Table 4.1 shows military spending for the three years prior to and the three years after the transition; it indicates that the military had little to fear from an aggressive policy by Sarney. The real challenge came from congress, where the armed forces salvaged much, but not all that they wanted, in the new constitution.

□ *Uruguay: Coexistence*

The new civilian government found itself in a position of rough parity vis-à-vis the armed forces. The military had been unable to compel a transition on its own terms but nevertheless managed to achieve a negotiated transition that secured vital military interests. Civilian parties were divided over what sort of military policy to pursue—the most contentious division was over how to handle human rights violations that occurred during the military regime. The Frente Amplio supported the prosecution of all violators, but the policy of President Sanguinetti (1985–1990) was one of coexistence. It was essentially two-pronged: to support the armed forces' demands for an amnesty for rights violators and to cut back on the power and prerogatives of the armed forces generally.

While the Uruguayan armed forces had been slow to develop a national security doctrine and the necessary institutions to apply it—witness the late development of its umbrella intelligence agency[56]—they had increased in size, and the military budget had grown apace during the 1973–1985 period of military rule. (See Table 4.2.) One of the president's first efforts was to reduce the size and budget of the military establishment to pre–military regime levels. This he was eventually able to do. In related matters, he attempted to impose discipline on military officers whom he viewed as speaking out of turn on essentially political questions. He forcibly retired three of the country's four most powerful generals for statements regarded as attacks on government policy.[57]

One of these incidents, which occurred during Sanguinetti's first six

Table 4.2 Uruguayan Armed Forces

Year	Uruguay Military Budget (1972 = 100)	Armed Forces (thousands)
1972	100	20
1973	108	20
1974	117	25
1975	118	25
1976	99	28
1977	107	28
1978	109	28
1979	121	28
1980	159	28
1981	216	28
1982	202	29
1983	150	30
1984	107	30

Source: United States Arms Control and Disarmament Agency

months in office, reveals the ambiguity of his stance vis-à-vis the armed forces. General Feola, a military region commander, had written a letter in response to legislative criticisms about the princely salaries of general officers. Feola was quickly cashiered by the president and by the defense minister, Hugo Medina, a retired general. Medina, however, scrupulous in applying regulations that mandated the successor, appointed a military hard-liner as Feola's replacement.[58]

The most serious rumblings of discontent have been over human rights prosecutions. Military refusals to appear before civilian courts, which began investigating rights abuses in October 1986, and threats of a new coup induced the legislature to enact an amnesty law by year's end. Coupled with the amnesty was the transfer of the national intelligence service from military control to the national defense ministry and the approval of civilians for high-ranking military appointments.[59] Passage of the law did not end the issue. Opponents of the amnesty, led by the FA were able to gather enough signatures to have the amnesty contested in a referendum.

The amnesty issue illustrates both the fragility of transition pacts and the tentativeness of military obedience to civilian authority. The Sanguinetti policy of limited change in the armed forces balanced by concession to the most sensitive issue of amnesty has yielded some positive results. The size of the armed forces and military budget has decreased and warnings about internal subversion have abated somewhat. Yet, in the final year of Sanguinetti's term, even though the army commander ruled out the possibility of a terrorist threat reemerging in the country and declared that there were no nostalgic army officers yearning for a return to military rule, rumors persisted about unrest in the armed forces and a split between the high command and their subordinates.[60]

□ *Chile*

The civilian government in Chile assumed power backed by a coalition of the left and center that, in light of past Chilean experience, had shown an amazing degree of cohesion during the 1988 and 1989 campaigns. Furthermore, the moderate right National Renovation (RN) seemed willing to cooperate with the government on at least a selective basis. Candidates and positions in sympathy with the armed forces, however, managed to gain more than 40 percent of the vote in the 1988 and 1989 elections. Moreover, General Pinochet remained as commander in chief of the army, had domestic intelligence transferred to his jurisdiction, and in the transition, purged leading professionalists (moderates who supported many elements of traditional professionalism) from the army high command.[61]

These conditions create a good deal of uncertainty about the civilian government's strategy and possible outcome. Key tests are likely to occur over the issue of amnesty and the continuance of Pinochet as army commander in chief. The resolution of these conflicts and the increasing marginalization of the leading terrorist group, the Frente Patriótico Manuel Rodríguez (Manuel Rodríguez Patriotic Front, or FPMR), could provide the basis for the government to assume a more aggressive policy of doctrinal change. The government has disappointed the armed forces by appointing a civilian defense minister and civilian service secretaries, although the government's first choice for navy secretary was vetoed by the military. The pre-1973 political tradition of Chile augurs well for such a development.

■ **CONCLUSIONS**

Civilian regimes are faced with the task of exorcising the ghost—and often much more than the ghost—of the former national security state. Their present position is the result of the fact that the armed forces have beaten a tactical retreat from outright political control. It is only a tactical retreat because important sectors of the armed forces have not given up pretensions associated with the national security doctrine and the new professionalism. Civilian governments must transform this tactical retreat into a strategic reorientation of the armed forces. Most of the post-transition governments have shown at least an implicit recognition of the need to do this, although their actions have often been cautious, except in cutting the military budget where they have manifested a slightly more aggressive posture. Even when civilians have taken active steps to transform the military establishment, as in Argentina and during the first half of García's term in Peru, the results have been limited because of civilian errors and military intransigence.

Nonetheless, a number of modest gains beyond budget cuts have been made. In almost all countries, senior military leaders have professed at least nominal loyalty to democratic procedures and obedience to constitutional authority. The nature of such protestations of support for the constitutional system must, of course, be viewed with caution. Support for the constitution or the national interest has been common justification for coups; and especially in the Chilean instance, the constitution in question may be, in part, a document of questionable democratic credentials. Nevertheless, legality is on the side of the civilian governments, and the armed forces appear to recognize that fact. A second gain is the curtailing of the military's national security role. While Peru represents a glaring exception to this pattern, the trajectory of development for military participation in policy matters and domestic administrative duties seems to be downward. At the very least, such involvement has become a serious political issue.

Over the last decade, civilian strategies for controlling the armed forces have tended to fall between civil-military coexistence and doctrinal change; but the success of any policy, well thought out or chosen by default, depends on the concrete, mundane, day-to-day execution of policy initiatives. Civilians must effectively counter active or passive military resistance on a number of fronts concerning a number of important issues. It is to these issues that we turn next.

■ NOTES

1. Machiavelli, 1977, bk. 12, pp. 35–36.
2. Rapaport, p. 74. See also Huntington, 1968, pp. 78–92.
3. Machiavelli, op. cit., p. 36.
4. Machiavelli, for example, sees the establishment of a new-model military system as a central part of founding a new regime that requires the systematic use of religion, nationalism, and extensive violence.
5. Rapaport, pp. 77–83.
6. An exception is Ballester et al.
7. My formulation of cadre army corresponds to what Rapaport calls the "cadre-conscript army," which is only the latest military instrument of what he terms the "civilian-military polity." This type of polity includes eighteenth-century European monarchies as well as other nondemocratic states. Rapaport's formulation is more global, mine more parochial in that it is restricted only to contemporary instances. Under the more inclusive formula, it would be incorrect to link cadrelike institutions with democracy.
8. Moskos and Wood, pp. 19–24.
9. José Nun, "The Middle-Class Coup Revisited," in Lowenthal and Fitch, p. 73.
10. Stepan, 1971, p. 61; Huntington, 1964, pp. 83–84.

11. Huntington, 1964, pp. 15–16. This view is disputed by such analysts as Abrahamsson, pp. 159–160. He argues that the apolitical character of the professional armed forces is accidental and not a necessary part of professionalism as such. Similarly, Finer, pp. 22–26, takes issue with Huntington. Citing incidents from twentieth-century European and US history, Finer argues that the military is often thrust into conflict with civilian authorities and has intervened politically in various ways. For a discussion of Huntington and his critics, see Welch, pp. 14–18.

12. "Complete Text of the Speech of the Commander-in-Chief Given on August 6, 1964 at West Point," *Revista Militar*, no. 721 (January–June 1989), pp. 80–81, 83 (emphasis added).

13. Alfred Stepan, "The New Professionalism of Internal Warfare and Military Role Expansion," in Lowenthal, pp. 247–249.

14. Potash, p. 8.

15. McCann, pp. 505–522, argues that the new professionalism is not really new at all but has well-established historical roots. Whether this professionalism is indeed new, a result of the national security doctrine developed since the 1960s, or whether it is better attributed to deeper historical causes within the region itself is not critical to my argument. It is sufficient to note that the concept of professionalism now current entails military control of at least some areas of policy normally recognized as within the civilian sphere under democratic regimes. It is precisely this reversal of the Western pattern of professionalism that renders the reestablishment of democracy in Latin America potentially tenuous.

16. Feit, pp. 171–172.

17. Huntington, 1964, pp. 80–85.

18. Nordlinger, pp. 10–18.

19. McKinlay, pp. 247–248.

20. Stepan, 1971, pp. 57–60.

21. This study reverses what might be considered the natural pattern of discussions of praetorianism, which focus on the armed forces as the subject and the civilian government as the object of political activity. See, for example, the schema developed in Christopher Clapham and George Philip, "Political Dilemma of Military Regimes," in Clapham and Philip, pp. 8–25. Clapham and Philip follow Huntington's categories in Huntington, 1968.

22. In Latin America, only Mexico, Cuba, and Costa Rica can claim to have employed the strategy of wholesale institutional restructuring.

23. The use of politicization here is different from that of McKinlay, op. cit., p. 255. McKinlay stresses "the inculcation of values" and the reformation of the polity, while politicization in the sense I am using it can involve values and a new vision of the polity. In my account, politicization is linked with narrow partisan and personal interests rather than broader interests of a class or well-organized and -disciplined party.

24. Margiotta, pp. 214–237; Wesson, pp. 160–164; Adolfo Aguilar Zinser, "Civil-Military Relations in Mexico," in Goodman et al., pp. 220–223.

25. Constantino Urcuyo, "Civil-Military Relations in Cost Rica: Militarization or Adaptation to New Circumstances," in Goodman et al., p. 241.

26. Felipe Agüero, "The Military and Democracy in Venezuela," in Goodman et al., p. 267.

27. Urcuyo, op. cit., p. 248.

28. Agüero, op. cit., p. 267.

29. For a slightly different account of clientism, see Clapham and Philip, op. cit., pp. 12–15. They subdivide clientism into two types: authoritarian

clientism, which more closely corresponds to my description of the civilian government as client, and factional clientism, which more closely corresponds to what I have denominated a coexistence strategy.

30. This division of activities is based on Clausewitz, bk. 1, chap. 1, no. 24, p. 119, and bk. 2, chap. 2, p. 173.

31. English, p. 369.

32. According to Americas Watch, the Belaúnde government failed to affirm democratic control over the military and "tolerated the human rights abuses which sectors of the security forces asserted to be a necessary concomitant of war." Americas Watch, 1988, p. 3.

33. FBIS, "Cuts Mirage Purchase to 13," Paris, AFP, July 30, 1985, FBIS-LAM-85-147, July 31, 1985, p. J2.

34. FBIS, "Attempted Republican Guard Mutiny Discovered," Paris, AFP, September 3, 1985, FBIS-LAM-85-172, September 5, 1985, p. J1.

35. "Alan García Challenges Army's Counter-Insurgency Methods," *Latin American Regional Reports: Andean Group Report*, October 4, 1985, p. 1.

36. FBIS, "Abram Cavallerino Installed as Armed Forces Head," Paris, AFP, September 17, 1985, FBIS-LAM-85-182, September 19, 1985, pp. J1–J2.

37. *Latin American Weekly Report* (85-48), p. 12; FBIS, "Army General Positions to Be Reduced," Lima, Panamericana Television Network, November 14, 1985, FBIS-LAM-85-221, November 15, 1985, pp. J2–J3.

38. "García Quashes Military Protest," *Latin American Weekly Report*, April 16, 1987, p. 9.

39. Americas Watch 1988, pp. 61–64.

40. "Peru: Officers Sentenced for Homicide," *Latin American Weekly Report*, December 21, 1989, p. 12.

41. Americas Watch 1988, p. 3.

42. FBIS, "Alfonsín Addresses Armed Forces Banquet," Buenos Aires, Domestic Service, July 6, 1985, FBIS-LAM-85-130, July 8, 1985, p. B3.

43. "Defence Law Bans Internal Action," *Latin American Weekly Report*, April 28, 1988, p. 2.

44. Joint Publications Research Service (JPRS), "Changes in Military Code," Buenos Aires, *La Nacion*, April 28, 1984, JPRS-LAM-84-068, June 4, 1984, pp. 35–37.

45. "Argentine Intelligence Undergoes Restructure," *Jane's Defence Weekly*, April 18, 1987, p. 693.

46. "President Alfonsín Signs 'Due Obedience' Law," *Jane's Defence Weekly*, 20 June 1987, p. 1293.

47. "Alfonsín Has Run-in with the Law," *Latin American Weekly Report*, June 25, 1987, p. 8.

48. FBIS, "President Alfonsín Speech on Due Obedience Bill," Buenos Aires, Domestic Service, May 14, 1987, FBIS-LAM-87-093, May 14, 1987, pp. B1–B6.

49. David Pion-Berlin, in an unpublished paper, makes a harsher analysis of Alfonsín's failure than that offered here. He argues that Alfonsín never really attempted to create a positive-sum game situation in his dealings with the military but relied on negative sanctions. My position, spelled out in more detail in Chapters 5 and 6, is that the armed forces share about equal blame because of their own hard-line response, especially on the issue of human rights.

50. FBIS, "Sarney Message to Congress Opening Session," São Paulo, *Folha de São Paulo*, March 2, 1986, FBIS-LAM-86-046, March 10, 1986, p. D19 (emphasis added).

51. The armed forces, however, were active in making their views on land

reform apparent, claiming that the land reform administration was dominated by leftists. (Josias de Souza, "Agrarian Reform Planners Investigated by SNI," São Paulo, *Folha de São Paulo*, July 17, 1986, FBIS-LAM-86-141, July 23, 1986, p. D1). According to Alfred Stepan, this military intervention had a significant impact on the drive for land reform. Stepan, 1988, p. 109.

52. Zagorski, pp. 45–64.

53. FBIS, "Sarney's Popularity Declines in Poll," São Paulo, *Folha de São Paulo*, March 13, 1988, FBIS-LAT-88-051, March 16, 1988, p. 21.

54. FBIS, "Poll Shows Business Opposition to Government," São Paulo, *Folha de São Paulo*, December 27, 1987, FBIS-LAT-87-249, December 29, 1987, p. 22.

55. "O for the Wings of a Government," *Economist*, November 21, 1987, pp. 40–41.

56. Stepan, 1988, p. 23.

57. "Uruguay: Sanguinetti Proposes Amnesty for Rights Offenders," *Latinamerica Press*, August 28, 1986, pp. 1–2.

58. "Outspoken General Gets the Sack," *Latin American Regional Reports: Southern Cone Report*, November 15, 1985, p. 5.

59. Kathryn Leger, "Shadow of Military Looms Large over Uruguayan Democracy," *Christian Science Monitor*, February 21, 1987, pp. 9, 11.

60. FBIS, "Army Commander Rules Out Terrorist Resurgence," Montevideo, Radio Carve Network, May 19, 1989, FBIS-LAT-89-099, May 24, 1989, p. 38; FBIS, "Defense Minister Denies Military Unrest," Montevideo Radio Carve, October 20, 1989, FBIS-LAT-89-203, October 23, 1989, p. 38.

61. "Marked Man," *Economist*, October 14, 1989, pp. 46, 49.

5■
Flashpoint I: Human Rights

Not all military interests are created equal. Similarly, the various means the armed forces can use to influence the political process differ in effectiveness and entail different risks. Hence, civil-military politics is a complex web of actions and counteractions concerning a variety of policies. This web, although complex, is not completely chaotic. In the five countries under study, there are four major policy areas—flashpoints—where military interests have come into conflict with the policies of civilian governments or the desires of significant segments of society. These flashpoints are: the establishment of protection for human rights and punishment for past rights violations; counterinsurgency and internal security; military reform; and reform of the state.

Although the immediate salience of these basic issues varies from country to country, the issues have been important in all five countries upon which this study focuses—indeed, in most of Latin America. They represent areas in which military practices and aspirations often run counter to the requisites for consolidating democracy. Democracy entails the rule of law and due-process guarantees for those accused of crimes; yet military governments frequently and egregiously ignored due-process guarantees and the armed forces often demand that the authorities ignore them when, in the armed forces' judgment, the safety and order of society are seriously threatened. Democracy requires that civilian officials make and implement virtually all domestic policy, but internal security theory and practice pose a serious challenge to this civilian dominance. If they are to survive, democratic regimes must become efficient and able to respond to popular demands, but the influence of the armed forces often is a check on political reform. Stable democracy requires obedient and professional armed forces, yet military institutions have often frustrated attempts at civilian control.

The following chapters provide an analysis of these four major flashpoints, illustrating the political dynamics involved by means of case studies. Each case study is drawn from one of the countries where the issue in question has had the greatest immediate importance.

■   THE NATURE OF THE HUMAN RIGHTS ISSUE

Human rights has been the most volatile flashpoint. There are a number of causes for this volatility. First, the scale of human rights violations in all five countries has been significant and has placed these countries under intense international scrutiny. Second, prosecution of rights violators is a challenge to the traditional prerogatives of the military justice system when charges are brought before civilian courts. Third, in some instances, there was extensive military involvement in rights violations, and these violations were explicitly or implicitly a matter of military policy. In these cases, rights prosecutions represent a challenge to the armed forces' continuity in sheer quantitative terms. Fourth, the rights issue strikes at the heart of the military's national security doctrine, which views repressive military measures as part of a justified war against internal subversion. According to this view, human rights violations by the armed forces are regrettable but should be treated with leniency while the violations by the enemy (in military eyes much more deplorable than their own) must not be countenanced. From this military point of view, the prosecution of human rights violators is an act of vengeance, not justice.

While the armed forces argue that rights violations are justified or excusable, the argument for prosecuting violators is at least as compelling. Rights violations constitute massive contraventions of legal norms and basic human standards of fair and equal treatment. A policy that ignores or excuses such violations undermines basic norms of civilized behavior and the principle of due process, whose establishment is an important task in democratic consolidation. It would establish a precedent that the armed forces—or agents of the state—are above the law and render such violations more likely in the future.

However, civilian governments are not faced with a choice of all or nothing in regard to establishing the rule of law. A range of actions, from minimal support to the complete and retrospective support of the principle, are possible. At the lower end of the scale, governments can encourage military prosecutions of future human rights violators. As a more forceful step, they can amend military codes to establish the principle that soldiers must follow the law and not the orders of superiors when the two are in conflict. Further, they can alter the jurisdiction of the court system to provide for civilian jurisdiction over military offenders. Finally, they can attempt to bring some or all of those responsible for past violations to justice.

Thus, governments are faced with conflicting claims of justice, but more importantly, with a question of political prudence. Although military claims that human rights prosecutions are simply *revanchismo* (revenge taking) can be substantially discounted, the fervor with which military officers hold this view cannot. Nor can governments afford to discount the ability of the armed forces to resist rights prosecutions. Governments must be able to judge the political strength and solidarity of the armed forces in opposing prosecutions and decide what measures are possible for furthering the rule of law.

■ THE SCOPE OF THE PROBLEM

Some idea of the scope of the human rights problem can be gathered from the country-by-country statistical breakdown in Table 5.1. Since methods of tabulation differ in each case and there are often multiple estimates, such a breakdown can provide only a rough estimate of the actual numbers involved. Nonetheless, they present some interesting ways of evaluating the hypotheses developed in Chapter 3.

Table 5.1 Rights Violations

Country	Political Murders/ Disappearances	Other Victims	Security Forces Involved	Military Amnesty
Argentina	9,000–30,000	N/A	1,000	Yes
Brazil	250[a]	20,000	40,000	Yes
Chile	2,000	320,000	200	Yes
Peru[b]	3,000–8,000	N/A	N/A	No
Uruguay	240	8,000–50,000	50–180	No

Sources: Amnesty International; Chilean Human Rights Commission; Vicariate of Solidarity; *Brasil, Nunca Mais*; United Nations Human Rights Commission; *Nunca Más*; Chilean Commission on Peace and Reconciliation.
Notes: Figures are rounded. a. Half of the political killings in Brazil took place in land struggles during the 1980s.
b. Peruvian figures are from the 1980s and are largely military rights violations under the civilian regime.

The intensity of military resistance on the rights issue can serve as a gauge of how profoundly the armed forces have internalized a key nostrum of the new professionalism: that praetorianism is, in fact, a symptom of internal war in which victory requires repressive military action. If activities associated with the new professionalism are a rather late or relatively unimportant addition to the complex of military interests, then these repressive activities should be defended less vigorously and by a narrower stratum of officers. Believers in Western professionalism would be more likely to regard rights violations as illegal and unprofessional behavior and would be more likely to tolerate rights prosecutions than supporters of the new professionalism. On the other hand, if the new professionalism has taken deep root, support for officers charged with rights violations ought to be widespread within the officer corps, regardless of other factors that might serve to limit the importance of the issue, such as a relatively small number of officers subject to prosecution.

In addition to the general hypotheses listed in Chapter 3, another hypothesis, specifically related to the human rights issue, should also be considered: *Hypothesis 5: Other factors being constant, the relative magnitude of rights violations serves as indication of the potential political support for rights trials.*[1] A small country like Uruguay, with two to three million people, is likely to be affected much more than twice as seriously by 50,000 rights violations than is Brazil (population 150 million) with 20,000. This would probably be so even though the higher Uruguayan figures include short-term detentions while the Brazilian figures tend to represent more serious actions.

If Hypothesis 4 (chances of civilian success are correlated to low armed forces prestige) and Hypothesis 5 are substantially correct, the level of conflict over human rights ought to vary directly with the level of violence and inversely with the prestige of the armed forces. (For a listing of predictions, see Table 5.2.)

Table 5.2 Potential for Conflict over Human Rights

Country	Level of Violence	Prestige of Armed Forces	Predicted Potential for Conflict
Argentina	High	Low	High
Brazil	Low	Moderate-High	Low
Uruguay	High	Moderate	Moderate
Peru	High	Moderate	Moderate
Chile	High	Moderate-High	Moderate

■ CASE STUDY—ARGENTINA: PROSECUTION AND REVOLT

Argentina is the country with the greatest prima facie potential for conflict over human rights. Disappearances in Argentina were numerous and particularly abhorrent in that they were out of proportion to the seriousness of the threat and included people who were not enemies of the regime.[2] Responsibility for rights violations was not localized in a national intelligence service or even in service intelligence agencies. Rather, the methodology used to fight the dirty war, as the struggle against subversives came to be called, provided for highly decentralized execution of the plan to eliminate the internal enemy. This entailed widespread involvement by all three armed services (although the army played a more important role than the others). Moreover, operational commands and their subordinate units often took an active part in the process.[3] The return of civilian government presaged a day of reckoning.

President Alfonsín's strategy in regard to the military was to reorient the institution without a wholesale purge. The human rights issue was the most delicate part of the problem he faced in dealing with the armed forces. The government wanted to accomplish two objectives that appeared to be contrary if not contradictory. First, it had to support in some effective manner, albeit ex post facto, the principles of due process and the legal accountability of the armed forces for violations of fundamental rights. Second, the government had to obtain a degree of voluntary acceptance of these norms by the armed forces themselves, for without such internalization by the military, Argentine democracy might be no more stable than it had been previously. The grounds upon which this was to be done were explained by Raúl Alfonsín in 1985:

> [There is a] distinction we must draw between the bad chiefs the army had and the army as an institution. A country cannot function without any army. We must ensure that it has the prestige it ought to have in any society. To the skeptics on the other side, to those who wonder how we can talk about the armed forces' prestige without holding new trials, I say: The armed forces' prestige is linked to the fact that the bad chiefs have been brought to trial. This is what makes it possible to clarify the matter with regard to the rest of the army.[4]

This distinction between the bad chiefs and the army as an institution was manifested in Alfonsín's notion of three levels of responsibility: those who planned the dirty war, developed its methodology, and supervised its execution; those who committed excesses in carrying out orders; and those who limited themselves to carrying out orders. The president wished to prosecute only the first two groups and exclude the third because the orders they received "were imparted in a context that was not free from pressure of the effects of intense and permanent propaganda inspired by the totalitarian doctrine of national security . . . [which] led those who received orders to believe they were legitimate."[5] Alfonsín seemed to be operating on the presumption that the national security doctrine and the new professionalism had not sunk deep roots into the Argentine military establishment.

◻ *The Holy Week Crisis*

Alfonsín's distinction between a good institution and bad leaders, however, satisfied neither the military nor human rights groups. The threat of trials for officers who might be included in one of the first two categories produced great unease in the armed forces, while rights groups were troubled by the fact that the lion's share of violators might escape prosecution altogether. Each group saw in the formulation the result it most feared and pressured for a definitive solution that conformed to its predilections.

Military reaction was unsatisfactory on a number of fronts. The military justice system was supposed to handle the trials of the members of the three military juntas and the military chief of the Buenos Aires police during the dirty war, but the military courts failed to cooperate. The Military Supreme Council (the highest military court) indirectly justified actions taken by those indicted for human rights violations, called the whole proceeding into question,[6] turned the trials over to the civilian courts (claiming it could not rule on the basis of incomplete evidence),[7] and finally resigned en masse.[8] In other areas of military reform as well, the armed forces did little to implement the government's programs for subordinating the armed forces to a democratically elected government.

As the trials of the junta members moved toward a conclusion in mid-1985, the government hinted at a definitive amnesty.[9] The need for an amnesty bill would have been obviated, however, had the courts invoked Alfonsín's distinction between those responsible for rights violations and those who were only following orders. When the civilian court that passed sentence on the junta members failed to cite this distinction,[10] it placed the question of a definitive amnesty squarely in the government's lap. Still caught between political pressure for trials and military pressure for amnesty, the government procrastinated another year. It was not until December 1986 that it introduced a bill establishing the principle of obedience to orders (*obediencia debida*) as grounds for exemption from prosecution for human rights violations. The same bill set a cut-off date—*punto final*—sixty days after enactment for final charges to be filed against human rights violators.[11] The hope that the bill would put an end to the issue was short-lived. Before the deadline expired, charges had been brought against nearly 170 officers and NCOs.[12] As was the case with Alfonsín's human rights policy in general, the punto final compromise satisfied neither political nor military sectors.

In the early months of 1987, it became clear that a rift was developing between senior and junior officers concerning the continuation of the trials. One illustration of that rift was a document prepared by active-duty officers titled "Proclamation to Argentine Society." Reportedly, it was a pronouncement that grew out of discussions in almost all army garrisons. The proclamation declared that the current trials were not the result of justice but political vengeance. It claimed that the service chiefs were presiding over a process that brought to trial subordinates who were only following orders and let those responsible escape; and it proclaimed that the dissidents were "prepared to defend with . . . [their] lives . . . comrades who are being sacrificed for a mistaken notion of justice."[13] Convicted members of the juntas incited their adherents from prison. General Ramon Camps, serving a life term, called on fellow officers to "avoid being fooled by the fallacy of subordination to political power." General Luciano Benjamin Menéndez, awaiting trial, encouraged citizens "to save Argentina from Communist aggression."[14] In the face of such challenges, Army Chief of Staff Ríos Ereñú's defense seemed much too phlegmatic to the officers worried about civilian vengeance:

> We waged a just and legitimate war against an aggressor, no Argentine will disagree with this; and when we say that there were mistakes and injustices made during this war, something which, moreover is characteristic of any war, we admit that mistakes were made. . . . We have agreed to let the courts and the state of right establish whether these mistakes and injustices deserve to be punished or sentenced by the courts.[15]

The situation came to a head on April 16 when an army major refused to report as directed to a civilian court to answer charges of human rights violations and sought refuge in the Fourteenth Airborne Infantry Regiment in Córdoba, thus sparking the Holy Week rebellion. Major Ernesto Barreiro had the tacit support of the regiment's commander, Lieutenant Colonel Luis Polo. After forty-eight hours, Barreiro was cashiered by the armed forces. Meanwhile at the Campo de Mayo military base, another lieutenant colonel, Aldo Rico, took over the infantry school. He was supported by some 150 officers and troops. General Ríos Ereñú dispatched troops to suppress the mutiny, but when they arrived on the scene, they refused to take any action against the rebels. (Throughout this process the navy chief of staff remained aloof while the air force chief tried to dissuade rebels.)[16] On the military level, there was a standoff.

Although Alfonsín was unable to get the military to act effectively against the rebels, civilian support for the government was significant. Leading civilian politicians supported the Alfonsín administration. Every national political party signed a statement supporting the defense of democracy against the military. The president's address to congress, attended even by the president's leading critic, union federation leader Saúl Ubaldini, received a standing ovation. And a total of one million civilians rallied outside of congress and the presidential palace in support of the government against the military rebels.[17]

The crisis was apparently resolved on April 19 after a meeting between President Alfonsín and the rebels. Although the government denied making a deal with the dissident officers, the government modified its military policy significantly. The army high command was reorganized—the chief of staff was removed, José Segundo Caridi (formerly number four in seniority) was appointed in his stead, and the ten most-senior generals were retired (with the exception of Caridi)—and the government decided to lift many of its human rights prosecutions.[18]

Even these compromises, which were sufficient to induce the surrender of the major rebel forces, were not universally accepted by officers sympathetic to the aims of the rebellion. In the northwest, 100 officers and troops refused to recognize the appointment of General Caridi as chief of staff—Caridi's retirement was demanded by the rebels—although they were placated by the appointment of General Fausto González, a favorite of the dissident officers, as deputy chief of staff. By the end of the rebellion, 383 officers and troops had participated and 16 general officers were forced into retirement.[19]

The results of the rebellion were mixed as far as the government was concerned. While it was clear that the civilian climate was not propitious to a full-fledged coup d'état, the government did not face the mutineers down as it claimed. The rebels had challenged the government on narrow, but portentous, issues: political control of senior military personnel and the imposition of discipline through the courts. They tried to claim this was not an attack on democracy or the political system as a whole. As they put it in a communiqué from the Campo de Mayo base, "This is not a coup, but an internal problem of the armed forces." Yet, the same communiqué challenged the constitutionality of human rights trials.[20] With few exceptions, however, civilian leaders did not adhere to this analysis.

Although the rebels did not attempt to seize control of the government, their actions represented a clear challenge to civilian control of the armed forces. Far from being an internal matter, the appointment of senior officers and their continuation in office is clearly a matter of political purview under the concept of professionalism typical of constitutional democracies. Eligibility for senior positions is determined by military regulations, but those appointed must have the confidence of their political superiors, not their military juniors. Certainly, the removal of senior officers is not controlled by their subordinates. Similar judgments can be made concerning the trial and punishment of military officers. Hence, the government's compromise with the rebels constituted a significant breech of its own military policy. The outgoing chief of staff noted that the crisis had direct political ramifications.[21]

The centerpiece of the government's concessions turned out to be a new amnesty known as the obediencia debida bill. The main points of this new legislation were: prohibition of evidence that a given junior officer had acted on his own in committing illegalities; prohibition of trials for junior officers for torture, kidnapping, or murder; and the introduction of the principle of coerción irresistible, which attributed rights violations to commanding officers. The text of the law exempted from prosecution all those who did not have decisionmaking authority unless they committed rape, committed crimes against minors, or stole property. Those who did not hold decisionmaking posts were automatically exempt unless a court held within thirty days that they actually had decisionmaking authority. Even those with the rank of brigadier general or above could avail themselves of the amnesty if they could demonstrate they did not have such authority.[22]

The law exempted virtually everyone below the rank of brigadier general from prosecution.[23] The effect on the number of officers liable to stand trial was dramatic. According to *The Economist*, the law exonerated most of the generals and left only a small number of the approximately 1,000 officers that the government's commission thought implicated in human rights violations still subject to prosecution.[24] According to Defense Ministry figures, out of a total of 380 individuals originally liable for prosecution, only 80 military officers (including just two on active duty) remained subject to the courts after enactment of the new law.[25] Among those benefiting from the law was the major whose defiance had triggered the mutiny, Ernesto Barreiro.[26] As a concession to the future accountability of officers, Alfonsín promised that Article 514 of the military code, which, he noted, "virtually establishes the rule of blind obedience," would be abolished.[27] On the issues of military prosecutions, the government had beaten a retreat.

The retreat was necessitated by the inability of the army leadership to enforce its and the government's authority over junior officers. This failure was compounded by intelligence failures: The civilian head of SIDE (the Secretariat of State for Intelligence, the umbrella intelligence agency) admitted that Major Barreiro and Colonel Rico's disaffections were known, but authorities did not know if they would act. Another rebel, Lieutenant Colonel Jorge Venturino, had actually been a member of military intelligence and had been dismissed from his post because of disagreement with the government over rights trials.[28] In none of the cases had effective preventive action been taken nor, apparently, was adequate warning given to the president. Ríos Ereñú's replacement meant that Alfonsín had four different army chiefs of staff in a period of less than four years.[29]

□ Caridi as Chief of Staff

The government's retreat on personnel policy was not so dramatic, yet it seemed that not much could be expected from a chief of staff whose closest deputy was forced upon him by the rebels and whose own personal record was tainted by charges of human rights violations. Nonetheless, José Caridi was adroit in consolidating his control of the army and furthering governmental policy.

Initial steps were slow. Some of the leaders of the mutiny got off lightly. Some two dozen captains were set back one year in their course at the War College. Colonel Rico was charged with rebellion, not sedition.[30] And, while there was no purge of those disloyal to the army leadership and civilian authority, as recommended by a number of former military officers favoring the democratic transition,[31] General González was removed from his position as assistant chief of staff when he reinstated Major Barreiro and Colonel Rico to active duty. González also stepped beyond the pale in assuring middle-ranking officers that they would be tried by military and not civilian courts. González was replaced by General Miguel Abbate, noted for his hard line against the mutineers.[32]

A number of officers (including three majors, two captains, and three lieutenants) were disciplined then removed from the service when they refused to swear a newly required oath to obey the constitution. One colonel was given thirty days' detention for inappropriate public statements.[33] Other senior officers, apparently in agreement with the ultimate aims but not the methods of the rebels, requested their retirement from the service.[34] Meanwhile, the chief of the armed forces joint staff, Brigadier General Teodoro Waldner, refused to allow a lieutenant colonel involved in the Holy Week incidents to assume his post with the staff because he was, in Waldner's words, a "controversial individual."[35] In another parallel development, the defense ministry decided not to act on promotions for individuals until their pending cases involving human rights violations had been resolved.[36]

Caridi took a harder line than his predecessor in stating the military's case before the government and the public, calling for political measures to allay the armed forces' unease. He even defended the tactics used during the dirty war.[37] In a secret telegram sent to army units, he linked his support for the demands of the military with a call for discipline in the ranks. In the telegram, he criticized officers who "disregarded ethics and adversely affected discipline" during Holy Week but said he would keep lines of communication open.[38] In effect, the new chief of staff attempted to assume the position of the army's man while his predecessor had been tagged as the government's spokesman to the armed forces.

Caridi attempted to follow a pattern of professional behavior that would win him the support of the officer corps and the continued confidence of the government. While he defended the subordination of the military to civilian authorities and the need for loyalty to democratic principles, he nonetheless served as a spokesman for the interests of the military as an institution and the professional concerns of a large number, if not a preponderant majority, of serving officers. This stance avoided linking the chief of staff too closely and too personally with the policies of the existing government, which would have caused the loss of military support for Caridi and which had the appearance of politicization to the armed forces. At the same time, Caridi attempted to impose discipline on the army itself, as demanded by the norms of professionalism. To do otherwise would have countenanced the politicization of the services from within.

Although not in agreement with the Alfonsín government's human rights policy, Caridi's notion of the professional role of the military dovetailed nicely with the president's own. Politicization of the military from within threatened the position of both the civilian government and the senior military leadership. Moreover, failure to respect the autonomy of the political and military spheres had been the bane of Argentine politics for over fifty years. While the president and chief of staff might not agree on the meaning of democracy and due process, military discipline served both their interests.

□ *Continued Unrest*

Restiveness in the army did not cease with the change in the high command and the due obedience law. Caridi appeared to lack the personal authority to make more drastic shifts in personnel that would have consolidated the officer corps behind the norms of professionalism he supported. His lack of personal authority emphasized the ambiguities underlying the concepts of professionalism, internal discipline, and civilian control. While the transfer of lower-ranking officers is largely the prerogative of the uniformed heads of the services and the appointment of the high command the right of civilian political authority, these functions had to be exercised with discretion. A wholesale transfer or retirement of officers could be interpreted as politicization of the armed forces. Although it was not legally essential to secure the tacit consensus of the officer corps to execute such a reorganization, it was politically prudent to do so lest such transfers or retirements provoke further rebellions and further embarrassment for both government and army leadership.

Military oppositionists took advantage of this lack of consensus to press their views. One individual of influence on the military right was Colonel Mohammed Alí Seineldín, a Catholic ultranationalist. Seineldín published an article in *El Expreso* magazine claiming to explain subversion's long-term strategy. In the piece, Colonel Seineldín described the struggle as one between truth or God's reign, on one side, and error or evil's reign, on the other. Included in the former were: the Catholic church, the Crusades, Scholasticism, the reconquest of Spain from the Moors, the Counter-Reformation, and papal encyclicals. Included in the latter were: heresies condemned by the church and certain contemporary social, political, cultural, and religious movements.[39] After the Holy Week revolt, Colonel Seineldín did not remain silent. Although he was stationed in Panama as a military attaché, an Argentine paper carried an interview with him in which he was cited as defending the use of torture during the dirty war and openly supporting the Holy Week mutinies. When challenged, he denied having given the interview, and the chief of staff responded by ordering an internal investigation.[40]

Another troublemaker was Major Barreiro, now removed from the service, whose act of indiscipline had sparked the mutinies. He produced a videotape on the revolts, collectively called Operation Dignity (Operación

Dignidad), and circulated it to various army garrisons. On the tape, he criticized General Caridi and the policies of the government and denied that anyone had actually disappeared during the dirty war. General Caridi banned the showing of the tape in army barracks. Investigations were begun against those responsible for showing the tape, but the former major continued to tour the provinces showing the tape himself. In an interview, he stated that Colonel Seineldín shared his views on Operation Dignity and asserted that the army was undergoing a period of assessment.[41]

While the government put on a bold face, with Alfonsín saying in an interview that "in Argentina there is no danger of institutional instability, nor will there be,"[42] it took steps to thwart a potential crisis. The president warned the armed services at an annual military dinner that they would become the target of a major psychological campaign to undermine discipline. He apparently feared the reemergence of alliances between civilian and military factions that had characterized successful coups in the past. He presented two defensive measures. Each service chief was to implement a special plan drawn up by its intelligence service, and each service chief was instructed to use "the most severe disciplinary sanctions on any personnel making political statements."[43] Reportedly, in a secret session of the Chamber of Deputies, the civilian head of SIDE admitted that agents were involved in bombings following the mutiny and noted that a cleanup of the agency and reduction of its personnel by one-third was being conducted.[44]

The army undertook a policy of retiring or removing from sensitive positions officers who had demonstrated sympathy for the Holy Week rebels. Two incidents in September tested this policy and seemed to indicate a potential for further armed revolt. There was a shoot-out at the ammunition dump close to where Colonel Rico was being held. The shots were later explained as part of an exercise, but no exercise had been announced previous to the incident. Some officials suspected that the gunfire was staged to provoke an unsettling effect.

A more serious outbreak occurred with the Third Infantry Regiment stationed at La Tablada. Upon hearing of the transfer of its commander before the end of the normal two-year rotation, the regiment confined itself to barracks in battle gear. Officers told the press they considered the transfer a violation of the agreement that brought an end to the Holy Week mutiny. Caridi cut the incident short by flying to the barracks and ordering the troops to desist. Disciplinary proceedings were instigated against the ringleaders.[45] A defense ministry official admitted that the ministry had been aware of the potential for revolt but noted that the transfer and retirement of thirty officers from the rank of captain to lieutenant colonel who had participated in the Holy Week uprising was part of a policy that assumed a calculated risk. The defense ministry indicated that the officers had been following a strategy of "tarnish[ing] the image" of General Caridi.[46] The continuation of the strategy of consolidation via personnel policy was further confirmed by reports that fifty-seven colonels remained on active duty without function, except to collect their pay.[47]

Unresolved problems continued into the Christmas season. Pay, low for all civil servants, was causing restiveness among military officers. The continued enforcement of sentences against senior commanders remained a source of irritation. And the trial and punishment of Rico was a serious issue. He had been declared a war hero by the president for his actions during the Malvinas conflict, and the determination of his eventual status was a thorny issue. This came to a head with the transfer of his case by the supreme court from civilian to military jurisdiction, allowing the restoration of his rank and a less rigorous confinement.[48]

The events that followed the transfer of the case precipitated yet another crisis. A military judge ordered Rico returned to rigorous detention, while, reportedly, Caridi offered the former rebel officer a decent way out via voluntary retirement. In reaction to the judge's order, Colonel Rico called together some of his close followers from the Buenos Aires area, where he was detained, and announced he no longer recognized the authority of Caridi as chief of staff. The army mobilized troops, but Rico was able to escape before they arrived at the scene and put Operation Dispersal (Operación Desparramo) into effect.

The plan involved the dispersal of Rico sympathizers to provincial units to persuade them to take part in a major uprising. Sympathizers found support in Santa Cruz, western San Luis, and Tucumán, but in Las Lajas, Neuquén, a Rico emissary was promptly arrested. Because many officers were on holiday at the time, Rico obtained support from officers no higher in rank than lieutenant colonel, primarily from lieutenants. Rico himself holed up in Monte Caseros and had its approaches mined. Although the holiday season and bad weather slowed the army response, troops were finally mobilized and sent to face the rebels, and after an exchange of fire, Rico—who had vowed never to surrender—agreed to give himself up. Other revolts were also put down, including a revolt at the Aeroparque air base in Buenos Aires.[49] Although over three hundred rebels were originally arrested, the number slated to stand trial fell by half within about a month.[50]

While Rico's supporters could charge that the entire episode was the result of bad faith on the part of Caridi,[51] Rico's second revolt placed him clearly beyond the pale of acceptable military politics even for some of those sympathetic to his basic position.[52] By mutinying against his military superiors, Rico tried to limit the scope of his action in the same way as the Holy Week communiqué: He could claim it was not an attempted coup against the government but a protest against the behavior and character of uniformed military personnel. Such a stance, however, had little success in placating the major civilian sectors or the military leadership. Caridi's policies and the government's Holy Week concessions had apparently satisfied a majority of the armed forces. The prospect of another Holy Week revolt galvanized the high command into action, and in suppressing the rebellion, the army leadership was able to take the ethical high ground in defense of the constitution and the "honor of real Argentine soldiers." Additionally, it took a swipe at the messianic ideological concept underlying the rebellion.[53]

The reaction of the government to the January rebellion differed significantly from its actions in the face of the Holy Week mutiny. In the earlier instance, the government had relied upon large-scale popular rallies to overawe the insurgents but found itself negotiating concessions with them. In January, Alfonsín used exclusively military means to suppress a military uprising. Latin American newsletters put the following analysis in Alfonsín's mouth:

> When this gentleman [Rico] mutinied last Easter, we had no loyal troops. Now we have them, and they are the overwhelming majority. Caridi will suppress this rebellion, and a new phase will begin. For four years we have always had to play a delicate balancing act. Now, for the first time, we are in a position of strength, with a high command committed to the constitutional order. . . . Popular mobilization is necessary when you don't have troops of your own.[54]

The rebellion also gave Caridi the opportunity to continue his purge of the officer corps. Brigadier General Auel, deputy chief of staff for operations, was removed from his post and eventually given ten days' house arrest for actions stemming from his failure to report for duty promptly during the rebellion.[55] Two brigade commanders were removed.[56] Numerous other officers were either removed from their posts or retired. Those purged included passive sympathizers as well as active participants in the rebellion.[57]

Although the air force chief of staff pledged his support to Caridi in suppressing the revolt and said that all things were calm in his service,[58] that did not prove to be the case. In fact, the air force portion of the revolt revealed an even more disturbing development than was immediately discernible in the army incidents: civilian involvement. This situation evoked memories of the traditional pattern of past Argentine coups. The military leader of the air force rebellion, a retired colonel, Luis Estrella, was seconded by a civilian rightist. Documents discovered after the failure of the plot revealed that it was far more than just a military mutiny against sectors of the air force high command. Besides plotting the assassination of the chief of staff and other high-ranking air force officers, the rebel leaders intended to assassinate Alfonsín and replace Caridi with a candidate of their own choosing.[59] The air force rebellion was crushed by a small unit of border guards, although rumors of dissatisfaction within the air force and an internal move to retire the air force chief of staff, Brigadier Horacio Crespo, persisted for months afterward.[60] The reformist faction of the Peronists warned that there were civilians supporting the military mutiny; the party's military expert claimed that a coup was being plotted for 1989 (the year of the next presidential election).[61]

Within a month after the suppression of the rebellion, the military high command met with President Alfonsín to review the situation within the armed forces. The chiefs of staff told the president that the military required $26 million to pay off existing debts to suppliers. Although the maintenance of equipment and level of training remained in a deplorable state, Alfonsín made no promise to increase the military budget. On military pay, the president and his advisers held that merit increases rather than a general increase should be the rule, while Defense Minister Horacio Jaunarena, a civilian, argued for an across-the-board increase as a reward for loyalty. Once the military had purged certain elements, the government indicated it would back the military's modernization demands.[62] Although the armed forces received little immediate monetary boost, it was later revealed that the military budget would not be cut as part of a plan to reduce public expenses, and the military was to be given a pay increase to bring military salaries in line with those of the judiciary.[63] Within five months, the chiefs of staff were each promoted to ranks vacant since the advent of the new civilian government in 1983.[64]

□ *The Seineldín Mutiny*

The second Rico mutiny was not the last such test that the Alfonsín government had to face. In December 1988, in the face of new human rights trials, Colonel Mohammed Alí Seineldín returned to Argentina from his post as a military adviser in Panama to lead yet another revolt. The colonel had been denied a promotion to general when a promotion board failed to make the necessary recommendation and was pending reassignment. The revolt was to shake the high command once again.

On December 1, five hundred rebels, led by Colonel Seineldín, seized the Campo de Mayo Infantry School, 20 miles from Buenos Aires. They sought amnesty, an end to rights trials, and an increased military budget. Loyalist troops failed to act promptly. Observers suspected that commanders were unwilling to cooperate or were afraid troops would be unwilling to attack the rebels. In a smaller-scale repetition of the Holy Week event, 100,000 people rallied in Buenos Aires in support of the government.[65] Seineldín had widespread support, with five bases openly favoring the rebels. The rebels' freedom of action was such that they were able to leave Campo de Mayo and travel to the Villa Martelli logistics base 6 miles to the south.[66] As before, the rebels attempted to portray the mutiny as an internal army matter and asserted their respect for the constitutional order.[67]

The government's announcement on the night of December 4 that the military rebellion was over and no deals were made was greeted with widespread skepticism. Regardless of disclaimers, government concessions to the rebels were significant. General Caridi was forced to resign; the armed forces won a significantly higher pay raise than had been planned in November (20 percent instead of 12 percent, plus a $100 lump-sum payment); and Defense Minister Jaunarena declared publicly that the dirty war had been necessary. These concessions seemed to open the door to more fundamental revisions of the government's military policy. Nonetheless, the president remained firm in his position that the military amnesty would not be extended.[68]

□ *The Menem Amnesty*

On October 7, 1989, the new president, Carlos Menem, issued a pardon that covered all but a handful of military officers and ex-guerrillas. All told, he pardoned 210 members of the military, 64 former guerrillas, and 5 civilians. This included 19 officers still awaiting judicial resolution of their cases and 174 military men involved in the three mutinies.[69] The president claimed that he was particularly qualified to grant a pardon because he had been incarcerated by the armed forces for years after the 1976 coup. However, his attempt at reconciliation was at least partly unsuccessful. In polls, 95 percent of the population disapproved of his pardon of the military and the Montoneros, the left-wing terrorists defeated in the dirty war.[70] In fact, negative reaction was so intense that Menem decided to postpone the second phase of the pardon, which was to have included the handful of generals and ex-guerrillas still in prison.[71]

□ *Summary*

While the human rights issue in Argentina did not provoke a coup, it provoked the next most dangerous thing: three barracks revolts. Unrest in the lower levels of the officer corps and repeated turmoil in the high command helped to stymie efforts at military reform in areas other than rights prosecutions. Moreover, the protracted struggle over rights trials helped generate, or at least reveal, fissures within the officer corps that were generational and ideological in character. Splits of this nature strike at the heart of military discipline and the viability of the chain of command. Moreover, they are not easily healed. Seineldín and Rico, now retired, continued to lead a military movement with a substantial following, hostile to the military hierarchy and based on extreme right-wing principles. Thus, the waffling of senior officers in suppressing the mutinies and applying quick and effective sanctions showed the importance of the human rights issue for the officer corps as a whole.

■ URUGUAY, BRAZIL, AND PERU

The struggle over human rights trials has not been nearly as intense in Uruguay, Brazil, and Peru. In Uruguay, the two dominant parties found themselves backing the retention of an amnesty law against attempts to overturn it in a referendum. In Brazil, the issue did not reach that level of political saliency, and the amnesty passed by the military government in 1978 has met with no significant political challenge.

□ *The Uruguayan Referendum*

The rights issue in Uruguay tested both the power of the military and the balance of political power inside and outside the government. Initially, the military did not favor a specific amnesty law because it would imply guilt on the part of military officers. However, as public opinion began to register support for rights trials similar to those in Argentina (85 percent in a Gallup poll in Montevideo), the armed forces and the political parties began to face the issue.[72] The military backed a general amnesty, while the president's ruling Colorado Party and the opposition seemed at one point to have agreed to a partial amnesty.

In the face of military recalcitrance, however, the president decided to support a general amnesty. This left congress with two alternative amnesty proposals: the president's and an opposition proposal similar to the president's original proposal. The bill supported by the opposition would have permitted prosecutions but only for homicide, grievous injury, disappearance, or rape. It would also have excluded human rights violations committed during the campaign against the Tupamaros (1967–1972), set sanctions for future coup attempts, exempted civilians from trial by military courts, and established torture as a crime. Forty-eight cases were excluded from the amnesty.[73]

Congress failed to approve either measure. Thus, President Sanguinetti faced a potential constitutional crisis when, in late 1986, the supreme court decided that civilian courts could try military offenders for violations of human rights during the dictatorship. The president could have been faced with ordering military officers not to appear when summoned by civilian courts.[74] Such a crisis was avoided when military pressure, reportedly including blackmail, forced a general amnesty through the legislature in late December, just hours before court proceedings were to resume.[75] While the passage of the bill avoided a constitutional crisis, it also established the capacity of the armed forces to pressure the politicians on this central issue.

The issue, however, was not quickly laid to rest. A signature-gathering campaign was begun to force a referendum on the amnesty. Although the leftist Broad Front (FA) was the only major political party/coalition backing the campaign, it managed to garner considerable support. After a series of legal challenges and delays, the electoral court verified that opponents of the law had the support of the legally required 25 percent of the electorate necessary to call a referendum. As in Argentina, during the referendum process some officers took the opportunity to vilify civilian authorities over their human rights stand. Military leaders cautioned about unrest within the institution and labeled the referendum a first step to discredit the military.[76] The April 1989 vote gave the proamnesty forces a 57 percent to 43 percent victory. While opponents carried Montevideo with 55 percent of the vote, proamnesty forces carried the interior.[77]

□ *Brazil*

In Brazil, a 1979 amnesty provided blanket protection for military officers and others accused of human rights violations. This amnesty has not met any serious challenges. In the analysis of one critic, the country has undergone a transition from above, based on a deal with the military that the civilian government will not investigate past crimes.[78] While the government occasionally ventured into the rights field, as in the establishment of a commission to investigate the disappearance of 125 people during the two decades of military rule,[79] such efforts remain largely stillborn. A manifestation of the military's traditional impunity came in mid-1989 when Army Minister Leonidas Pires Gonçalves informed his subordinates that he would not allow members of the military to testify in an investigation into the killing of four strikers by soldiers at the Volta Redonda steel mill in 1988. Other generals who took part in the meeting of the high command reportedly rejected as outrageous the attempt to "put the military in the dock" and warned that "there will be no Argentinization of Brazil."[80]

It appears unlikely that a serious challenge to the 1979 amnesty law will arise. It has survived for too long without meaningful efforts to overturn it, and it was part of a brokered deal to lessen political repression. Moreover, even a left-leaning government would face issues of greater currency and would likely be adverse to spending the political capital necessary to reopen the issue.

□ *Peru*

While the Belaúnde administration saw the beginning of the war with Sendero Luminoso and significant human rights violations by the armed forces, the advent of the García administration seemed to change the picture. The government retired four hundred military and lower-ranking police officers as part of its moralization campaign,[81] and it made significant improvements in enforcing respect for human rights. International response was generally positive.

Americas Watch initially praised the García administration, saying Peru experienced dramatic changes regarding human rights during García's first year. It noted that the president and his closest advisers had frequently taken responsibility for correcting rights abuses and had rejected a purely military solution to the war with the Sendero insurgents. It further pointed to a noticeable decrease in disappearances, extrajudicial executions, and indiscriminate killings attributable to the security forces. It observed, however, that even with prosecutors doing a better job of working on complaints of disappearances compared to the Belaúnde period, little progress was being made in applying sanctions. It further indicated that the military had not readily accepted the authority of the civilian government. In sensitive matters, such as prosecutions of officers, they continued to exert a considerable amount of pressure. Furthermore, the military often blurred the distinction between armed groups and other leftist organizations.[82]

By the middle of the administration, international observers had changed their assessment. A United Nations Rights Commission report found that there were 170 forced disappearances in Peru in 1988, nearly half of the world's total.[83] According to an Amnesty International report, both the government and its adversaries routinely tortured, mutilated, and murdered their captives. Further, the military courts were accused of a tendency to issue rulings exonerating the armed forces.[84] The picture was not totally negative, however. In a departure from previous practice, the supreme council of military justices sentenced a colonel to fifteen years in prison and a lieutenant to seven for qualified homicide for ordering their forces to kill 124 inmates at the Lurigancho prison after they surrendered in the 1986 mutiny; but another seventy-six members of the national police and army were acquitted after they pleaded they had merely followed orders.[85]

Despite the number of rights violations involved, the issue of human rights prosecutions appears to have little saliency within Peruvian politics. While the military and security forces have engaged in extensive roundups and the seizure of property in the major cities, most of the more serious abuses of authority are confined to the countryside, where the guerrilla insurgents are strongest. The government and armed forces of Peru found themselves more hard-pressed by foreign than domestic critics. During the Belaúnde government and the latter part of the García administration, the typical government response was to defend the military by assailing the bias of critics and their failure to criticize rights violations by the insurgents. Thus, although the García administration reorganized military commands when it took office in part for the stated purpose of attaining better military adherence to human rights standards, little progress was made overall.

■ CONCLUSIONS

The cases discussed above provide mixed results for our hypotheses.

Hypothesis 1: The armed forces will vigorously defend their fundamental interest—the armed forces' survival as an institution. The armed forces will defend other interests only to the degree that they are necessary for survival or the maintenance of core interests. Military resistance on the human rights issue has been intense. The armed forces in Brazil, Uruguay, Peru, and Chile seemed to regard the issue as equally significant but were in a position to defend their interests much more easily. The solidarity shown by the officer corps as a whole on the human rights issue, especially in Argentina, supports the notion that norms of the new professionalism have been internalized. The new professionalism has assumed a degree of importance verging on the fundamental. There is no indication that the officer corps broke ranks over the rights issue. From the very first, the military courts refused to prosecute violations even under political pressure. At most, some members of the armed forces remained passively on the sidelines in the face of military revolts. This passivity says much about their limited support for due process and their disciplined obedience to the chain of command when these principles conflict with the national security doctrine.

Hypothesis 2: The more fundamental the interest, the greater the likelihood of the high command's involvement in or tolerance of potentially risky or costly means of resistance. In all cases, the high command did not stand on the sidelines as far as human rights prosecutions were concerned. Foreclosing the possibility of prosecutions was a key objective of the transition process. Even in Argentina, where the armed forces and the high command were in a much more difficult position, the generals attempted to show as much solidarity as they could for demands for an end to human rights prosecutions. Lacking the prestige and political support for a coup, or enough internal support to impose strict discipline, the high command was forced to tolerate dissident activity within the armed forces that undermined their position and the chain of command.

Hypothesis 3: The more uniform the interest across the various sectors of the armed forces, the more likely the success of the armed forces' action in defense of this interest. Although the numbers of military officers liable to prosecution varied considerably from country to country, there was no indication of a significant breaking of ranks in regard to the rights issue. Officers were at best reluctant to suppress mutinies and at worst supportive of their colleagues' illegal actions to the point of joining mutinies themselves. There appears to be no significant fault line, similar to that between hard- and soft-liners in the transition period, insofar as human rights prosecutions are concerned. If interest is to be understood in terms of narrow career or branch interests, lack of uniformity of interest had virtually no effect on the solidarity of the officer corps. This hypothesis is not supported. In fact, the converse appears to be true.

Hypothesis 4: The lower the prestige of the armed forces and the higher the prestige of the civilian government, the more likely the success of the civilian authorities' efforts to reform the military. This hypothesis receives only limited support from the cases discussed. Only in Argentina did the military possess such low prestige as to open the way to systematic action against human rights violators. Even in the case of Argentina, where the military began with a very weakened position, there was a substantial effort to stem the course of rights prosecutions. This single instance yielded mixed results. The Alfonsín government brought members of the junta to trial and, having obtained guilty verdicts, imprisoned them; but the Menem government freed almost all of those convicted and pardoned military mutineers in the bargain. Nonetheless, the result is hardly a clear-cut victory for the armed forces. While they came close to obtaining their ultimate goal, the cost for the armed forces as an institution was significant. If their position was vindicated, such a vindication provides scant assurance of immunity in applying dirty-war techniques in the future. Moreover, the failure of the Alfonsín policy may be due more to tactical errors on the government's part than to the intrinsic difficulty of the task. Had Alfonsín acted quickly to bring some people to justice and pardon the rest, a lingering crisis might have been avoided. Furthermore, had he acted early in his term to resolve the situation definitively, he could have dealt with the armed forces while they were weakest.[86] The jury is still out on this hypothesis.

Hypothesis 5: Other factors being constant, the relative magnitude of rights violations serves as indication of the potential political support for rights trials. The relative magnitude of violations, especially when more than disappearances are taken into account, explains part of the behavior of civilian governments. Yet, other factors are also important. One of these other factors that must be taken into account is who the disappeared are. The disappearance of members of the middle class, politically prominent individuals, and urban workers associated with political movements is likely to have a significant political impact. The disappearance of Indian campesinos (a significant portion of the Peruvian total) is not as likely to arouse widespread outrage in the politically more significant urban areas. Another factor likely to affect the political impact of disappearances is the context in which they occurred. In the cases of Argentina, Brazil, Chile, and Uruguay, human rights violations took place under military governments, and initially the population remained largely passive. In Peru, the most serious rights violations have continued to occur in the context of a war against Sendero Luminoso and other guerrilla groups, to whom the population is not generally sympathetic. Moreover, this struggle has been authorized by the civilian government. To date, the Peruvian armed forces have faced no serious domestic movement advocating systematic civilian prosecution of military human rights violators, as have the armed forces in the other countries. In sum, this hypothesis appears to be supported by events, but the significance of the other factors that need to be held constant limits its importance.

Taken together, the predictive value of Hypotheses 4 and 5 holds in only three of four cases. Argentina, Uruguay, and Brazil conform to expectations, but Peru does not. The failure in the case of Peru can be attributed to a lack of precision in Hypothesis 5. Had the targets of official violence been considered along with the level of violence, the prediction might have conformed better to the actual course of events. However, we should not place too much stress on deterministic propositions; the different course of development of the rights issue in Argentina and Uruguay demonstrates that political leaders can significantly affect how the issue is resolved.

Although there is no assurance that Latin America (or even Chile) will follow patterns established in the four cases discussed, generalizations drawn from these cases do provide some guidance about the parameters of the human rights problem. First, even when a newly established civilian regime seems to be in a very favorable position vis-à-vis the military, the government may find it difficult to bring members of the armed forces to trial for rights violations. The armed forces have recourse to a number of tactics short of an outright coup d'état. A coup in the face of widespread popular resistance, in fact, is probably the least desirable alternative for the armed forces. Instead, they can put pressure on politicians through noncooperation, threats, blackmail, and mutinies. The cumulative effect of these actions can be serious, and the effectiveness may be enhanced rather than weakened by the fact that it is often not coordinated by the high command but represents reactions, more or less spontaneous, of a broad stratum of the officer corps.

Second, when human rights violations become a matter of intense popular interest, that interest is likely to produce divisions within the political community. While many political leaders—politicians from the mainline, centrist, and right-wing political parties—may wish to avoid confrontation with the military, the reaction of sectors of the general public may make that difficult. In Chile, for instance, a division between the Aylwin administration and many of its supporters seemed to be developing as of early 1990.

Third, the passage of an amnesty law may provide at least the possibility of a legal closure to the rights issue. When issued by a civilian regime, an amnesty is probably definitive. Self-amnesties by the military will probably be respected only if the armed forces have managed to maintain their prestige during the transition process. That prestige translates into civilian support or acquiescence. Again, in Chile, where the rights issue seemed to be emerging, the capacity of Pinochet and progovernment candidates to garner a solid 40 percent of the vote in two electoral tests presages great difficulty for any effort to overturn the 1978 amnesty or even to bring post-1978 violators to justice.

In summary, if democratic governments attempt to punish past human rights violations thoroughly and systematically, they will probably be able to do so only in a political environment where the military is largely discredited. This need not render human rights and due process a dead issue in other circumstances, however. The establishment of a viable legal system to assure due process is a daunting political task, and agitation on the rights issue may help sustain political pressure to establish such a system. In short, the prognosis for the full application of legal penalties for past human rights violations under military regimes is not good. Any substantial improvement of these possibilities seems to rest on the success of more basic and less-threatening changes in the structure of civilian authority and military responsibilities.

■ NOTES

1. This is Alfred Stepan's contention. He argues that the difference in the figure of disappeared per 100,000 people (32.0 for Argentina, 1.0 for Uruguay, and 0.1 for Brazil) explains the saliency of the rights issues in each country. Stepan, 1988, pp. 69–72.

2. Pion-Berlin, 1989a, pp. 5–7.

3. Ibid., pp. 102–104.

4. FBIS, "Alfonsín Discusses Junta Trials, Economy," Paris, *Le Monde*, September 17, 1985, FBIS-LAM-85-184, September 23, 1985, p. B3.

5. FBIS, "Alfonsín National Address on State of Law," Buenos Aires, Agentina Televisor Color Network, December 14, 1983, FBIS-LAM-83-241, December 14, 1983, p. B2.

6. FBIS, "Military Council Justifies Juntas' Actions," Buenos Aires, *Noticias Argentinas*, September 25, 1984, FBIS-LAM-84-188, September 26, 1984, pp. B5–B7.

7. FBIS, "Council Will Not Issue Verdict on Junta Members," Buenos Aires, TELAM, September 24, 1984, FBIS-LAM-84-187, September 25, 1984, p. B14.

8. FBIS, "Entire Armed Forces Supreme Council Resigns," Buenos Aires, TELAM, November 14, 1987, FBIS-LAM-84-222, November 15, 1984, p. B1.

9. "Alfonsín Turns to the Army," *Latin American Weekly Report*, July 19, 1985, p. 9.

10. "Argentina's Juntas Sentenced; Touchier Second Phase Begins," *Latin American Weekly Report*, December 13, 1985, p. 1.

11. "The Disappeared Disappear," *Economist*, December 13, 1986, p. 42.

12. FBIS, "Defense Secretary Musso [sic] Defends Court Summonses," Buenos Aires, *Noticias Argentinas*, March 5, 1987, FBIS-LAT-87-044, March 6, 1987, p. B1.

13. FBIS, "Army Officers Document on Human Rights Trials," Buenos Aires, DYN, March 9, 1987, FBIS-LAM-87-046, March 10, 1987, pp. B1–B3.

14. "Officers Become More Assertive," *Latin American Weekly Report*, April 2, 1987, p. 9.

15. FBIS, "Army Chief of Staff Warns of Social Conflict," Buenos Aires, *Noticias Argentinas*, March 5, 1987, FBIS-LAM-87-045, March 9, 1987, pp. B2–B3.

16. "Alfonsín Overcomes Army Challenge," *Latin American Weekly Report*, May 7, 1988, p. 8.

17. Ibid.

18. Clara Germani, "Argentine's Need to Redefine Military's Role in Society," *Christian Science Monitor*, April 23, 1987, pp. 9, 11.

19. "Alfonsín Overcomes Army Challenge," *Latin American Weekly Report*, May 7, 1988, p. 8.

20. FBIS, "Rebels Release Note," Buenos Aires, *Noticias Argentinas*, April 17, 1987, FBIS-LAM-87-075, April 20, 1987, pp. B3–B4.

21. FBIS, "Former COS Ereñú on Military Crisis, Reconciliation," Buenos

Aires, *Noticias Argentinas*, April 23, 1987, FBIS-LAM-87-079, April 24, 1987, p. B3.

22. FBIS, "Passage, 'Text' of Due Obedience Law Reported," Buenos Aires, *Noticias Argentinas*, June 5, 1987, FBIS-LAT-87-109, June 8, 1987, pp. K1–K2.

23. "President Alfonsín Signs 'Due Obedience' Law," *Jane's Defence Weekly*, June 20, 1987, p. 1293.

24. "The Dirty War Gets Laundered," *Economist*, June 6, 1987, p. 36.

25. "Alfonsín Sticks to His Guns," *Latin American Weekly Report*, June 4, 1987, p. 9.

26. FBIS, "Former Rebel Army Major Barreiro Released," Buenos Aires, TELAM, June 25, 1987, FBIS-LAT-87-123, June 26, 1987, p. K2.

27. "Obediencia Debidia Bill to End Some Trials, Continue Others," *Latin American Regional Reports: Southern Cone Report*, May 28, 1987, p. 1.

28. FBIS, "SIDE Leader Suarez Discusses Easter Rebellion," Buenos Aires, *Noticias Argentinas*, April 23, 1987, FBIS-LAM-87-079, April 24, 1987, pp. B4–B5.

29. "'Traumatised' Army Is Restructured," *Latin American Regional Reports: Southern Cone Report*, May 28, 1987, p. 2.

30. "Some Mutineers Off Hook," *Latin American Weekly Report*, May 21, 1987, p. 8.

31. Clara Germani, "Broad Reforms Necessary for Argentine Military, Ex-Officers Say," *Christian Science Monitor*, May 1, 1987, p. 13.

32. Andrew McLeod, "Argentine Chief Replaces Assistant over 'Differences'" *Jane's Defence Weekly*, July 25, 1987, p. 131.

33. "Argentine Senate Weighs Relief for Junior Officers," *Christian Science Monitor*, May 28, 1987, p. 2; "The Military Factor," *Latin American Weekly Report*, July 2, 1987, p. 5.

34. Generals Santarrosa (the army's institutional affairs director, fourth in the chain of command) and Ramallo requested retirement. Santarrosa had made a previous request immediately after the Holy Week incidents. "Argentine Army Reshuffle," *Jane's Defence Weekly*, September 12, 1987, p. 513.

35. FBIS, "Joint Staff Head Prevents Officer's Posting," Buenos Aires, DYN, May 28, 1987, FBIS-LAM-87-103, May 29, 1987, p. B2.

36. FBIS, "Armed Forces Sale for Reorganization," Buenos Aires, *Noticias Argentinas*, August 29, 1988, FBIS-LAT-87-107, September 2, 1987, pp. 14–15.

37. "Radicals Concerned About Poll Chances," *Latin American Weekly Report*, June 11, 1987, pp. 8–9.

38. FBIS, "Army Chief Caridi Discusses Military Discipline," Buenos Aires, *Noticias Argentinas*, May 21, 1987, FBIS-LAM-87-099, May 22, 1987, pp. B1–B2.

39. Dafne S. de Plou, "Armed Forces' 'Savior Complex' Threatens Argentine Democracy," *Latinamerica Press*, June 18, 1987, pp. 1–2.

40. "Postscript," *Latin American Weekly Report*, August 20, 1987, p. 12.

41. FBIS, "Caridi Orders Video on Military Confiscated," Buenos Aires, Domestic Service, September 15, 1987, FBIS-LAT-87-180, September 17, 1987, pp. 18–19; FBIS, "Army Maj. Barreiro Tours with Holy Week Video," Buenos Aires, Domestic Service, September 22, 1987, FBIS-LAT-87-184, September 23, 1987, p. 20.

42. Clara Germani, "Argentine Leader Sees Debt Crisis as Main Threat to Democratic Progress," *Christian Science Monitor*, June 25, 1987, pp. 9–10.

43. "Alfonsín: Officers to Be Kept in Line," *Latin American Weekly Report*, July 23, 1987, p. 2.

44. FBIS, "Intelligence Agents Participate in UCR Bombings," Buenos

Aires, *Noticias Argentinas*, July 8, 1987, FBIS-LAT-87-132, July 10, 1987, p. K2.

45. "Incidents Test Alfonsín's Army Policy," *Latin American Regional Reports: Southern Cone Report*, October 15, 1987, pp. 4–5.

46. FBIS, "Government Said Aware of Threat," Buenos Aires, *Noticias Argentinas*, September 28, 1987, FBIS-LAT-87-190, October 1, 1987, pp. 28–29.

47. FBIS, "Commentary Discusses Military 'Crisis,'" Buenos Aires, *La Prensa*, December 6–7, 1987, FBIS-LAT-87-238, December 11, 1987, pp. 22–23.

48. "Postscript," *Latin American Weekly Report*, January 14, 1988, p. 12.

49. "How Rico's Revolt Rose and Collapsed," *Latin American Weekly Report*, January 28, 1988, pp. 2–3.

50. "Amnesty Dismissed; Charges Dropped," *Latin American Weekly Report*, February 18, 1988, p. 8.

51. FBIS, "'Unofficial Spokesman' Cited," Buenos Aires, DYN, January 14, 1988, FBIS-LAT-88-010, January 15, 1988, pp. 21–22.

52. "Argentine Army Commanders Appointed," *Jane's Defence Weekly*, February 6, 1988, p. 199.

53. FBIS, "Communiqué on Rebels Issued," Buenos Aires, DYN, January 17, 1988, FBIS-LAT-88-011, January 19, 1988, pp. 53–54.

54. "Suppression of Rico Rebellion Shows Extent of Change in Argentina," *Latin American Weekly Report*, January 28, 1988, p. 1.

55. FBIS, "General Punished for Not Observing Regulations," Buenos Aires, *Noticias Argentinas*, March 3, 1988, FBIS-LAT-88-043, March 4, 1988, p. 25.

56. "Argentine Army, Air Force Shake-ups," *Jane's Defence Weekly*, February 13, 1988, p. 248.

57. FBIS, "Army Chief of Staff Retires Five Officers," Buenos Aires, *Noticias Argentinas*, March 9, 1988, FBIS-LAT-88-047, March 10, 1988, p. 24; "Mutineers Booted," *Latin American Weekly Report*, March 3, 1988, p. 9.

58. FBIS, "Air Force Chief Vows Support," Buenos Aires, TELAM, January 17, 1988, FBIS-LAT-88-011, January 19, 1988, p. 55.

59. Joe Schneider, "Alfonsín Looks to Safeguard Argentina's Democracy," *Jane's Defence Weekly*, February 20, 1988, p. 310.

60. FBIS, "Officers Deny Questioning Crespo's Term," Buenos Aires, *Noticias Argentinas*, April 27, 1988, FBIS-LAT-88-081, April 27, 1988, pp. 31–32.

61. "Gauging the Extent of the Rico Revolt," *Latin American Weekly Report*, February 4, 1988, p. 2.

62. Schneider, op. cit., p. 301.

63. FBIS, "Government, Army Say Situation Normal," Buenos Aires, Domestic Service, March 25, 1988, FBIS-LAT-88-059, March 28, 1988, p. 36.

64. FBIS, "Senate Approves Top Military Promotions," Buenos Aires, *Noticias Argentinas*, June 8, 1988, FBIS-LAT-88-114, June 14, 1988, p. 22.

65. Peter Ford, "Argentine Mutineers Sought Respect for Military," *Christian Science Monitor*, December 5, 1988, pp. 9–10, and "Waiting for Answers in Argentina," *Christian Science Monitor*, December 6, 1988, p. 10.

66. Adrian English, "Mounting Army Threat to Argentine Government," *Jane's Defence Weekly*, December 17, 1988, p. 1556.

67. FBIS, "Rebel Spokesman Interviewed," Buenos Aires, *Noticias Argentinas*, December 2, 1988, FBIS-LAT-88-233, December 5, 1988, pp. 27–28.

68. Peter Ford, "Argentine Calls for Mending Civil-Military Rift," *Christian Science Monitor*, December 23, 1988, p. 7.

69. "Army Mutineers, Dirty War Chiefs, Ex-Guerrillas Pardoned by Menem," *Latin American Weekly Report*, October 19, 1989, p. 1.

70. María Laura Avignolo, "Argentina: Ex-Montoneros Are Repentant After Pardon," *Latinamerica Press*, November 9, 1989, p. 3.

71. "Argentina," *Times of the Americas*, November 29, 1989, p. 9.

72. *Latin American Regional Reports: Southern Cone Report*, January 31, 1986, pp. 4–5; *Latin American Weekly Report*, May 30, 1986, p. 9.

73. "Congress Agrees on an Amnesty," *Latin American Weekly Report*, October 9, 1986, p. 9.

74. "Sanguinetti Faces Serious Clash with Supreme Court and Congress," *Latin American Weekly Report*, November 27, 1986, p. 1.

75. Tim Coone, "Uruguay Human Rights Amnesty Shows the Fragility of Civilian Rule, *Christian Science Monitor*, December 30, 1986, p. 10.

76. FBIS, "Campaign to Discredit Military Alleged," September 18, 1987, FBIS-LAT-87-190, October 1, 1987, p. 36.

77. *Latin American Weekly Report*, April 27, 1989, p. 9.

78. "Alleged Torturers Remain Unpunished," *Latin American Regional Reports: Brazil Report*, June 4, 1987, p. 2.

79. "Postscript," *Latin American Weekly Report*, December 25, 1986, p. 12.

80. "Officers Ordered Not to Testify," *Latin American Weekly Report*, June 29, 1989, p. 5.

81. "Postscript," *Latin American Regional Reports*, January 29, 1987, p. 8.

82. Americas Watch 1986, pp. 2ff.

83. "Human Rights Watch—February," *Latinamerica Press*, March 9, 1989, p. 7.

84. "Blanket Killings Are Policy Once More," *Latin American Weekly Report*, August 31, 1989, p. 9.

85. "Peru: Officers Sentenced for Homicide," *Latin American Weekly Report*, December 21, 1989, p. 12.

86. For example, a poll taken by Lynch, Menéndez y Nivel in December 1986 revealed that negative opinions on the armed forces outnumbered positive opinions almost two to one. By March 1989, however, they were evenly balanced. Public concern over the military issue also waned during that same period. Fraga, p. 137.

6■

Flashpoint II: Internal Security

Since their inception, Latin American military organizations have been involved in enforcing domestic order. Yet, the second half of the twentieth century saw the development of a new version of this domestic role—internal security—which sets contemporary practice apart from what occurred earlier. Internal security is different because it is a systematic, theory-based response to the problem of internal order, while past practice had largely been ad hoc and interventions were initiated primarily on the basis of personal judgment. In the earlier period, military intervention was a response to social, economic, and political circumstances; today, military involvement in enforcing domestic order has its roots in military doctrine as well. As such, it is more than an objective, sociological phenomenon; it is also a matter of subjective perception and intellectual conviction.

■ NATIONAL SECURITY AND THE QUESTION OF INTERNAL WAR

The military understanding of the problem of internal security is usually articulated in what is called a national security doctrine or a doctrine of national security and development. Titles and formulations vary, but virtually all such theories share a number of common perceptions and basic policy recommendations. As the expression *national* security implies, these doctrines are part of a global approach to the issue of national defense. From a nonmilitary, police perspective, the problem of internal security is the narrow, albeit often complicated, one of maintaining law and order. When the armed forces become involved, law and order becomes associated with national power, defense against foreign enemies, and the military practice of formulating comprehensive strategies. The police focus on apprehending lawbreakers; the armed forces focus on planning or fighting battles, campaigns, and wars. Where the police officer sees a criminal, the military officer is likely to see an organized threat to the continuance of the nation.

To restate the matter, the armed forces traditionally direct their attention not simply to the neutralization of the individual enemy soldier but to the destruction of the enemy's capacity to make war. Hence, from a global perception of the internal security threat grow global prescriptions. The armed forces come to see political, economic, and social changes as necessary to eliminate the systemic bases of internal security threats. Individuals and groups acting directly against the internal security interest of the country must be neutralized. So too must the network that provides them intelligence, logistical support, and recruits. Military structures must be developed to accomplish these tasks.

The risk of abuse implicit in such an orientation is fairly obvious, yet few developing countries are in a position simply to ignore the possibility or reality of organized, internal threats aimed at the violent overthrow of the state. Thus, governments must find methods of countering such threats while minimizing the risk of abuse. The difficulties involved are manifest, as can be seen from an examination of the civilian-oriented approach of the United States to internal security, which has had a significant influence in Latin America.[1]

□ Major Tenets of US Doctrine

Although it is probably an exaggeration to say that US internal security doctrine finds itself trapped between the horns of a dilemma, it is certainly correct that it finds itself tugged in two directions. On the one hand, the doctrine is meant to protect democratic governments and, consequently, civilian control of the military. On the other hand, the logic of the doctrine seems to lead to the militarization of politics and the expansion of military roles.

As is typical with other military approaches to national security, US doctrine defines the threat broadly. Terrorism, subversion, and insurgencies are only possible because lack of development and serious inequities within the society make it susceptible to such threats. The active agent who attempts to overthrow the state is just one part of a more complex and larger picture. Likewise, foreign assistance, when it plays a role, would be ineffective were it not for the underlying internal factors that make insurgency possible.[2]

US doctrine views insurgency as a multiphased process that is the result of a conscious plan. Insurgency—guerrilla war aimed at the conquest of state power—requires not only a susceptible society but also a subversive organization and detailed preparation. A communist party, or a similar organization, is assumed to be the core of the subversive apparatus. The path of insurgency is chosen, for whatever reason, over other illegal or quasi-legal methods of gaining power.[3]

In an attempt to recapitulate Mao Zedong's three stages of protracted people's war, US doctrine calls the initial stage a latent or incipient insurgency. In this phase, the party's choice of guerrilla war is not readily apparent because the armed clashes are few and the party devotes its energy to organizing, both politically and militarily, and undermining the authority of the government. A network of sympathizers and supporters, some connected to front organizations, develops. The doctrine views the growth of terrorism, increased antiregime propaganda, and mass illegal strikes, protests, and demonstrations as indicators of a first-stage insurgency.[4]

It is only with the second phase—guerrilla war—that the political violence, which has escalated during the first phase, reaches sufficient intensity to be characterized as a full-fledged insurgency. Military targets are attacked as the insurgent military organization becomes extensive and sophisticated. On the political level, the insurgents continue to use agitation and propaganda to induce or coerce support. They eventually establish a shadow government in liberated zones, from which they can mobilize still more resources to fight the government. The insurgents, however, do not attempt the systematic defense of liberated zones, although limited defense of such zones may be conducted. Their main military focus is the conduct of hit-and-run attacks in a campaign of attrition against government forces.[5]

Only when the balance of forces is altered sufficiently in the guerrillas' favor can stage three—a conventional campaign to seize the centers of national power and defeat the government's armed forces in open combat—begin. With the successful completion of this stage, the insurgents become the new government of the country.[6]

□ *Some Worrisome Implications*

The problem with this picture of reality is that it is unnuanced. It clarifies what is—and ought to remain—obscure. Greater unity, planning, and fixity of purpose are assumed than seem to be the case in the Latin American context. Moreover, the model, drawn from Asian experience, has a poor fit with most Latin American insurgent movements of the 1960s and 1970s, the period in which insurgency was an intermittent threat in a number of countries. In the 1980s, Peru's Sendero Luminoso and the Frente Farabundo Martí de Liberación Nacional (Farabundo Martí National Liberation Front, or FMLN) are the only major groups seriously committed to such a model. Thus, the doctrine is likely to give the wrong cues. What may be disorganized expressions of widespread opposition or the acts of a handful of extremists take on the color of a systematic, extensive conspiracy. Just how quickly this perspective can lead to an attitude supporting a no-holds-barred war against subversion can be seen in the remarks of retired Chilean General Luis Danús, once considered a moderate.

> We are trained to take action against regular forces. In fact, if an adversary is not wearing insignias, is not wearing a uniform, he is regarded as an irregular and can be shot on the spot. The laws of war say so, and the Geneva Convention accepts it. So, these soldiers from the

outside, these individuals, who are trained in universities or in special groups in the Soviet Union, come to fight against us, and we have to regard them as external enemies. And we can't be so naive in acting against them as to go around just like the traditional soldiers in Napoleonic wars. We have to have other tools: [the intelligence services and equivalent weapons].[7]

In reality, insurgent and counterinsurgent strategic perspectives frequently reverse the Clausewitzian dictum that war is politics by other means. In so doing, they have the potential for displacing attitudes necessary for the peaceful conduct of politics. Once political dissent and low-level turmoil are viewed as a potential military problem, certain habits of mind typical of military organizations begin to have a decided impact. Military organizations plan by assessing threats rather than intentions. For reasons of bureaucratic aggrandizement as well as simple prudence, they prefer to prepare for worst-case possibilities.[8] It is not surprising, then, that the military approach to the problem of actual or potential subversion is quite different than the approach of most mainline politicians.

The paradigm of internal war underlies internal security/national security doctrines. It assumes that illegal, violent actions will be preceded by legal or quasi-legal attempts to organize an insurgent movement and spread its influence. Counterinsurgency strategy, in turn, assumes that it is best and easiest to neutralize an insurgent movement when the insurgency is in its incipient stages, otherwise such neutralization may be extremely costly or even impossible. In effect, the specter of full-scale guerrilla war often shapes the military approach to internal security matters; and threat assessment becomes an ideological surrogate.

The sort of national security orientation just described presents a concrete problem for civilian control. If the doctrine's analysis of the threat provides a false clarity, its assignment of roles to the armed forces creates ambiguity where clarity ought to be the norm. Objective civilian control requires that military missions be defined in terms restricting the armed forces to activities directly related to the management of coercion.[9] Yet, the internal security doctrine assigns the military various roles that traditionally have been only tangentially related to the management of coercion. These roles include: conducting psychological operations that target the country's own population; population and resource control (normally police functions); domestic intelligence; and civic action (service activities provided by the armed forces to the local community).

Indeed, the doctrine stresses the integration of purely military means with broader political means. In theory, the formulation of general strategy and the execution of that strategy, even at the local level, is to be directed by civilians.[10] But what should happen if civilian authorities do not understand the nature of the threat? What if incompetent civilian authorities are part of the problem? This integrated approach leaves open the door to the ad hoc assumption of governmental functions by the armed forces. Military involvement in domestic intelligence gathering, psychological operations, and other political and economic measures, even if only on a temporary basis, raises the possibility of military subversion of the political process. Nonetheless, it is difficult to dismiss entirely the need for counterinsurgency operations in Latin America.

■ CASE STUDY—PERU'S MILITARY AND SENDERO LUMINOSO

As dangerous as the integrated, military-political approach to counterinsurgency might appear to be for democracy and civilian control of the military, it has recently been criticized as not integrated enough. A critique authored by two US military officers argues that low-intensity conflict (the current official term for counterinsurgency) is both improperly understood and misnamed. Current doctrine, it argues, attempts to fit counterinsurgency into the traditional Western military mold, where combat occurs between recognized armed forces and war occurs between politically stable states for politically defined objectives. The fit is not a good one. Low-intensity conflict arises in unstable states, among populations of uncertain political commitment, and is part of an ongoing social process. It is not a low-level conflict; it is total war for the reshaping and control of an entire society. In this context, traditional distinctions—combatant versus noncombatant, military versus political, economic versus social—need to be rethought.[11] The implementation of the changes implied in this criticism would probably further undermine restrictions necessary for objective civilian control.

Unfortunately, the analysis may be correct, at least in certain contexts. If sheer effectiveness in suppressing insurgencies is the measure, an integrated approach seems a promising strategy, as opposed to one that stresses a clear demarcation between the political and military fields and limits the armed forces to the conduct of combat operations. Two recent examples of success against fairly well developed insurgent organizations are worth noting. In Guatemala, the armed forces have been able to repress and substantially contain an insurgent organization that posed a serious threat in the early 1980s. Going further afield, in Thailand, the military was able to eradicate an insurgency and obtain the surrender of most of the active participants. Both the qualified Guatemalan success and the unqualified success in Thailand were the result of a strategy involving military penetration of village life and the development of local militia and political structures under military tutelage.[12]

Further, the Guatemalan experience reveals a link between insurgency and military rule. From the late 1950s through the mid-1980s, the country had a succession of military governments that fought a succession of insurgencies. When a civilian regime was reestablished in the mid-1980s, the armed forces continued to control counterinsurgency policy and exercised important vetoes over human rights investigations and political liberalization.[13] The Christian Democratic government was largely a client/hostage of the military. Thailand, as well, was and remains a government under military tutelage.

The course of the insurgent war in Peru provides further grist for the mill.

□ *Sendero Luminoso in Peru*

Since the mid-1980s the Peruvian government has faced a serious challenge to its authority from a number of guerrilla movements. The most important and innovative of these is Sendero Luminoso. Sendero's approach represents a creative adaptation of the methods of Mao Zedong to the conditions of the Peruvian Andes. It avoids the rigid orthodoxy typical of many Marxist-Leninist movements, learns from practice, and allows concrete experience to reshape theory.

The Ideology. Perhaps the best example of Sendero's abandonment of orthodoxies is its ideology—a mixture of Mao Zedong thought and the ideology of Peruvian Marxist José Mariateguí, intended to appeal to the Indian population.[14] While this approach may seem peculiar to First World Marxists, it has strong precedents in the development of Mao's thought. The key for Mao, as for Abimael Guzmán (Comrade Gonzalo), Sendero's founder and chief ideologist, was to discover the most revolutionary stratum of society. While others believed China's minuscule working class would serve as the base for revolution, Mao made clear, in his *Report from Hunan*, that the poorest of the peasantry was the only viable revolutionary base. In a parallel fashion, Sendero has cultivated the poorest, most dispossessed stratum of Indian campesinos, appealing to their historic rejection of Hispanic culture and white and mestizo exploitation.[15] Sendero's efforts to acculturate itself to the Indian stand in counterpoint to the approach of the second largest guerrilla group, Movimiento Revolucionario Tupac Amarú (Tupac Amarú Revolutionary Movement, or MRTA), whose ideology and approach remains largely influenced by the dominant white culture.

On the issue of the method of struggle, Sendero also takes its cue from Chinese experience. In his *Report*, Mao rejected the orthodox Comintern policy of alliance with certain strata of the bourgeoisie in favor of an all-out struggle of the poorest against almost everyone else. He believed this struggle was developing more or less spontaneously, and the party had to learn from the practice of the ideologically untutored. In the same way, Sendero views as class enemies people other observers might classify as dispossessed. Campesino cooperatives and smallholders have not been immune from attack. Essentially, Sendero's goal is radicalization and polarization.

The revolutionary process culminates in the creation of a new society, not in a transformation—even a revolutionary transformation—of old structures. That society will be puritanical in its tastes and Spartan in its living conditions. Sendero constitutes its present-day nucleus.

The Strategy. Sendero has followed the strategy of a classic people's war. It began preparation for open warfare in 1970 with organizational activity in the Ayacucho region. In May 1980, when the organization was ready to begin open war, it followed the tactic of replacing the established government's representatives. A Sendero column would be sent into a village to spread propaganda and dispense revolutionary justice. The first column would be followed by a second, composed of better-indoctrinated Senderistas who could create new structures in an authoritarian fashion. Since any meaningful government vanished as local officials were killed or forced to resign, revolutionary justice could easily be dispensed not only to political enemies but to thieves, rustlers, small traders, and those guilty of drunkenness and adultery. Harsh justice went hand in hand with the reestablishment of the ancient practice of participation of the whole village in communal tasks. Then Sendero would introduce new organs of government, popular committees, two-thirds of whose members would be Sendero loyalists or poor peasants.[16]

Typical of a people's war, Sendero has extended control to areas outside its original Ayacucho base, northward toward Lima and in to the coca-growing areas even further north in the upper Huallaga valley. This inkblot strategy puts the government under greater and greater constraints. If it is successful, the military will be hemmed in by an ever-increasing Sendero presence in the countryside and in the poorest shantytowns of the capital as well. The civilian government will be unable to function or conduct credible national elections. A military coup could, at some point, polarize the situation still further and bolster the uprising.

Government Response and Sendero Counter-response. For the first two years of the insurgency, the government of President Fernando Belaúnde Terry allowed the problem to fester. Sendero faced only police forces that were largely ineffectual. While the military chafed at the bit, demanding a larger role, the president was unwilling to permit it. Finally, in late December 1982, spurred by expanding Sendero attacks, Belaúnde authorized the army to assume political and military control of Ayacucho Department.[17] The military campaign in the new emergency zone, while more successful than previous efforts, drove the guerrillas to expand into other areas. Moreover, the army's response seemed to be to fight fire with fire. Sendero terrorist tactics were met with military terrorist tactics as fatalities escalated.[18] The violence appeared to have little lasting impact on the government's fortunes. In mid-1984, Sendero could claim 100,000 people living under its new political order.[19] Furthermore, Sendero had the capacity to make its presence felt in the developed parts of the country. It was able to carry out selective assassinations and disrupt power distribution in Lima by blowing up electricity pylons in the network carrying electric power to the capital.

In mid-1985, the newly elected Alan García administration promised a change in counterinsurgency policy. García presided over a series of personnel changes in military and police commands and demanded that the armed forces improve their tactics and respect human rights.[20] By the end of the year, the minister of defense said that 80 percent of the emergency zone had been pacified,[21] yet the existence of any significant change could be doubted. Early in 1986, a state of emergency was imposed in Lima, and for the entire year, terrorist incidents in the country were up by over 50 percent. By 1987, six of Peru's twenty-four departments, including one-third of the country's population, were under military control.[22]

By the late 1980s, in part because of pressure elsewhere, the guerrillas had concentrated most of their forces in the coca-growing areas. Intelligence reports indicated that Sendero and the second largest guerrilla group, MRTA, had 80 percent of their guerrillas in the area loosely defined as the middle and upper Huallaga valley. There were few reliable estimates of the strength of the units, though one weekly suggested that Sendero may have had as many as two thousand guerrillas in the area.[23] Meanwhile, Sendero formed an alliance with the small-peasant coca producers to protect them against the government and drug middlemen.

This alliance proved difficult for the military to break. A drug enforcement policy pushed by the United States and the US Drug Enforcement Administration (DEA) ran counter to military efforts to win support from the local population. Coca cultivation offered campesinos a readily marketable cash crop promising higher incomes than legal crops. Government destruction of coca plants drove the campesinos further into the arms of the guerrillas, and crop substitution programs were poorly funded and did not produce a viable alternative to coca cultivation as far as small growers were concerned. Eventually, the armed forces countenanced coca production. In a striking example of this, the military-political governor of Army Sub-Zone Eight (mainly the upper Huallaga valley) addressed twenty thousand assembled coca growers as fellow *cocaleros* and told them he was there to protect them. The tactic was meant to win people over against Sendero by not disturbing the coca growers, only disturbing Sendero and those who buy and process the growers' crops.[24] This may be the only antiterrorist policy that has any hope of success.

The early months of 1989 saw the government forces compelled to assume a position of passivity because of budget and other problems. These problems were highlighted by a successful guerrilla attack on a government garrison to which troops nearby failed to respond.[25] The government responded to the problems with a cabinet reorganization and new attempts to coordinate counterinsurgency efforts. In order to increase firepower and mobility, it also acquired $21 million worth of arms and began negotiating for the purchase of Soviet troop-lift helicopters.[26]

To deal with the continuing and growing Sendero threat based on the guerrilla–drug producer alliance in the upper Huallaga valley, the government opted for a military solution. President García bowed to military pressure and allowed the military to take part in the repression of drug trafficking. In mid-1989, the military launched a major offensive against Sendero's jungle bases. Fighter-bomber attacks devastated at least three training camps, and the follow-up by ground forces allowed the government, for the first time since the internal war began, to claim it inflicted four hundred casualties on Sendero. Army field commanders had also been given a free hand to act politically in a bid to drive a wedge between Sendero and its drug base. This meant offering coca-planting campesinos—though not the drug mafia's transportation and processing operations—virtual immunity if they cooperated against Sendero or remained neutral. The guerrillas responded by blowing up nineteen power pylons.[27]

In the midst of the violence of the 1980s, grassroots organizations called *rondas* sprang up in thirteen of Peru's twenty-five departments. Their rise appeared to be spontaneous and induced by a lack of trust in the authorities and their inability to keep order. The rondas were directed mainly against known thieves; they apprehended, tried, and punished by means of popular courts. They also got involved in matters of wife beating and other crimes. APRA tried to co-opt the groups by passing a law to put them under official control and by encouraging its own activists to supplant them. In mid-1989, the government decided to give one thousand M-1 rifles to the rondas.[28] Meanwhile, the military in the southern emergency zones formed its own civil patrols, which were supposedly voluntary. The patrols were placed under strict military control.[29]

By the end of the decade, the balance sheet did not look good. The committee in the Peruvian senate that monitors political violence reported that 15,811 killings had been recorded since Sendero began operations in May 1980. In 1989, the committee recorded 2,117 attacks, of which 1,632 were attributed to Sendero. Sendero was reported to have five thousand active fighters and to operate in all but five of the country's twenty-four departments. Fifty-two mayors and ninety-two governors, judges, and other officials were killed, mainly by Sendero attacks.[30] The human rights picture was hardly reassuring either. According to Amnesty International, the military continued to use the same terrorist tactics as Sendero. It noted that three thousand people taken into custody disappeared in the last seven years of the decade and at least another three thousand were estimated killed by security forces in mass executions. The report says that security forces terrorized women in the emergency zones (males between the ages of fourteen and forty being largely absent). Violations included rape and torture for their husbands' actions and their own community-organizing activities.[31] By 1989, 60 percent of Peruvians lived in emergency zones.[32]

Analysis. While Sendero's strategy is unquestionably effective in certain regions, it seems to be self-limiting. Without a substantial base in urban areas, where much of the population lives, it appears to be unlikely to defeat the government outright. The roadblock to Sendero's urban advance is largely political: the existence of a strong, though factious left, grouped until late 1989 under Izquierda Unida (United Left, or IU). Sendero has attempted to discredit IU and attack its cadres so as to supplant it as the natural repository for the support of the urban poor. Sendero was unable to make substantial progress in this regard in the 1980s. Moreover, an urban environment presents much more formidable problems for guerrillas than does a rural area.

In effect, Sendero Luminoso's ultimate hope seems to be a military coup that would remove any political alternative between a military and a guerrilla dictatorship. According to one Peruvian specialist, however, the armed forces are unlikely to intervene because they have accurately assessed the likely cost—a civil war—and do not want to undertake such a risk.[33] Thus, the military, while playing a substantial role in the formulation and execution of counterinsurgency strategy, is politically constrained by the likely reaction should it seize political power. To use Maoist terminology, the people's war seems to have reached a strategic stalemate. Unlike conditions in revolutionary China, the initiative—to take successful action or blunder—rests with the established government as Peru enters the 1990s. This is an odd reversal of the classic Maoist description.

□ The Transferability of the Peruvian Experience

The notion that an insurgency is really an internal war has a certain credence given the experience of Peru, as well as that of Guatemala and Thailand. The saving grace, as far as the possibility of democratic control in Latin America is concerned, is that these examples have limited applicability. All three insurgencies began in relatively backward areas or countries. Thailand in the mid-1960s, Guatemala in the 1970s and 1980s, and the Peruvian highlands in the 1980s hardly typify the situation in most South American countries. Moreover, the rebels focused their agitation and propaganda on the neglect these rural areas had suffered, and in the case of Guatemala and Peru, on the cultural oppression suffered by the Indian campesinos.

A comparison of Latin American countries reveals an interesting pattern (Table 6.1). Political violence, especially insurgent activity, is concentrated in countries with a GNP per capita of under $1,500 and a relatively poor showing insofar as other developmental indicators are concerned. Furthermore, the only two active insurgencies in countries with GNPs per capita greater than $1,000—Peru and Colombia—appear to have special factors that help account for the emergence or continuation of such conflicts

Table 6.1 Socioeconomic Indicators and Political Violence

Country	GNP per Capita (US$)	Life Expectancy (years)	Population/ Doctor	% in Secondary School	% Urban	Political Violence
Bolivia	580	53	1,540	37	50	
Dominican Republic	730	66	1,760	47	58	
Honduras	810	64	1,510	36	42	some terrorism
Nicaragua	830	63	1,500	42	58	insurgency
Thailand	850	64	6,290	29	21	insurgency (defeated)
El Salvador	860	62	2,830	24	44	insurgency
Guatemala	950	62	2,180	20	33	insurgency
Paraguay	990	67	1,460	30	46	
Ecuador	1,040	65	830	55	55	insurgency (defeated)
Colombia	1,240	66	1,190	56	69	insurgency, terrorism
Chile	1,310	72	1,230	70	85	terrorism
Peru	1,470	61	1,040	65	69	insurgency
Costa Rica	1,610	74	960	42	45	
Mexico	1,830	69	1,240	55	71	
Brazil	2,020	65	1,080	36	75	
Uruguay	2,190	71	510	71	85	
Panama	2,240	72	980	59	54	
Argentina	2,390	71	370	74	85	some terrorism
Venezuela	3,230	70	700	46	83	

Source: IBRD

there. Colombia has a history of political violence going back to at least the 1950s, and Peru's insurgencies, as noted, were started principally among the Indian population. While special circumstances in other countries may yet provide opportunities for insurgent movements, it nonetheless appears that there are few additional breeding grounds for the classic Maoist-style insurgency that an integrated counterinsurgency strategy is designed to defeat. Moreover, a classic people's war based on the campesino would often seem to have, as noted in Peru, self-limiting features. Where that population is relatively small or limited to areas geographically remote from centers of population and economic activity, insurgents may lack a potential mass base large enough to conduct a guerrilla war successfully. The more-developed Latin American countries fit this urbanized profile.

The applicability of an integrated counterinsurgency strategy is also made less relevant by the fact that in recent history most Latin American insurgent movements have not followed the classic pattern the strategy is designed to counter. The 1960s saw the rise of numerous guerrilla movements based on the Cuban model. This model, elaborated in Che Guevara's *Guerrilla Warfare* and Régis Debray's *Revolution in the Revolution*, was a self-conscious break with the classic pattern and an attempt to formulate an insurrectionist strategy. It replaced the party with the guerrilla band, or *foco*, and eschewed the establishment of liberated areas or an elaborate shadow government. Unlike its Asian predecessors that retained the orthodox Marxist-Leninist attention to objective conditions necessary for revolution and the need for their painstaking cultivation, it simply assumed that the objective conditions for revolution already existed. Besides being a misreading of the Cuban experience, this strategy was well-nigh bankrupt by the time of Guevara's capture and death in Bolivia in 1967. In the late 1960s and 1970s, urban guerrilla movements made further attempts to rehabilitate the insurrectionist approach.[34] However, the most successful representatives of this strategy, movements in Brazil, Uruguay, and Argentina, were decisively crushed by the end of the 1970s.

□ *Some Tentative Conclusions*

The threat of guerrilla war, though great for some Latin American countries, is not great for the more-developed parts of Latin America. Governments and military organizations would be wise to alter their planning accordingly. Where there is a guerrilla threat, are Latin American countries faced with the inevitability of the increasing militarization of politics? On the basis of experience in major Latin American countries, the record is mixed.

Colombia has found itself beset by various guerrilla movements. It has been unable to neutralize the guerrillas' appeal or to fully control its own armed forces. Various governments have followed what amounted to a coexistence strategy, tacitly permitting the armed forces a good deal of authority in zones where a variety of insurgent movements operated. Only since the 1980s have civilian administrations begun to depart from this pattern. President Betancur (1982–1986) opened negotiations with the guerrillas that eventually resulted in the partial reincorporation of one movement into the political process. This move, however, was opposed by the military. Betancur's successor, Vigilio Barco (1986–1990), also embarked upon a policy of negotiations with the guerrillas, along with limited administrative decentralization and democratization.

A more hopeful example for successfully coupling democratic control with a counterinsurgency struggle comes from Venezuela in the early 1960s. There, the newly installed democratic regime faced erstwhile political allies who, feeling betrayed by the political moderation of the government, embarked upon a guerrilla struggle. The Venezuelan armed forces followed a policy so closely paralleling US doctrine that it has served as a case study for the US armed forces. The guerrillas, who followed an insurrectionist (foco) strategy, were quickly contained. The Venezuelan military continues to have a significant influence in certain rural areas and has followed a prophylactic strategy to prevent the development of further insurgencies. Thus, even where guerrilla conflict is a credible threat, the picture is not totally bleak.

■ CURRENT THREATS AND PERCEPTIONS

How do Latin American armed forces actually view the potential for political violence and the means necessary to counter it? One answer comes from a hemisphere-wide army conference held in late 1987. Leaked documents present a picture of military thinking that seems to have matured politically very little since the early 1960s. For example, Agreement Number 15 stated that the communist threat had not changed for twenty-eight years and asserted that the International Communist Movement (MCI) continued to pose the main threat to all American countries. It recommended that the military participate temporarily in development and asserted that security depended on integrated strategic actions in four forms of power: political, military, economic, and psychological. Furthermore, it recommended "a thorough evaluation of studies that will allow the implementation of a political-strategic policy for the armies of the Americas" in the "spirit of continental integration." Although the report recommended that action outside the military area not be permanent, it did recommend that a continental intelligence center be established and action taken to counter the psychological advantages the MCI had in the media.[35]

While the documents did not name organizations associated with the MCI, other leaked working papers indicated that some participants considered organizations demanding better living conditions as the enemy, including the American Association of Jurists, the Latin American Association for Human Rights, the Latin American Council of Churches, and the Latin American Federation of Family Members of the Disappeared. Several of these organizations received funds from institutions such as Bread for the World, the Ford Foundation, and the World Council of Churches. These funds were purportedly distributed "to support activities that fit within the strategy of the international communist movement." These papers also attacked liberation theology as a tool of international communism.[36]

Alarmist views of the potential for political violence, or a seizure of power by the left, are also prevalent in four of our five countries without an active insurgency. In all but one of the four, the numbers of militants in leftist organizations that have engaged in political violence are minimal (Table 6.2), and civilian efforts to bring the intelligence services to heel have been limited.

Table 6.2 Insurgent/Terrorist Groups

Country	Number of Members
Peru	3,800–4,400
Chile	1,400
Argentina	50–200
Uruguay	———
Brazil	———

Sources: United States Army Southern Command, Centro de Estudios Unión para la Nueva Mayoría

□ *Uruguay*

Since the transfer of power to civilians in the mid-1980s, Uruguay has faced little in the way of a terrorist threat. Nonetheless, the left has made an impact on national politics. Popular mobilization over the amnesty issue was extensive, and the leftist Broad Front has gained a significant share of the vote, making it a competitor with the two major parties, especially in the Montevideo metropolitan area. Clearly, this development worries the armed forces, which warned President Sanguinetti that the Marxists might take over by a peaceful election.[37]

By all indications, the military has not abandoned its domestic intelligence role, continuing to engage in surveillance of union members and the political opposition. The military attitude about the risk of political violence is mixed. While the army commander, General Carlos Berois, said that according to intelligence information there was no indication of a possible terrorist resurgence in Uruguay,[38] the minister of defense, General (retired) Hugo Medina put a different gloss on the phenomenon:

> If terrorists are inactive here it only means the timing is not right for them, or that their international leaders do not think terrorist action would be to their benefit or lucrative enough at this particular moment. When they decide that the time is ripe, here or anywhere else, they will

strike, and we need to be ready. It would be inexcusable not to be prepared. The raison d'être of an army is to be ready to defend the country from internal or external threats.[39]

Though the Sanguinetti government has taken a firm hand in trimming the military budget, it has been less than resilient in dealing with the armed forces on other political issues.

□ *Brazil*

As is the case with Uruguay, the Brazilian armed forces are concerned with developments in organized labor and in a newly emergent left-wing political party—the Workers' Party (PT)—but what outright political violence has transpired may be the work of provocateurs. Again, as in Uruguay, the armed forces have sent mixed signals. In the wake of significant gains for the PT in the 1988 municipal elections, including capturing the office of mayor in São Paulo, the army minister remarked: "Playing the opposition for the outside is easy; the PT will now discover how tough it is to be on the other side of the fence."[40] Yet during the same period, Aeronautics Minister Brigadier Octavio Moreira Lima, generally considered a moderate, labeled a wave of work stoppages evidence of "an inadmissible and irresponsible strike which is totally disrespectful of society." "I am amazed," he said, "to see how the working class lets itself become involved in movements which are harmful to its members and are conducted by absolute minorities." In the opinion of the military, this wave of strikes dated back to the Volta Redonda and Manesmann strikes in 1988, when the armed forces detected the use of urban guerrilla techniques.[41]

In dealing with the earlier strikes, the armed forces took the initiative, in effect ignoring the president. The army minister and the head of the national intelligence service were reputedly the ones who ordered the suppression of the Volta Redonda strike and the settlement with striking oilworkers. Apparently, the military was most worried about the spread of strike action to essential areas of the economy. Further blurring the line between civilian and military policy roles, national intelligence service reports criticized the president of the labor appeals court for authorizing wage increases in the public section contrary to government guidelines. In dealing with strikes, the military believed that toughness pays off.[42]

With the advent of the new administration in March 1990, however, there was a dramatic organizational change in the National Intelligence Service (SNI). President Collor de Mello carried through on his commitment to disband the SNI. The agency was replaced by the Secretaria de Assuntos Estratégicos (SAE), which took over the rump of the SNI. The SAE will function as a planning secretariat. The account for secret operations was closed, and the operations department, known for its proficiency in wiretapping, was deactivated as well. Its stock of microphones and tape recorders was distributed to other ministries. The old Escola Nacional de Informaçoes was slated for transformation into an academy for training intelligence technicians. Aspirants (civilian and military) were to be recruited via public competition from university graduates.[43]

In summary, the armed forces have retained a significant degree of autonomy and have had a disproportionate influence in the executive branch under the Sarney administration, especially in its latter phases. Part of this may be due to the political weakness of Sarney, which in turn may have furthered the reemergence of traditional patterns of Brazilian civil-military relations. It remains to be seen whether Collor de Mello's initial reforms will culminate in effective civilian oversight of military intelligence and other internal security activities.

□ Argentina

The threat of political violence in Argentina probably comes more from the right than from the left. Even though the only full-scale attack on a military installation, in early 1989, was lead by a Trotskyist group, a number of bombing incidents have been attributed to the right, and rightist arms caches have been uncovered. Followers of or sympathizers with Rico and Seineldín seem to be behind the rightist violence. However, some riots did occur in mid-1989 and again about six months later during bursts of hyperinflation, but the looting of food stores, the principal form of those disorders, appeared to be spontaneous.

The government has been only partially successful in curbing the armed forces' involvement in internal security matters. Plans by the Alfonsín administration to remove the internal security function from the armed forces were partially defeated by the government itself. After disagreements with the legislature, the government finally passed a defense bill in 1988 despite persistent military objections that the powers granted to the armed forces in reference to internal security were too limited. The armed forces wanted assurances that military intelligence could engage in domestic surveillance and that military forces could be used in an internal security role.[44] This the new law did not do. The defense law explicitly barred the armed forces from intervening in domestic civil conflicts and said that "matters related to the country's domestic politics cannot, in any case, constitute working hypotheses for military intelligence organisms."[45] Moreover, the armed forces were not to act on their own. The president as commander in chief and the entire civilian national defense council were the mechanisms by which control of the military was to be established. A civilian was in charge of intelligence operations.

However, the reliability of civilian control could easily be doubted. According to reports, the civilian head of the umbrella state intelligence secretariat, with nominal control over military intelligence, admitted to the Chamber of Deputies in a secret session that intelligence service personnel were involved in bombings.[46] On a later occasion, he also admitted that his organization used wiretaps but, he said, only with court orders permitting the investigation of internal subversion.[47]

The attack on the La Tablada barracks in February 1989 further turned the situation in the military's favor. President Alfonsín signed a decree creating an internal security committee to "prevent and combat the appearance of activities of armed groups capable of endangering constitutional rule, or attacking the life, freedom, property or safety of the nation's inhabitants."[48] The decree empowered the armed forces to participate in internal intelligence matters and repress subversive action in case the police and security forces were overwhelmed by a terrorist attack. Thus, what the armed forces had been unable to gain in the national defense law, they largely recovered by presidential decree.

Furthermore, in February 1990, faced with renewed supermarket sackings and other disturbances, President Menem issued a decree empowering the armed forces to participate in maintaining domestic order.[49]

□ *Chile*

Of the four countries without an insurgency, Chile represents the only case where an active terrorist group has been able to make its presence felt in more than a sporadic fashion. The Manuel Rodríguez Patriotic Front (FPMR), associated with the Chilean Communist Party (PCCh), has been able over a period of years to engage in assassinations and bombings and came close to assassinating Pinochet in 1987.

The PCCh, the largest nonruling communist party in the hemisphere, had been unwilling to sever its links to the FPMR, even while engaging in the campaign for the 1988 plebiscite and 1989 general election. In line with this attitude, the party had been ambivalent about abandoning its position favoring mass popular rebellion that it came to assume under the Pinochet dictatorship. However, with the success of the communist-supported opposition in the plebiscite and prospects for further success in the 1989 general election, the party began to reinterpret its position. According to the then newly elected secretary-general, Volodia Teitelboim, "We will engage in electoral activity, and this, too, is an expression of popular mass rebellion, because it adapts to new conditions."[50] It was not until January 1990, following the electoral rebuff of communist legislative candidates, that the party modified its line, abandoning violence as a means of struggle.[51]

With the transition to democracy, the FPMR has assumed an ambiguous posture. While it retains the capability to continue violent attacks on the establishment, it has tried to distinguish between attacks against the armed forces and attacks against the repressive apparatus carried over from the military government and the newly elected civilian government.[52] The assassination attempt on General Gustavo Leigh, former commander of the Chilean air force during the first period of the military government, fit this pattern. The autonomous faction of the FPMR claimed responsibility for the incident, saying Leigh was targeted for his role in the 1973 repression.[53]

If the FPMR seemed reluctant to abandon the violent option, the Pinochet government was unstinting in its support for the continuance of the military's internal security function. Although the transition to civilian government provoked an organizational change in the security services, that change was more cosmetic than real. In fact, it had the effect of shielding intelligence operations from civilian control. In the decade prior to the transfer of power, the chief organ for domestic intelligence operations had been the Central Nacional de Informaciones (National Information Center, or CNI). But even before the presidential election in December 1989, the minister of defense announced that the CNI would close before the inauguration of a civilian president on March 11, 1990, and destroy its files. Since this would be tantamount to destroying evidence that might be used in future human rights prosecutions, the opposition protested.[54] As it transpired, the internal intelligence service was not being disbanded; it was being transferred to the army. There, it would continue under the direct control of General Pinochet, who was constitutionally guaranteed his position as army commander.

The CNI had long been a focal point of criticism. It came into existence in 1978, replacing a predecessor that had been responsible for carrying out repression during the first phase of the dictatorship. The CNI was on a somewhat shorter leash than its predecessor, but even so, its record of repression has been extensive. According to critics, the CNI has been responsible for assassinating 170 people, torturing 1,300, illegally detaining 2,000, and threatening and keeping track of another 4,000. While its predecessor was covered by the amnesty that was passed in conjunction with the reorganization, the CNI was not. However, the same day the reorganization of the CNI was announced, the judge who had been investigating charges against the CNI was removed from the bench by the supreme court on the grounds he failed to recognize the validity of the agency's claim that he lacked jurisdiction.[55]

The possibility of meaningful change leading to civilian control over the intelligence service will hinge on the attitude of the National Renovation (RN), the most moderate of the former regime's supporters. RN has the balance of power in the senate. It holds enough seats to block the formation of a progovernment majority or to give the government the necessary two-thirds majority to amend the constitution. Having its roots in the pre-Pinochet National Party, RN has been more pragmatic and less ideological than the other major right-wing party, the Unión Democrática Independiente (Independent Democratic Union, or UDI). The RN is clearly open to more constitutional revision than the armed forces have been hitherto willing to concede.

■ CONCLUSIONS

Internal security is a sensitive issue. First, it impinges on the power of a democratically elected government to make policy in response to its perception of the majority's wishes. Second, it inhibits the ability of society to organize and, thus, raises questions about the true wishes of the majority. Third, it directly affects military claims to professional expertise and its claim to have the moral responsibility to defend the nation. Fourth, and most fundamentally, disagreement over the internal security issue appears to be intractable, at least in the short run, because it involves decidedly different perceptions. As for the military, these perceptions are rooted more in an organizational mentality than an explicit ideology, and as such, they are difficult to alter. In short, it is in the internal security area that the requirements for consolidating democracy come most into conflict with the military's post–national security state prerogatives.

Hypothesis 1: The armed forces will vigorously defend their fundamental interest—the armed forces' survival as an institution. The armed forces will defend other interests only to the degree that they are necessary for survival or the maintenance of core interests. The Latin American military has a deep institutional bias that tends to overrate subversive threats. This tendency produced national security doctrines and the belief that internal security is a primary military mission. The military has resisted efforts to change this orientation. Such resistance has taken the form of obstructing civilian oversight in the limited number of cases where that oversight was systematically attempted. Where an active insurgency does exist and the security of the state does seem to be threatened (Peru), the armed forces have repeatedly been able to influence the civilian government to extend the authority of the armed forces.

Hypothesis 2: The more fundamental the interest, the greater the likelihood of the high command's involvement in or tolerance of potentially risky or costly means of resistance. The internal security issue provides little data to test this hypothesis. In internal security matters, the armed forces and the high command have the upper hand. Bureaucratic inertia and the difficulty of establishing civilian oversight over a host of military activities besides internal security conspired to provide few challenges to the aspirations of the armed forces to continue an internal security role.

Hypothesis 3: The more uniform the interest across the various sectors of the armed forces, the more likely the success of the armed forces' action in defense of this interest. Again, little direct evidence is provided for this hypothesis. Although there are obvious branch and service divisions that seem pertinent here, they are more latent than patent. While a hard-line versus soft-line split within the armed forces characterized the transition period, that division has not been openly mimicked. This may well be because the armed forces have not been subject to the internal strains and external pressures over internal security that they faced during the final phases of the military regime. Thus, although this hypothesis remains plausible, any divisions are likely to become important only in the face of consistent civilian pressure to reform internal security operations.

Hypothesis 4: The lower the prestige of the armed forces and the higher the prestige of the civilian government, the more likely the success of the civilian authorities' efforts to reform the military. Of the four instances where enough time has elapsed to provide some assessment of civilian policy and its success, we have observed that only the Argentine government (the one most favorably situated) had attempted to face the problem directly and systematically and then, in the face of a largely isolated left-wing threat, backpedaled. In Peru, an initial attempt by the García government to regularize internal security activities and subject them to due-process restrictions faded away as the government lost political popularity. Hence, the prognosis for stringent limitations on military involvement in internal security is not encouraging. The military's influence grew as the actual situation came to resemble the situation as perceived by the armed forces.

The gradual self-modification of the military's internal security views may be possible when there is no serious threat of political violence for an extended period of time. Yet, it is more likely that a civilian government that persistently avoids the problem of direct confrontation over these military prerogatives will achieve very little. Institutional perceptions are largely self-perpetuating, and as we have seen, the perception of a latent threat has little to do with the existence of an actual threat. Moreover, military organizations and operations tend to be opaque to civilians not schooled in military affairs; and intelligence operations with their inherent secrecy are even more so. Budgetary control will probably be of little use alone. Besides fiscal subterfuge, civilian authorities have to face the fact that some intelligence operations may actually be self-financing.[56]

The effective alteration of internal security practices will probably require the skills of bureaucratic guerrilla warfare. Unless civilian authorities can develop the expertise and marshal the will to undertake such a protracted endeavor, the armed forces' internal security operations will have a chilling effect on democratic practices and on democratic consolidation. In most circumstances, it would probably be impolitic and probably unsound policy to attempt to remove the armed forces totally from internal security matters, as the Alfonsín government in Argentina proposed. It would probably be wiser to use the military as a backup, riot-control force under the control of other agencies, while removing domestic intelligence as much as possible from the military's purview. In cases of actual insurgency, civilians will have to take the initiative to assure that the armed forces do not direct and shape the response. In either case, it will be necessary to develop the proper civilian structures and train both civilian and military personnel in roles appropriate to each. Such a long-range solution may be the only practical one.

■ NOTES

1. Aside from representing a kind of best-case example, US doctrine is particularly apropos given the influence, or at least high degree of visibility, the United States has in the region. From 1961 to 1975, the United States trained 71,651 Latin American military personnel in counterinsurgency and supplied the region with $2.5 billion worth of weapons. Mary Rose Donnelly, "Dictators Eclipsed by Democrats but Terror Apparatus Still Intact," *Latinamerica Press*, March 26, 1987, p. 2. For a discussion of the range of Latin American doctrines, including that of Argentina, which is heavily influenced by French counterinsurgency doctrine, see Pion-Berlin, 1989b, pp. 411–429.

2. United States Army, pp. 17–25. Earlier editions of this manual present essentially the same analysis and doctrine.

3. Ibid., pp. 35–37. Other methods include: a rightist strategy to infiltrate existing organizations and a leftist strategy to prepare an insurgent military organization capable of provoking or taking advantage of mass outbursts. Most importantly, the doctrine implies the choice as a matter of expediency rather than principle. Ibid., pp. 29–31.

4. Ibid., pp. 32–33.

5. Ibid., p. 34.

6. Ibid.

7. FBIS, "Opposition, Conservatives Discuss Military Role," Santiago, *El Mercurio*, September 3, 1989, FBIS-LAT-89-208, October 31, 1989, p. 59.

8. For a discussion of this tendency he dubs "alarmism," see Abrahamsson, pp. 87–92.

9. Welch and Smith, p. 44.

10. United States Army, pp. 46–57.

11. Lane and Weisenbloom, pp. 35–39.

12. Slade, pp. 21–25.

13. Ebel.

14. Favre, pp. 3–28.

15. Ronald H. Berg, "*Sendero Luminoso* and Peasants of Andahuaylas," *Journal of Interamerican Studies and World Affairs*, 28, no. 4 (Winter 1986–1987):187–189.

16. *Latin American Weekly Report*, October 12, 1989, pp. 4–5.

17. FBIS, "President Gives Order," Buenos Aires, TELAM, December 29, 1982, FBIS-LAM-82-251, December 30, 1982, p. H1.

18. Official figures place the death toll in the first half of 1983 at 900 compared to less than 150 for the 1980–1982 period. Caitlin Randall, "Peru Finds 'Small' Guerrilla Band Is Hard to Crush," *Christian Science Monitor*, June 27, 1983, p. 7.

19. "Sendero Organisation and Objectives," *Latin American Regional Reports: Andean Group Report*, April 5, 1985, p. 4.

20. "Alan García Challenges Army's Counter-Insurgency Methods," *Latin American Regional Reports: Andean Group Report*, October 4, 1985, p. 1.

21. Michael L. Smith, "Progress in Peru—Maybe," *Washington Post National Weekly Edition*, December 30, 1985, p. 15.

22. Kathryn Leger, "García Enlists Each Peruvian in Battle Against Terrorism," *Christian Science Monitor*, February 11, 1987, pp. 9, 12.

23. "Guerrillas Extend Their Influence," *Latin American Weekly Report*, March 2, 1989, p. 4.

24. "The General and the Cocaleros," *Economist*, December 9, 1989, pp. 40–41.

25. "Peru's Insurgency Policy Flaws," *Latin American Weekly Report*, May 11, 1989, pp. 6–7.

26. Chris Kline, "Peruvian Government Steps Up Counterinsurgency Campaign," *Times of the Americas*, March 22, 1989, p. 4.

27. "Alan García Opts for Last-Minute Shift in His Policy Toward Sendero Insurgency," *Latin American Weekly Report*, August 10, 1989, p. 1.

28. "Postscript," *Latin American Weekly Report*, June 1, 1989, p. 12.

29. "Peru: 'Rondas Campesinas' Carry Out Rural Justice," *Latinamerica Press*, November 27, 1986, pp. 6–7; Elsa Chanduví, "Peru: Peasant Farmers Resent Government Move to Control Self-Defense Patrols," *Latinamerica Press*, June 10, 1988, p. 5.

30. "Steep Rise in Political Killings in Peru," *Latin American Regional Reports: Andean Group Report*, February 1, 1990, pp. 4–5.

31. "Rights Group Report on Peru Shows Rising Tide of Abuses," *New York Times*, August 24, 1989, p. 6.

32. Chris Kline, "Peruvian Government Steps Up Counterinsurgency Campaign," *Times of the Americas*, March 22, 1989, p. 4.

33. McClintock, pp. 136–137.

34. For the classic statement of its methods, see Marighella.

35. FBIS, "'Text' of Armies Conference Agreement No. 15," *Folha de São Paulo*, September 25, 1988, FBIS-LAT-88-189, September 29, 1988, p. 1; Clovis Rossi, "Pact Between 'Armies of America' Leaked," *Folha de São Paulo*, September 25, 1988, FBIS-LAT-88-187, September 27, 1988, pp. 1–2.

36. Samuel Blixen, "Latin America: Armies Draw Up Continent-wide Security Doctrine," *Latinamerica Press*, December 1, 1988, pp. 1–2.

37. "Officials Prepare for Referendum," *Latin American Weekly Report*, October 29, 1987, p. 2.

38. FBIS, "Army Commander Rules Out Terrorist Resurgence," Montevideo, Radio Carve Network, May 19, 1989, FBIS-LAT-89-099, May 24, 1989, p. 38.

39. Boeker, p. 83.

40. José Pedro S. Martins, "Brazil's Leftist Presidential Candidates Reach Out to Pacify Armed Forces," *Latinamerica Press*, February 2, 1989, p. 5.

41. FBIS, "Strikes Alarm Military," Rio de Janeiro, *O Globo*, April 7, 1989, FBIS-LAT-89-084, May 3, 1989, p. 40.

42. "Generals Impose New Tough Line," *Latin American Weekly Report*, December 8, 1988, p. 4.

43. "Unveiling Secrets of the SNI," *Latin American Weekly Report*, May 3, 1990, p. 9.

44. "Defence Bill Debate," *Latin American Weekly Report*, September 4, 1986, p. 8.

45. "Defence Law Bans Internal Action," *Latin American Regional Reports: Southern Cone Report*, April 28, 1988, p. 2.

46. FBIS, "Intelligence Agents Participate in UCR Bombings," Buenos Aires, *Noticias Argentinas*, July 8, 1987, FBIS-LAT-87-132, July 10, 1990, p. K2.

47. FBIS, "SIDE Chief on New Role of Intelligence," Buenos Aires, *Ambito Financiero*, July 19, 1989, FBIS-LAT-89-045, March 9, 1989, pp. 36–40.

48. FBIS, "Alfonsín Creates 'Internal Security Committee,'" *Buenos Aires Herald*, March 11, 1989, FBIS-LAT-89-048, March 14, 1989, p. 43.

49. Michael Soltys, "Menem Throws Mace at Congress," *Buenos Aires Herald*, March 11, 1990, p. 3.

50. "Rebellion via Polls, Says Teitelboim," *Latin American Weekly Report*, June 1, 1989, pp. 4–5.

51. FBIS, "PCCh Announces End of Rebellion of the Masses," Madrid, EFE, January 14, 1990, FBIS-LAT-90-010, January 16, 1990, pp. 40–41.

52. FBIS, "FPMR to Continue with Violent Policy," Santiago, Domestic Service, December 26, 1989, FBIS-LAT-89-247, December 27, 1989, p. 48.

53. "Two Groups Claim Attack on General," *Latin American Weekly Report*, April 5, 1990, p. 10.

54. "Secret Files to Be Destroyed," *Latin American Weekly Report*, November 30, 1989, p. 12.

55. María Laura Avignolo, "Chile's Secret Police Disbanded," *Latinamerica Press*, January 18, 1990, p. 3.

56. FBIS, "Alfonsín Signs Secret Decree; Army Benefits," *Buenos Aires Herald*, July 7, 1988, FBIS-LAT-88-131, July 8, 1988, pp. 19–20. A decree signed by the president legalized military involvement in business operations, whose proceeds were to continue unreported to state auditors. The armed forces, however, denied the significance of such self-financing, claiming that it provided less than 1 percent of the intelligence budget.

7■

Flashpoint III: Military Reform

Civilian control of the armed forces is necessary for democracy. As with other political dictates, this is easy to state but hard to fulfill. The difficulty arises from the fact that such control requires both knowledge and power; and in this case—Francis Bacon notwithstanding—the two are different. Knowledge implies a degree of understanding of military affairs sufficient to formulate viable and credible policies. This understanding entails the comprehension of military affairs in general, as well as familiarity with one's own country's armed forces. Power implies the legal authority to compel and political capacity to induce compliance.

In most of Latin America, effective civilian control does not yet exist. Civilian control can be established only through effective military reform. Any reform worthy of the name would consist in either a wholesale restructuring of the institution—for example, establishing a nation-in-arms or constabulary armed forces in place of a cadre-type force—or doctrinal change. In the case of our five countries, reform would also be premised on strengthening mechanisms of objective civilian control. The armed forces of these countries do not seem susceptible to effective subjective control, which seems possible only under specific circumstances. For example, Welch and Smith cite a number of types of cases in which subjective methods of control (what they term "fragmented boundaries" between military and civilian roles) work. These cases involve the penetration of the officer corps by individuals who owe their primary allegiance to other organizations or groups such as: the communist party; an ethnic group, tribe, or region; the society at large with incompatible civilian values of egalitarianism, pacifism, or the ethic of the citizen-soldier; or a ruler or ruling elite.[1] These cases do not fit the pattern of our countries, or most Latin American countries, very well, and further, some are non- or even antidemocratic.

■ OBJECTIVE CONTROL: ISSUES AND AMBIGUITIES

The goal of objective civilian control is to foster the loyalty of the armed forces to the regime while preserving the military institution's professionalism, autonomy, and corporateness. Civilian control is exercised through the chain of command, while the armed forces have a narrowly defined sphere of competence. Thus, objective control is external control accepted willingly.

One question arises, however: What matters are internal to the armed forces, over which the preservation of military control is essential to assure autonomy, and what matters are external and require political direction to ensure civilian control? Although the principle that military officers should be "constrained from participating as a group in the sphere of political activity not directly associated with the management of coercion,"[2] adds some precision, it does not foreclose debate. Leaving aside the issue of internal security, the management of coercion is an open-ended concept and the principle itself leaves other questions unanswered.

It is these partially unanswered questions that create a potential for conflict between civilian officials and the military. Although most may agree on the basic principles involved in democratic control of professional armed forces, debate quickly arises about the exact meanings and implications of these principles. What one side sees as democratic and compatible with the norms of professionalism, the other may view as unjustified politicization.

□ *Assigning vs. Executing Missions*

It is a dictum of strategy from the time of Clausewitz that the purpose of war is to serve the ends of politics—the political leadership assigns the mission, the armed forces decide how to execute it. In other words, the general designation of objectives is provided by the former; the specific implementation of policies to accomplish the objectives is the realm of the latter. Yet, the objective applies to politically directed grand strategy as well as to tactics, unquestionably the province of the armed forces. This ambiguity is more than semantic. Should political authority be too general in establishing the objectives or missions of the armed forces, it virtually abdicates responsibility to the armed forces. Should political authority be too specific, it risks micromanaging defense matters and politicizing the armed forces.

Parallel problems exist with the notion that the military professionals advise and the political leadership decides on policies. Is the failure to follow advice an indirect attack on the professional competence of the advisers? Does supposedly technical advice really mask an underlying nontechnical political orientation? Does competence in the management of coercion entail expertise in the setting of related foreign and domestic policy priorities? There are no a priori answers to such questions. Answers necessarily depend on the context and are frequently not clear-cut.

□ *The Issue of Personnel Assignment*

Additional ambiguities surround the notion that promotion and assignment of military personnel should be done in a manner commensurate with professionalism. Professionalism implies that these personnel actions will be made on the basis of objective criteria beyond the reach of political manipulation. Promotion is supposed to be based on seniority and merit, assignment on appropriate rank and experience. At all but the highest levels—in most cases that of general officers—political authorities simply defer to the military establishment in these matters. At the highest levels however, where execution of policy is most likely to shade into policymaking, political discretion on the promotion and assignment of officers is the norm, provided professional criteria are respected. But discretion opens the door for charges of politicization.

Assignments outside the narrow military sphere also raise questions about proper personnel policy. Should officers be assigned to nonmilitary posts in parastatal corporations or other parts of the executive branch? Is their military expertise transferable? Should military education attempt to cultivate expertise in other areas besides the military sphere so that at least some officers possess professional competence in areas such as foreign affairs, economics, and administration? Should civilians fill those positions in the defense establishment not absolutely requiring a uniformed officer? What control should civilian authorities have over military education?

□ *Some Consequences*

These questions have serious, practical import in that they provide fertile soil for day-to-day civil-military disputes. Professionalism, even of the more traditional sort, can provide a pretext for policymaking by the military. Establishing meaningful objective control looks more like guerrilla warfare, with small victories and tactical retreats, than a grand battle of Napoleonic proportions.

■ SOME ASPECTS OF LATIN AMERICA'S MILITARY TRADITION

The ambiguity of professionalism and its inadequacy in providing exact guidance on military policy affect all governments attempting to implement objective civilian control. In Latin America, the struggle to establish civilian control over the armed forces is also a struggle against established traditions and organizational prejudices largely peculiar to the region. These regional factors compound the problem of establishing civilian control by giving the military additional motives and pretexts for resisting its civilian superiors. Two of the most pertinent of these factors are the persistence of outdated threat analyses and continuing intellectual isolation of the officer corps from other social sectors.

□ Cross-Border Threats

In the 1980s, the armed forces of Latin America seemed to have few significant external defense missions in comparison to their European or North American counterparts. The South American continent faced no credible, extrahemispheric, conventional threat comparable to the Soviet threat to Western Europe in the 1980s. Further, the possibility of wars between regional powers was also remote given the experience of the past century. There had not been any major international war in Latin America since the Gran Chaco conflict of the 1930s and only two minor ones—Peru-Ecuador (1941) and El Salvador–Honduras (1969). The most recent war that involved more that two powers was the War of the Pacific over a century ago. Yet military organizations habitually prepare for worst-case scenarios. This tendency is reinforced by the study of geopolitics typical of Latin American militaries.

Although there are differences between the various national schools of geopolitical thought, all possess a number of underlying characteristics that have largely underpinned geopolitical thought since its inception in the late nineteenth century. International politics is seen as a struggle for survival between states. The states themselves are organic entities with an internal dynamic more important than the idiosyncrasies of their component parts—their citizens or subjects. Just as with other living organisms, the state needs resources to grow and survive. Hence, international politics is the struggle for these resources—territory—among states. And power, not right, is the major weapon in this struggle.[3] Geopolitics gives a theoretical rationale for territorial disputes and traditional antagonisms between neighboring states. Such disagreements are seen as the result of fundamentally divergent national interests, not the expressions of irrational and ultimately self-defeating jingoism.

The geopolitical perspective provides intellectual support for hard-line nationalist attitudes toward international disputes. A number of disputes exist among the five countries upon which we are focusing.

Bolivian Exit to the Sea. Since the loss of its seacoast as a result of the War of the Pacific, Bolivia has long sought to reestablish an exit to the sea. The problem is compounded by the fact that the conflict was three-sided—Peru, as well as Bolivia, lost territory to Chile; and the 1929 treaty governing potential settlement requires the three powers to agree if any prospective adjustment involves territory that formerly belonged to Peru. Furthermore, the geopolitical debate over whether insecure frontiers should be developed and fully incorporated into the rest of the state has impelled both Chile and Peru to develop free-trade zones in the region to further the incorporation process. This has had the effect of raising the stakes. As recently as October 1989, a meeting between President García of Peru and President Paz Zamora of Bolivia further inflamed the controversy. The adverse reaction from Chile, and even some sectors in Peru, demonstrated once again the sensitivity of the issue.[4]

Regional Oceans and Antarctic Claims. Perhaps the most confused and confusing set of territorial issues arises from the conflicting claims made by various Latin American states to Antarctica and the waters of the Antarctic and Atlantic oceans. These claims involve a host of states, extraregional powers, and international organizations. National positions are based on conflicting theories of international law and varying definitions of territorial seas. The most notable dispute, but certainly not the only one, is between Chile and Argentina involving the attempt by Chile to define its territorial sea in terms that extend it into waters claimed by Argentina. Chile, Argentina, Brazil, and Peru have mounted polar expeditions; and Chile and Argentina have established a permanent presence on the continent. Many advocates of the exploitation of Antarctica see the continent and the surrounding seas as possessing immense economic potential.[5]

Brazil's Living Borders and Argentina's Anxiety. Although no outstanding border disputes serve as its basis, perhaps the key geopolitical rivalry in South America is that between Argentina and Brazil. The real issue is economic and political dynamism rather than the future possibility of a Brazilian seizure of Argentine territory. Brazilian economic influence in Paraguay and Uruguay—the historical buffer states between the two giants of South America—and the infiltration of Brazilian settlers into these areas and northern Argentina constitute a challenge to Argentina's power. Argentina is acutely aware that in terms of size of territory and population it is outclassed by its larger neighbor, and for the past several decades, Brazilian economic growth has outstripped Argentina's by a large margin as well.

Argentine geopoliticians see a favorite Brazilian theory, that of living borders, as sanctioning the penetration, assimilation, and eventual outright seizure of Argentine territory. This theory was adapted to Brazilian conditions by General Golbery do Couto e Silva, a leading figure in Brazil's military regime as well as an influential geopolitical theorist. This theory asserts that frontiers are dynamic realities, not merely static demarcations on political maps. The migration of people, the expansion of their economic activity, and an area's link with the rest of the country provide the real basis, in terms of actual power, of determining the border between states. And without the power to support them, political demarcations are susceptible to alteration.[6]

It is not surprising, then, that Argentine military geopoliticians are suspicious of Brazilian intentions and see integration differently from many of their civilian counterparts. From a civilian geopolitical perspective, integration of Spanish-speaking states in the region is a positive benefit. Only then can Brazilian power be balanced. Once balanced, regional integration as a whole can be put on the agenda. However, this has not been the thrust of civilian efforts at economic and political integration in the region.

☐ *Intellectual and Social Isolation*
of the Armed Forces

Modern Latin American armed forces have been largely isolated from many of the intellectual and political currents in their society. Military officers are professionals, neither citizen-soldiers nor short-service reservists. Most countries commission their officer corps only from military academy graduates, and the curriculum of these academies bears little resemblance to the curriculum of civilian universities. Civilian institutions reinforce this voluntary estrangement. On the one hand, Latin America lacks the range of research institutes or university programs on strategic studies found in the United States, and many people who study the military treat the institution more as a social pathology than one whose policies and analyses are worthy of serious study in their own right. On the other hand, civilian geopoliticians and graduates of senior military schools, such as the Brazilian Superior War College (ESG), do little to rectify the situation. They too often are proponents of the military outlook rather than thoughtful critics of existing organizations and strategies. While the armed forces' intellectual isolation is not absolute, it is nonetheless significant.

This isolation is further enhanced by the social structure of the armed forces. Latin American armed forces are largely structured on what Charles Moscos terms the "institutional" rather than the "occupational" model. The institutional model stresses organizational attributes much different from most civilian professions. It also stresses a generalist rather than a specialist orientation. Military skills have little application outside the armed forces. The individual takes his reference from those above him in the military hierarchy rather than from similar groups in civilian society. Work and residence are adjacent; military rather than civilian housing is the norm. Personnel retain military status upon retirement. The occupational model, on the contrary, stresses the opposite features: specialist orientations compatible with civilian skills, a concomitant civilian reference group, and a life-style and retirement more nearly comparable with civilian practice.[7] The effect of the institutional social structure upon civil-military communication is obvious.

The intellectual and social isolation of the armed forces promotes a sense of autonomy on the part of the armed forces and an attitude of malign neglect from civilians. Certain military programs and policies may arouse intense civilian interest when they have a direct impact on the population—witness the human rights issues. Others may be of interest only to selected civilian sectors, as is the case with the military's arms industries. A whole range of activities and programs, such as various strategic weapons programs, are the source of occasional scandals but fail to arouse persistent interest from politicians or the general public.

■ **CASE STUDY:**
   MILITARY REFORM IN ARGENTINA

During the decade of the 1980s, the efforts of the Alfonsín administration (1983–1989) were the most systematic attempt at military reform in our five countries. The history of these efforts illustrates how attempts at military reform can provoke charges by the armed forces that the government is politicizing the military and ignoring the country's national interest.

Alfonsín's reform strategy operated on two levels. On the national level, it attempted to implement norms of objective civilian control and induce the military to rethink its strategy and organization in light of new international conditions. On the international level, Alfonsín tried to further regional military cooperation as part of a more thoroughgoing integration process. Regionwide defense was to have priority over defense against historic, regional rivals (primarily Chile and Brazil). In line with the general policy of regional cooperation, Alfonsín took steps to render his country's nuclear program less provocative.

The Alfonsín government came into office in propitious circumstances for initiating a policy of military reform insofar as the power and prestige of the armed forces were concerned. The armed forces were politically demoralized, but the government faced a host of other problems that tended to make military reform one issue among many. The most troubling of these other issues, and the one that eventually forced the president to voluntarily turn power over to his successor early, was the economy.

□ *Government Policy*

Aside from human rights prosecutions, the major thrust of the Alfonsín government's military policy was the attempt to reorient the military toward external defense missions and to increase civilian oversight. Civilians were appointed to the top posts of a unified defense ministry, and a strategic review was begun.

The government's endeavor to promote military rethinking of basic defense issues came at a propitious time. The military itself began extensive self-criticism after the Falklands/Malvinas debacle. These critiques took note of the conventional inadequacies of the armed forces. In budgetary terms, the military government had become heavily committed to external defense as a direct aftermath of the war. According to one estimate, defense spending rose dramatically from 2.9 percent of GDP in 1981 to 6.4 percent of GDP in 1982, the year of the conflict.[8] The military government began the procurement of new equipment essential to the modernization of all three services.

The Alfonsín government proposed to give the modernization process a further twist by reorganizing the military and making changes in the curricula of military schools. Military strategy and planning were to become a function of the president and his cabinet and not the sole prerogative of uniformed military personnel. The military was to recognize the legitimacy of ideological pluralism and avoid espousing any principles that would imply the need for ideological conformity.[9] The defense ministry issued a directive specifying a timetable for the reorganization of the armed services.[10] It was a three-staged process designed to culminate in 1988. Proposed elements of the reorganization included: abolition of some of the existing branch schools, reorganization of the branches along more modern lines, the creation of new branches such as rocketry and armor, and interservice merging to comply with new technology.[11] In line with this changed concept of the military's mission, the defense ministry ordered unprecedented joint exercises.[12]

The Alfonsín administration also began asserting civilian control over the defense industries formerly controlled by the various armed services. Military industries represented a significant portion of the Argentine economy; they included the largest industrial group in the country and a 99 percent interest in the country's largest steel mill.[13] By the time of the Alfonsín government, they also represented a considerable drain on governmental resources. The government initiated a policy of shifting control of defense industries from the separate services to the defense ministry as a whole and attempted to privatize some of the industries. In a related matter, the government planned to sell eight military bases in the greater Buenos Aires area, putting the land into more productive economic use and removing military garrisons from key political, transportation, and communications centers.[14]

The privileges of the military as a corporate entity, many of which extend back to the Spanish colonial period, were reduced. A new military code abolished certain legal exemptions enjoyed by members of the military caste, specifically the right of officers to be tried exclusively by military courts. The revised military code gave jurisdiction over military officers to civilian courts when officers faced civilian criminal charges. Military courts retained jurisdiction only over those crimes that affected the military as an institution.[15]

In sum, the Alfonsín government undertook a multifaceted program to assert civilian control of the military. While the policy's objectives were not extraordinary within the Western democratic context, within the Argentinian context they would have meant a major revision of the status quo. The president attempted to reconcile the military to their changed role and status but did not attempt a purge or wholesale restructuring of the institution. His efforts, however, did not result in a real dialogue with the armed forces.

□ *Military Reaction*

Members of the armed forces, while clearly on the political defensive, engaged in passive and in some cases active resistance against the government's reforms. These acts ranged from bureaucratic obstructionism to acts of violence and coup threats. Resistance was predictable, given the substantial nature of the change in the role and privileges of the military undertaken by the government. Some interests of the institution as a whole and certain sectional interests within it were threatened by the changes. The drive to establish traditional professionalism challenged the military's largely self-assumed, internal security mission and its aspiration to be a key actor in many civilian policy areas. Reorganization threatened a number of the branches and those officers who made their careers serving within them. Privatization of defense industries, or placing them under civilian control within the defense ministry, damaged the influence of the individual services. It has likewise limited career opportunities for numerous officers.

Most importantly, budgetary stringency had a decided impact on morale and on the ability of the armed forces to prepare satisfactorily for external defense missions. This stringency was partly a matter of necessity, partly a matter of policy to promote military cooperation. At first, cuts in the military budget did not affect the procurement of new equipment, and the military was urged to act imaginatively to make the best use of their limited funds. Cutbacks were made in the number of conscripts taken into the service and the extent and scale of maneuvers; also, a significant portion of equipment was mothballed in order to lower costs.[16] By late 1985, however, it became apparent that these changes would not be sufficient and plans were laid for the sale of some of the recently acquired equipment.[17]

The army revolts of 1987 and 1988 embittered military-government relations, which had been testy at best. While senior officers had been very correct in their official bearing toward the president, they remained quietly uncooperative. The president reciprocated. The budgetary limits, which became more stringent after the revolts, seemed to belie the government's public expression of esteem for the military and the importance of its revised mission. Financial constraints had an impact on the stability of the officer and NCO corps. The number of officers and NCO's fell by 35 percent between 1983 and 1986; the number of entrants in military schools dropped from 250 in 1985 to 40 in 1986; and some of that year's conscripts were discharged early because of financial exigencies.[18]

Lower defense budgets also resulted in a decline in the purchasing power of officers' salaries. In the latter part of 1986, the government was forced to grant a 35 percent salary increase to the armed forces, whose real income had been in constant decline since the inauguration of the government's Austral Plan in June 1985.[19] Still, salaries in August 1988 were at 44 percent of what they had been when Alfonsín assumed office.[20] Although the data reveal that the sharp decline in the purchasing power of officers' salaries (Table 7.1) and erosion in the defense budget (Table 7.2) started long before the advent of the new government, military officers held the president responsible.

Table 7.1 Purchasing Power of Argentine Officers' Salaries (1975 = 100)

	Year									
	1975	1976	1977	1978	1979	1980	1981	1982	1983	1984–IQ
Index	100	81	61	55	56	66	65	48	45	46

Source: Luis F. Torres, "Military Takes Steps to Meet Impost Financial Constraints," Buenos Aires, *Somos*, April, 27, 1984, JPRS-LAM-84-68, June 4, 1984, pp. 39–43

Table 7.2 Argentine Defense Budget

	Years							
	1970–75	1976–80	1981–83	1984	1985	1986	1987	1988
Military budget as percent of GDP	2.4	3.6	4.4	2.8	2.4	2.3	2.4	2.5

Source: Centro de Estudios Unión para la Nueva Mayoría

□ Strategic Programs

Prior to the Alfonsín administration, the armed forces had begun a number of strategic weapons programs. Budgetary restrictions had a decided impact on these programs, but discussion of their relevance to the promised new defense posture never materialized. Major strategic programs fell into three categories.

The nuclear project had been underway since the late 1970s, and by the end of the 1980s, the country developed the capacity to reprocess plutonium.

The Ezeiza plant operated under International Atomic Energy Agency (IAEA) safeguards, but Argentina reserved the right to operate it without IAEA inspection. The Pilcaniyeu uranium enrichment plant will reportedly produce only slightly enriched material but have the capacity to produce 220 pounds of 90 percent enriched uranium per year. Although the Alfonsín government took some initial steps to bring the nuclear program under full civilian control, the armed forces remained largely unaccountable in this area.[21]

Argentina's premier missile project was the Cóndor II, which was undertaken with the cooperation of a number of Middle Eastern states. The missile, an Argentine-developed, solid-fuel rocket, reputedly had a range in excess of 500 miles and a payload of over 750 pounds. The Cóndor II project was an attempt to upgrade an earlier version of the missile by developing a second stage with precision guidance. The first stage had a range of 300 miles and was first tested in October 1986. It lacked a precision guidance system. According to the US Department of State, guidance systems may have been offered by China and Israel,[22] and the guidance problem may have been partially solved by late 1989.[23]

The details of the project's financing and the source of its technical assistance are much disputed. Argentina and its partners, Egypt and Iraq, are said to have used a variety of legal and illegal mechanisms to obtain technology and circumvent the Missile Technology Control Regime (MTCR). Iraq reportedly received up to $1.7 billion in financing from an Italian bank, a large part of which supposedly went to the Cóndor project.[24] Argentine denials about these arrangements and about the capabilities of the missile have been belied by military comments on the country's capability in the ballistic missile field.[25] Iraq and Argentina have been involved in the project since 1984, although Argentina's role is understood to have diminished.

The project may, in fact, have become a bargaining chip with the passing of the Alfonsín administration. A number of quid pro quos have been suggested for Argentina's dropping the project: US purchase of the Pampa military trainer aircraft and Argentine membership in MTCR, now exclusively composed of Western powers.[26] This may seem an attractive trade-off, given reports that the project has run into serious difficulties.[27] Details of civilian oversight or approval of the Cóndor project during the Alfonsín administration remain murky, but Carlos Menem's second defense minister publicly blamed the project and its Iraqi connection on a decision of the Alfonsín government.[28]

Although the Argentine military expressed interest in constructing a nuclear-powered submarine, little progress was made in this endeavor because of budgetary problems. Government sources denied rumors that such a submarine was under construction.[29] As was the case with the other strategic programs, the details of the submarine program remained secret. The government encouraged neither public discussion nor legislative oversight.

Strategic programs continued, if they did not prosper, during the Alfonsín government. They escaped effective oversight, and there is no indication that the government ever addressed their role within the proposed new defense policy.

□ *Regional Cooperation*

President Alfonsín did take advantage of opportunities on the international level to promote a change in military orientation. These efforts ran against a strong current of military opinion, which continued to be distrustful of the power and intentions of the country's major neighbors.

Background. Efforts at military cooperation had their origins in the 1970s and were shaped by a bellicose, Cold War perspective, but the evolution of proposals for cooperation have demonstrated the growing independence of the region from East-West politics. A longtime backwater in East-West competition, the South Atlantic gained greater strategic prominence in the mid-1970s and became the focal point for efforts at military integration because of a number of developments. Perhaps the most important underlying trend was the marked increase in Soviet naval power that began after the Cuban missile crisis. Exacerbating this declining margin of US naval superiority was the aging of the US fleet and the retirement of many World War II–era warships that the United States could not afford to replace. The US defeat in Vietnam in the mid-1970s, and Soviet-supported leftist victories in Africa thereafter, added to the picture of US decline.

For hard-line advocates of a Cold War strategy in the United States and elsewhere, these were the worst of times. Cold War strategists, however, were soon proposing a South Atlantic Treaty Organization (SATO) that would parallel NATO and secure NATO's vulnerable South Atlantic flank. A precursor Ocean Venture 81, a joint US Navy exercise with the Argentine, Brazilian, Colombian, Uruguayan, and Venezuelan navies, was established to coincide with NATO maneuvers in the North Atlantic.[30]

Although the SATO proposal seemed to square nicely with much Latin American geopolitical analysis about the importance of the South Atlantic, it ran afoul of regional interests in other ways. It ignored traditional rivalries between Brazil and Argentina. It failed to take into account that Argentina was unwilling to cooperate with the United Kingdom after the Falklands/Malvinas conflict of 1982; such cooperation was essential, given Britain's control of strategic islands in the region. It also flew in the face of Brazil's growing attempt to woo black African states. SATO would have required the participation of South Africa, which would have effectively scuttled Brazil's efforts in the rest of the continent. In the final analysis, a reintegration into the Western system premised on the increase of East-West tensions promised to be more deleterious than helpful in advancing regional interests. As the Brazilian foreign minister noted before a conference of senior military officers, the re-bipolarization of international politics monopolized diplomatic energy around superpower issues, thus weakening efforts to advance other issues.[31]

Steps Toward Cooperation. It is not surprising, therefore, that Brazil advanced a South Atlantic Zone of Peace resolution in the United Nations as a means of subtly shifting the focus of international debate. The resolution, passed by the United Nations General Assembly in 1986, called for regional cooperation, economic development, and the elimination of apartheid in South Africa. Specifically in regard to military matters, it called

> upon all other States of all other regions, in particular the militarily significant States, scrupulously to respect the region of the South Atlantic as a zone of peace and cooperation, especially through the *reduction and eventual elimination of their military presence there*, the non-introduction of nuclear weapons or other weapons of mass destruction and non-extension into the region of rivalries and conflicts that are foreign to it.[32]

Although the language appears decisive, there is no timetable or method of enforcement suggested for the removal of nonregional military forces.

In addition, the resolution called "upon all States of the region and of all other regions to cooperate in the elimination of all sources of tension in the zone, to respect national unity, sovereignty, political independence and territorial integrity of every State therein."[33] Thus, in typical diplomatic language, the resolution is vague regarding points that could be seen as bearing directly on the disputed claims over the Falklands/Malvinas.

President Alfonsín took full advantage of Brazil's openness to regional cooperation and the willingness of his Brazilian counterpart to engage in a round of summit meetings. Alfonsín and Sarney exchanged visits to one another's nuclear installations and promoted expanded formal contacts between the two countries' armed forces. As a result of the agreement signed by the presidents in 1985, the two militaries have held a number of joint conferences on strategic studies. The first was held in Buenos Aires in 1987. One of the participants, retired Vice Admiral Armando Ferreira Vidigal of Brazil, argued that Brazil and Argentina should cooperate further in the nuclear field. A joint venture for producing a nuclear submarine was suggested in order to capitalize on Brazil's engineering capacity and Argentina's progress in mastering the nuclear fuel cycle. Cooperation, he asserted, was manifest destiny. In the same conference, an Argentine colonel proposed a military alliance. The proposal was not accepted, in part because it would be seen as threatening to third parties.

Common interests, according to a paper by two Argentine officers, included avoiding militarization of the South Atlantic by extraregional powers. Retired Rear Admiral Mario Eduardo Olmos, a member of the

Argentine navy's center for strategic studies, identified the following common interests: regional political integration to strengthen negotiating capacity with extraregional interests, maintenance and consolidation of pluralist political systems, preservation of the South Atlantic as a zone of peace, and defense of interests in Antarctica. In the military area, he noted a number of areas suitable for cooperative efforts: agreement on a reasonable level of parity between their military forces, development of joint programs for the production of materiel, and joint use of force in regional conflicts that may affect common interests.[34]

At the second conference the following year in São Paulo, Vice Admiral Ferreira again appealed for defense production integration, asserting that it was possible in the short term. He argued that it was important to prevent dependence on foreign suppliers such as Argentina suffered from during the Malvinas conflict, when it could not get spare parts for its Exocet missiles.[35]

The third conference took place in 1989 with Uruguay also in attendance. In his closing remarks, Argentine Defense Minister Horacio Jaunarena took note of the fact that serious difficulties continued to block cooperation. To achieve real integration, he said, the participating countries needed to "exorcise ghosts and cruel specters of old and stubborn enmities," referring to antagonistic geopolitical doctrines. Moreover, he noted, "It is not just a matter of integrating technocratic apparatuses; we need to integrate two societies that have different characteristics"—an oblique reference to Argentina's substantial trade deficit with Brazil. He argued that integration would require a firm will and a democratic consensus.[36]

As part of the integration process, Argentina and Brazil agreed to cooperate in building a nineteen-passenger, turboprop, twin-engine plane. The agreement involves the air forces of both countries.[37] The new plane, the CBA-123, would replace the Bandeirante and Xingu aircraft, which have been exported regionally and on the international market for several years by Brazil's Embraer. The plane will be able to fly at 400 miles per hour. Its development was estimated to cost $300 million.[38]

The two governments have also taken some encouraging steps in the nuclear field. Nuclear rivalry between the two was especially important because both were among the handful of threshold states with the technical capacity to develop nuclear weapons within the foreseeable future. Further, neither had ratified the Non-Proliferation Treaty (NPT) or its regional variant, the Tlatelolco Pact. The new civilian governments led the move toward nuclear cooperation against the wishes of their reluctant military establishments. While neither civilian president was strong enough to overrule nationalist and military opinion against ratifying the NPT or Tlatelolco treaty, the presidents took steps to move their countries away from a nuclear arms production race.

A series of agreements provided for cooperation on the joint production of a nuclear reactor,[39] cooperation on uranium enrichment,[40] and an agreement to exchange enriched uranium.[41] Although Brazil rejected a clause including nuclear inspections as part of the 1986 economic integration treaty, presidents Sarney and Alfonsín exchanged visits at closely restricted nuclear facilities.[42] A pact signed on April 8, 1988, committed the two countries to the peaceful use of nuclear energy and regular exchanges of information on technology with the aim of allaying fears about nuclear weapons development. It was hailed as the most important accord ever reached between the two countries.[43] Later the same year, the Argentine-Brazilian Permanent Committee on Nuclear Policy agreed on nuclear integration and the promotion of fast-breeder reactors.[44]

Joint military exercises in the South Atlantic involving Argentina and Brazil had been held for over a decade. The eleventh edition of the Fraterno maneuvers took place in early 1989.[45] Although these maneuvers were premised, in part, on the Zone of Peace resolution, they have not prevented Brazilian participation in the annual Unitas exercises involving the US Navy and navies from various Latin American states. Nor has it prevented either Brazil or Argentina from participating in other joint naval exercises with the United States in the region.[46]

All in all, steps toward military integration remained largely symbolic. Cooperative efforts did not really change the underlying distrust the two national military establishments had for one another. While the armed forces did not resist their respective presidents vocally, their lack of enthusiasm was manifested by the fact that the most sensitive issue of nuclear proliferation was set aside. Further, the governments devoted only limited resources to and invested even less prestige in military integration.

□ *Assessment*

The Alfonsín program of military reform was unbalanced. The effort to restructure the armed forces and establish a new grand strategy for the country bogged down in mutual recriminations between the military sector and the Radical Party. Military prestige projects (the strategic weapons programs) were allowed to continue leading lives of their own. Had the development of regional cooperation been integrated with real military restructuring—as was the case with Spain and its integration into NATO during the 1980s[47]—it could have provided much more substantial benefits. As it was, regional cooperation, arguably the most successful part of the reform program, remained largely symbolic. The Alfonsín government broke new ground but was far from making real progress in erecting new military structures.

Whether the changes initiated by the Alfonsín government will be consolidated is still an open question. It is clear that the armed forces regarded the administration as the enemy. Some officers believed that the president was responsible for what a document prepared by a clandestine group in 1984 termed the "psychological campaign" against the armed forces.[48] According to one Argentine military analyst, the second half of the 1980s saw a historic transformation: The Radicals replaced the Peronists as the armed forces' principal domestic adversary.[49] The government was beset by active and passive resistance. Alfonsín had four defense ministers during his brief tenure in office; one had to resign in the wake of legislative investigations into an apparent attempt by military personnel to assassinate the president. The timetable for military reorganization met with repeated delays until it was quietly abandoned.

At first, Alfonsín was beset by open, mainly symbolic, acts of military insubordination. As detailed in Chapter 5, resistance to the government became more than symbolic in April 1987, when officers at a number of garrisons rebelled in support of colleagues who refused to obey summonses by civilian courts to appear and answer charges of human rights violations. This and the two subsequent revolts tested the government's and the high command's control over the army's officer corps.

The balance sheet by the end of the Alfonsín administration was mixed. Integration of the armed services remained more theoretical than real; only the third joint exercise was held in November 1988.[50] The readiness of the armed forces remained at low levels. Officer-to-soldier ratios climbed from 1:10 in 1982 to 1:5 in 1988. In a report to the defense minister, the army chief of staff indicated that operational capability was down to 40 to 50 percent for half the force and at a minimal level for the rest. Half the helicopters were out of service, and 30 percent of the tanks—World War II–era Shermans—had to have their drive trains refurbished. One-quarter of the artillery pieces were out of service, and 25 percent of those in service (1928 vintage) would have to be replaced. Modernization, new air defense artillery, helicopters, armored vehicles, and ammunition would require $1.55 billion. The navy would need $350 million, and the air force $150 million to modernize. On the positive side, the reform of the military academies and their curricula and the transfer of control over the defense industry from the armed forces to the defense ministry have been the most successful changes under the new policy. Also, ministry control over promotions and discipline has been legally established.[51]

The program of military reform foundered on the rocks of financial exigency and mutiny over the human rights issue. Yet, the breadth of hard-core support for extremists within the officer corps may be limited to as few as three to four hundred junior officers and NCOs, and this support may be largely confined to the army.[52] If these optimistic assessments are correct, a purge of the military and economic improvement could yet provide the wherewithal to substantially advance the changes initiated under Alfonsín.

■ MILITARY REFORM IN OTHER COUNTRIES

If military reform in Argentina foundered, military reform in the other countries died for want of a second. Governments shied away from addressing military issues in anything approaching a comprehensive manner. Military restructuring and strategic rethinking, when it was done at all, was executed chiefly by the armed forces.

□ *Brazil*

The Brazilian armed forces took the initiative during the waning years of the last military government in the early 1980s to initiate force modernization. The army, the senior service, was the major beneficiary of this modernization program. Part of this program, Land Force 1990 (TF-90), was directed at improving the army's capacity in the frontier region.

The program, estimated to cost about $100 million annually into the 1990s, included both reorganization of commands and the purchase and integration of new equipment. Reorganization of commands involved the creation of a new western military command and the consequent creation of a new headquarters. Also included in the reorganization was the creation of a rapid deployment force and the creation of an army aviation element.[53] New vehicles, produced in Brazil, were to replace horse cavalry hitherto used in the interior. Troop strength would be increased by about 100,000, so the ground forces would eventually total 280,000. The program also involved the building of roads in border areas.[54]

Besides the establishment of a new western military command, the army attempted to extend control over border regions, hitherto largely neglected. The threat of a border war between Venezuela and Suriname and the existence of foreign guerrilla bases in the same general region gave rise to a Brazilian program to strengthen the military presence in the northern border area from Colombia to Guyana. The project, denominated Calha Norte, was recommended by an interministry committee to President Sarney on June 19, 1985. It encompasses a region 1,400 miles in length and 100 miles deep. Within the affected region, the government planned to construct land and air bases and strengthen river patrols. The project also included the development of the transportation and hydraulic infrastructure and an attempt to promote government-Indian cooperation, although Indian leaders and the church remained skeptical of the project, whose planning was kept secret. (An estimated 55,000 Indians live in the region.)[55]

While leaders have been coy about the country's intention to build a nuclear bomb, the military has been systematically developing the capacity to do so independent of international controls and sanctions. Brazil was a signatory of neither the NPT nor the regional Tlatelolco Pact; hence, it was free from direct treaty restraints on its own nuclear program. However, Brazil was bound indirectly by the NPT when it purchased nuclear technology from signatory nations, the major source of such technology. To avoid these restraints, Brazil had two nuclear programs. Its official program, which included the purchase of nuclear reactor technology from the Germans, was coupled with the secret, multifaceted, parallel research and development program largely under the control of the military.

According to *Veja*, for almost a decade the parallel nuclear program employed three thousand people and had an annual budget of $1–3 billion. One scientist estimated the two uranium enrichment projects would cost a total of $3.5 billion. Reportedly, the program changed little under the Sarney administration from what it had been under the military government. CNEN, the article charged, is "a civilian front for the parallel program."[56]

A major part of the effort in the parallel program was directed toward the mastery of the fuel cycle. The program pursued a number of routes to acquiring mastery over the fuel cycle, including laser ray stimulation (a purely theoretical technique) and jet nozzle techniques.[57] Brazil's ability to produce highly enriched fuel is disputed. While some government sources claim Brazil had already mastered the fuel cycle by 1986,[58] other sources insist that the country's progress has been strictly limited.[59] In 1987, military spokesmen claimed Brazil could make a bomb within the span of two years. As with mastery of the fuel cycle, other experts dispute such a possibility.[60] Although at least one important officer has openly advocated the production of the bomb,[61] for the most part the armed forces, in their public pronouncements, have deferred to the civilian government. This deference should probably be discounted.

As another part of the nuclear effort, the navy has undertaken a program to produce a nuclear-powered submarine by the early 1990s. This project involved the initial purchase of West German submarine technology, further development in Brazil, and the production of a domestic nuclear reactor to power the submarine. Brazil also has a developmental program to produce rockets for its space program as well as for military applications. Such medium-range rockets are well suited for the delivery of nuclear warheads but are not cost-effective for conventional munitions.

The Sarney administration did little to reform the armed forces. Yet, there is a potential for military reform in Brazil. The armed forces are open to modernization and restructuring. The connection between the armed forces and civilian society has historically been greater in Brazil than in other Latin American countries. And Brazil possesses one of the region's few strategic studies centers at the University of Campinas. An administration less beholden to the armed forces, with more enduring political support than that of José Sarney, may yet be able to initiate effective military reform.

□ *Peru*

The prognosis for substantial military reform in Peru is bleak. The persistence of deep-seated economic and social problems—insurgency, drug trafficking, economic stagnation—limits the resources and popularity available to any government. It is unlikely there will be anything beyond piecemeal improvements in such areas as personnel policy, technical competence, weapons procurement, and tactical capability in counter-insurgency until the guerrilla threat is countered.

□ Uruguay

Uruguay is in a peculiar situation. A rational evaluation of the country's strategic requirements may lead to the conclusion that it requires little more than a constabulary force on land, and air and sea forces capable of coast guard functions. Uruguay's small size and population render defense against its neighbors as futile as the need for such a defense is remote. While the Sanguinetti government has been able to reduce the size of the armed forces, a reformulation of their structure and mission would likely meet significant resistance.

□ Chile

In one respect Chile is unique. Unlike other countries, resistance to military reform in Chile is closely associated with one man. Augusto Pinochet, former president and commander of the army with a guaranteed eight-year term, stands as a symbol of the past and an obstacle to change. In thirteen years as head of the government, he managed to gain extraordinary power over the promotion of senior military personnel, especially those in the army. Only one officer, General Pinochet himself, has been exempt from normal retirement regulations. All other active generals rose from the middle ranks during Pinochet's tenure as president cum chief of staff and were vetted at various points in their careers by Pinochet.[62] As a result, it is not surprising that the high command has a strong representation of Pinochet loyalists. The constitutional power of the civilian president to refuse nominations for promotion to general does not appear to give the president much leverage to further military reform. Passage of military reform legislation is also difficult because of elected and appointed conservative strength in the Chilean senate. During the transition, however, other officers were open to dialogue with the civilian opposition; thus, there may be some flexibility in the military's position should Pinochet pass from the scene.

■ CONCLUSIONS

The military reactions to reform measures provide limited support for the hypotheses.

Hypothesis 1: The armed forces will vigorously defend their fundamental interest—the armed forces' survival as an institution. The armed forces will defend other interests only to the degree that they are necessary for survival or the maintenance of core interests. Resistance to military reform is based on an institutional preference for known and well-established procedures. The two countries where reform was either attempted by the government (Argentina) or restructuring was undertaken by the armed forces themselves (Brazil) do not provide clear-cut tests of the degree to which the military will resist reform. The resistance to military reform in Argentina appeared to be based on a perceived threat to the institution. The human rights controversy adversely affected the military's perception of government motives; the government's use of budget restraints as a political lever further confirmed this perception. Had the rights issue been absent, it is possible results could have been considerably different. In Brazil, the military itself planned reorganization and a reorientation of missions. It is tempting to imagine what a politically skilled president not dependent on the armed forces, as was Sarney, might have accomplished. These contrafactual scenarios, however, are impossible to evaluate.

Hypothesis 2: The more fundamental the interest, the greater the likelihood of the high command's involvement in or tolerance of potentially risky or costly means of resistance. In no case was the survival of the armed forces as an institution in jeopardy. In no case did the high command express open insubordination to civilian authority. The armed forces' ability to resist change by ordinary bureaucratic methods seemed more than sufficient. Some Alfonsín reforms were put into practice; senior generals accepted the legality of budgetary restrictions they protested in private. They recognized significant limits to their resistance.

Hypothesis 3: The more uniform the interest across the various sectors of the armed forces, the more likely the success of the armed forces' action in defense of this interest. Thorough military reform impinges on an array of military interests. In Argentina, the junior services created fewer problems for the government, but the negative impact of financial stringencies seemed to overcome any real possibility of the government's building a military reform coalition with more modern and democratic sectors of the officer corps. If that potential really existed, it was not effectively exploited. Moreover, in Argentina, divisions within the armed forces appeared to be more generational in nature, with some junior and field grade officers taking a radical line opposed to their superiors' cautious response. The Argentine case tends to invalidate the hypothesis.

Hypothesis 4: The lower the prestige of the armed forces and the higher the prestige of the civilian government, the more likely the success of the civilian authorities' efforts to reform the military. This hypothesis seems to be borne out if only weakly. Civilians have attempted military reform only where the military's prestige was lowest—in Argentina. By and large, civilians have addressed military reform either tentatively or unskillfully if at all.

The burden of this chapter is that civilian governments have yet to acquire a facility for dealing with military affairs. Military reform has foundered, or not been attempted, because governments lacked both knowledge and power. If democracy is to be consolidated, civilians must assume ultimate control of the armed forces, and they must provide the armed forces with credible, new missions. Governments' lack of knowledge compounds their lack of effective political power over the armed forces. In this respect, the intellectual isolation of the armed forces has a double effect. It not only weakens the armed forces' ability to establish a dialogue with civilians, it also curtails the ability of civilians to influence the armed forces. Issues involved in military reform become technical and arcane—the privileged bailiwick of the officer corps. In a regime where obedience to democratic authority has not been consolidated, mere legal authority may not be sufficient for effective, as opposed to nominal, control; civilian authorities must be able to persuade as well as order. To do so, they must be credible to their military subordinates. The executive should gain and exercise with discretion the right to appoint senior officers. Working relationships should be formed on the basis of shared views on military policy rather than on political convenience or ideological dictates because even the appearance of politicization has provoked unrest in the officer corps.

Credibility also requires the provision of adequate financial resources to carry out new missions. Governments have yet to link effective budgetary decisions to prior decisions about military missions and levels of threat. The military budget cannot be used as an instrument of rational control unless questions about the size and structure of the armed forces, and the arming and recruitment of the forces, are answered first. These answers depend, in turn, on answers to more fundamental questions about national strategy and foreign policy.

The armed forces have remained the dominant sector in formulating these military issues; within the armed forces, interservice planning and cooperation have been limited at best. This tends to make each of the armed services a proponent of its own interests rather than a participant in a debate about a truly national strategy. Such behavior is certainly not limited to Latin American armed forces, but bureaucratic inertia will probably be more pernicious there in the 1990s than at other times in other regions. If regional defense and the securing of maritime resources are serious new missions, force structures will have to be altered to address them properly. The army-dominated military institutions are frequently too large and too technologically unsophisticated for these tasks. It is unlikely, therefore, that the armed forces can or will change rapidly enough on their own. In sum, while military reforms can be ignored, ignoring them will, almost assuredly, entail the waste of scarce resources and the diminution of civilian authority. Governments would do well to direct the activity of their armed forces into areas that pose little challenge to the consolidation of democracy and where there exists a real need for military activity.

■ **NOTES**

1. Welch and Smith, pp. 48–51.

2. Ibid., p. 44.

3. For a summary of major themes and the major national schools of thought, see Child, 1979, pp. 89–111.

4. "Sudden Flare-up of Old Border Row," *Latin American Weekly Report*, November 2, 1989, p. 2.

5. Child, 1989, pp. 31–44.

6. For a good example of the Argentine analysis of living frontiers and related issues, see Guglialmelli, pp. 1–29.

7. Charles C. Moskos, "Institutional and Occupational Trends in the Armed Forces," in Moskos and Wood, pp. 15–25.

8. Stockholm International Peace Research Institute, 1984.

9. FBIS, "New National Defense Doctrine Under Study," Madrid, EFE, March 24, 1985, FBIS-LAM-85-058, March 26, 1985, p. B1.

10. FBIS, "Defense Ministry Issues Directive to Armed Forces," Buenos Aires, *Noticias Argentinas*, September 11, 1985, FBIS-LAM-85-181, September 18, 1985, pp. B1–B2.

11. FBIS, "Armed Forces Reorganization Plan Criticized," Buenos Aires, TELAM, September 29, 1985, FBIS-LAM-85-191, October 2, 1985, pp. B2–B3.

12. JPRS, "Proposed Joint Maneuvers to Foster Armed Forces Unity," Buenos Aires, *La Prensa*, January 23, 1984, JPRS-LAM-84-028, March 2, 1984, pp. 26–27.

13. JPRS, "Military to Retain Selected Enterprises," Buenos Aires, *La Nacion*, December 24, 1983, JPRS-LAM-84-028, March 2, 1984, pp. 24–25.

14. "Professional Roles Found for Forces," *Latin American Weekly Report*, January 15, 1987, p. 8; "Punto Final Paves Way for Reform," *Latin American Regional Reports: Southern Cone Report*, February 5, 1987, p. 6.

15. German J. Bidart, "Change in Military Code," *La Nacion*, April 28, 1984, JPRS-LAM-84-068, June 4, 1984, pp. 37–39.

16. FBIS, "Budget Cuts Limit Armed Forces Vehicle Use," Buenos Aires, DYN, December 19, 1984, FBIS-LAM-84-247, December 21, 1984, pp. B1–B2.

17. FBIS, "Government to Sell Tanks, Aircraft, Submarines," *Buenos Aires Herald*, October 18, 1985, FBIS-LAM-85-204, October 22, 1985, p. B2.

18. "Army Says Enough," *Latin American Weekly Report*, July 31, 1986, p. 8.

19. "Postscript," *Latin American Weekly Report*, September 18, 1986, p. 12.

20. Fraga, p. 136.

21. Spector, pp. 182–183.

22. "Cóndor II Rocket Headlined Again," *Latin American Weekly Report*, October 6, 1988, p. 2.

23. FBIS, "Cavallo Acknowledges Rocket Vector Technology," Buenos Aires, *Noticias Argentinas*, October 29, 1989, FBIS-LAT-89-208, October 30, 1989, p. 58.

24. James Bruce, "Assessing Iraq's Missile Technology," *Jane's Defence Weekly*, December 23, 1989, pp. 1371, 1374.

25. FBIS, "Crespo Says Missile Construction Feasible," Buenos Aires, Domestic Service, May 24, 1988, FBIS-LAT-88-101, May 25, 1988, p. 20; FBIS, "Military Sources on Rocket," Buenos Aires, TELAM, September 20, 1988, FBIS-LAT-88-183, September 21, 1988, p. 22.

26. *Latin American Weekly Report*, November 2, 1989, p. 9; "Condor II in

the News," *Latin American Regional Reports: Southern Cone Report*, November 16, 1989, p. 8.

27. Duncan Lennox, "The Global Proliferation of Ballistic Missiles," *Jane's Defence Weekly*, December 23, 1989, pp. 1384–1385.

28. FBIS, "Defense Minister on Gulf, Condor Missile," Buenos Aires, *Noticias Argentinas*, September 21, 1990, FBIS-LAT-90-185, September 24, 1990, p. 20.

29. FBIS, "CNEA Denies Construction of Nuclear Submarine," Buenos Aires, TELAM, August 17, 1988, FBIS-LAT-88-160, August 18, 1988, p. 31.

30. Charles Lambelin, Reuters, July 27, 1981.

31. Saraiva Guerreiro, p. 132.

32. United Nations, p. 16. Emphasis added.

33. Ibid.

34. "Proposal for Closer Ties with Argentina," *Latin American Weekly Report*, April 23, 1987, p. 9.

35. FBIS, "Defense Integration with Argentina Viewed," Madrid, EFE, April 5, 1988, FBIS-LAT-88-067, April 7, 1988, pp. 22–23.

36. FBIS, "Defense Minister on Integration with Brazil," Buenos Aires, *Noticias Argentinas*, April 27, 1989, FBIS-LAT-89-082, May 1, 1989, pp. 40–41.

37. FBIS, "Agreement Signed with Argentina to Build Plane," Buenos Aires, TELAM, May 22, 1987, FBIS-LAM-87-106, June 3, 1987, p. M7.

38. FBIS, "New Plane Developed in Project with Argentina," Buenos Aires, TELAM, September 16, 1988, FBIS-LAT-88-181, September 19, 1988, p. 41.

39. FBIS, "Sarney, Alfonsín Visit Mine, Confer in Carajas," Brasília, Radio Nacional da Amazonia Network, December 9, 1986, FBIS-LAM-86-237, December 10, 1986, pp. D1–D4.

40. FBIS, "Official Admits Research in Nuclear Fuel Cycle," Madrid, EFE, September 9, 1986, FBIS-LAM-86-176, September 11, 1986, p. D1.

41. FBIS, "Foreign Secretary on Nuclear Projects, Iran," Buenos Aires, *Noticias Argentinas*, September 16, 1987, FBIS-LAT-87-180, September 17, 1987, p. 18.

42. "In Search of Enrichment," *Economist*, March 5, 1988, p. 86.

43. Tyler Bridges, "Brazilian-Argentine Summit Yields Nuclear Power Pact," *Christian Science Monitor*, April 4, 1988, p. 11.

44. FBIS, "Nuclear Committee with Brazil Meets," Buenos Aires, TELAM, July 4, 1988, FBIS-LAT-88-153, August 9, 1988, pp. 26–27.

45. FBIS, "Navy to Hold Exercises with Brazil, Spain," Buenos Aires, TELAM, January 26, 1989, FBIS-LAT-89-017, January 27, 1989, p. 24.

46. "South American Naval Exercise," *Jane's Defence Weekly*, May 21, 1988, p. 1003.

47. For a discussion of the Spanish case, see Agüero, pp. 23–49.

48. FBIS, "Army Document Replies to 'Antimilitary Stance,'" Buenos Aires, DYN, November 15, 1984, FBIS-LAM-84-224, November 19, 1984, pp. B2–B4.

49. Fraga, p. 137.

50. FBIS, "Jaunarena Observes Military Exercises in South," *Buenos Aires Herald*, November 18, 1988, FBIS-LAT-88-224, November 21, 1988, pp. 35–36; *Jane's Defence Weekly*, December 10, 1988, p. 1477.

51. Míguez, pp. 1581–1584.

52. "Former Mutineers Challenge Menem," *Latin American Weekly Report*, January 25, 1990, pp. 6–7. Less optimistic assessments based on the level of

participation in the December 1988 revolt would place the number at approximately one thousand. Fraga, p. 119.

53. FBIS, "Army Restructured; Rapid Deployment Force Formed," December 22, 1985, FBIS-LAM-85-248, December 26, 1985, pp. D2–D4.

54. "Army Set for Major Modernisation," *Latin American Regional Reports: Brazil Report*, January 3, 1986, p. 5; FBIS, "Brasilsat to Be Used in Army Modernization," January 6, 1986, FBIS-LAM-86-005, January 8, 1986, p. D1.

55. FBIS, "Government to Implement 'Calha Norte' Project," FBIS-LAM-86-213, November 4, 1986, p. D3; "Brazil: Native Groups Protest Plan to Militarize the Amazon," *Latinamerica Press*, February 19, 1987, pp. 1–2; FBIS, "Military to Strengthen Border Against Traffickers," March 30, 1987, FBIS-LAM-87-063, April 2, 1987, pp. D2–D3.

56. FBIS, "Newspaper Comments on Parallel Nuclear Program," São Paulo, *Veja*, April 22, 1987, FBIS-LAM-87-090, May 11, 1987, pp. 1–6.

57. JPRS, "Uranium to Be Enriched by Jet-Nozzle by 1989," *O Estado de São Paulo*, July 24, 1985, JPRS-TND-85-014, August 21, 1985, pp. 55–56.

58. FBIS, "Navy Masters Complete Nuclear Fuels Cycle," Paris, AFP, September 21, 1986, FBIS-LAM-86-183, September 22, 1986, p. D1.

59. FBIS, "Article Questions Nuclear Submarine Possibility," *Folha de São Paulo*, April 19, 1987, FBIS-LAM-87-078, April 23, 1987, pp. D2–D3.

60. FBIS, "Experts Discuss Development of Nuclear Bomb," *Folha de São Paulo*, March 23, 1987, FBIS-LAM-87-057, March 25, 1987, pp. D1–D3. The director of CNEN said in 1989 that if the decision were made to build atomic weapons, the construction of a bomb would take ten years. FBIS, "Nazere on Inability to Make Bomb for 10 Years," *O Estado de São Paulo*, October 22, 1989, FBIS-LAT-89-231, December 4, 1989, pp. 51–52.

61. FBIS, "Former Navy Minister Advocates Atomic Bomb," Paris, AFP, September 5, 1986, FBIS-LAM-86-173, September 8, 1986, p. D2.

62. Genaro Arriagada Herrera, "The Legal and Institutional Framework of the Armed Forces in Chile," in Valenzuela and Valenzuela, pp. 117–143.

8 ■
Flashpoint IV:
Reform of the State

By almost all accounts, Latin American state governmental and administrative structures suffer from a profound malaise. Government accounts show that expenditures far outrun revenues, and the ensuing deficits contribute to inflation and sometimes hyperinflation. Political corruption seems to be epidemic. An executive with extensive formal powers and an ample term but with no ability to succeed himself is often stalemated by an opposition legislature. Governments appear to be unresponsive to popular needs, and democracy at the local level may be nonexistent, rudimentary, or handicapped by lack of resources.

The contribution of the armed forces to this complex of problems is not insignificant. Large military outlays help bust governmental budgets. Military hyper-representation in the councils of government distorts policy formulation and execution. Military autonomy undermines government initiatives such as arms control, land reform, and environmental protection. Reform is not easy. Some, if not all, reforms entail political bias; predicting the actual effects of reform proposals, if implemented, is difficult; and reformers must counter bureaucratic inertia and entrenched opposition from those favoring the status quo.

■ REFORM PROPOSALS

Reform agendas are varied, but the following are proposals that frequently appear. Their political effects, especially upon the armed forces, are what concern us here, not their viability as true reforms.

□ *Establishing a Parliamentary System*

Unlike most democracies that use the parliamentary system, Latin American countries typically have a constitution based on a formal separation of powers similar to that of the United States. Such a separation can lead to a deadlock between the executive and the legislature. Further, since there is no method whereby a vote of no confidence can remove the executive, the deadlock can be a prolonged one. Most Latin American constitutions also prohibit the chief executive from serving consecutive terms. Such provisions were first established to counter the tendency toward *continuismo*, whereby an executive, once in power, used the opportunities provided by the office— both legal and illegal—to continue in office indefinitely. This seems to be a provision that has outlived its usefulness. Today, Latin American democracies are more threatened by lack of continuity in policy than by a single individual monopolizing power.

A parliamentary system, or some version of it, could alleviate some of the difficulties inherent in the system of formal separation of powers. A complete parliamentary system would make the chief executive subordinate to the legislature. The chief executive would be elected by the legislature, and it would be empowered to remove him from office for political reasons. The cabinet would be subject to such provisions also, and the conduct of ministers would be scrutinized on a regular basis by the legislature. A less radical reform would establish a mixed parliamentary-presidential system based on the French model. In this system, an elected president, whose most important powers deal with foreign policy and defense, would be independent of the legislature, but a prime minister and cabinet would operate as they otherwise would under a parliamentary system. Allowing the president to serve consecutive terms might have a limited benefit. The president could then translate any enduring political popularity into administrative continuity.

From the perspective of the military, however, a parliamentary system is not very appealing. The legislative scrutiny normally entailed in parliamentary systems is a risk without any compensating advantage. Moreover, the practice of ministerial responsibility to parliament, if applied to the military ministries, would undercut the tradition of most Latin American countries of military portfolios going to uniformed officers—at times, the most senior active officer.

□ *Privatization*

Since 1982, state and parastatal corporations have been increasingly seen as a burden. The operating deficits of these corporations strained the ability of the rest of the economy to support them.[1] Reformers with a right-wing bias have generally favored privatization of state-owned enterprises. They argue that the public sector is inefficient and that public regulation of the private sector is worse than inefficient—it penalizes entrepreneurs and the whole economy and damages the state by leading to widespread tax evasion.[2] By various estimates, the so-called black or informal economy amounts to a significant portion of the total.[3] Privatizers rely on market forces, hence they also favor the encouragement of foreign investment and foreign trade and the paring back of the size of the bureaucracy.

Such reforms adversely affect public-sector employees of state enterprises, civil servants, and beneficiaries of existing subsidies, at least in the short run. The armed forces could find their state-owned arms and related industries on the auction block. If fiscal discipline becomes the norm, military budgets and salaries may be unable to escape its stringencies. In effect, the military is torn in two directions. It supports national power, which requires a strong and efficient state, yet its sector interests may run counter to policies designed to enhance that strength and efficiency.

□ *Decentralization*

Many Latin American countries are beset with a concentration of power in their central governments and a concentration of population in their capital cities. Hence, decentralization has a twofold aspect. One element is governmental decentralization—the attempt to establish some degree of local autonomy or control over matters presently directed from the center. Elected governments should be established at the local level where they do not exist. Existing local governments should be provided with adequate resources. Governmental decentralization promises greater democracy because it would provide new opportunities for public opinion to affect public policy at the local level. This type of decentralization may sometimes be linked with a relaxation of rules for forming parties and running candidates.

The second element is geographic decentralization. In its most dramatic form, it entails the transfer of the national capital to a more central location, as happened in Brazil in 1960 and was proposed by President Alfonsín for Argentina in the mid-1980s. Less elaborate and costly programs of this same guise include the extension and improvement of transportation and communications networks in the interior and efforts to establish duty-free zones to spur development in areas hitherto largely neglected. Geographic decentralization offers the opportunity for greater national integration and faster economic development because of the exploitation of underused resources.

The financial cost of reform and the opposition of politicians whose influence is likely to be curtailed by reform stand as the greatest roadblocks to a thoroughgoing decentralization of either type. Such reforms may threaten the interests of the armed forces more marginally, yet as we shall observe below, the threats are not necessarily trivial.

■ CASE STUDY: BRAZIL'S CONSTITUTIONAL REFORM

Reform of the state has a wide range of potential effects upon the armed forces. How do the armed forces' interests and state reform get played out in actual practice? The Brazilian Constituent Assembly is the most important case from the 1980s where systematic efforts at state reform faced a number of military challenges. As such, the Brazilian experience can provide some guidance about military perceptions of its interests and the mechanisms it has available to defend it when circumstances peculiar to Brazil in the mid-1980s are taken into account.

□ *The Military Role and Influence in the State*

The Brazilian armed forces had significant institutional interests to protect. They emerged from the transition with as strong a position as that of any military in the five countries we are studying.

Military Influence in the Executive Branch. The military had managed to institutionalize its general preference for a strong executive in relation to the legislature but controlled in key ways by the armed forces. A National Security Council was in place, and it had a central role in policies affecting internal security, broadly defined. While the central role of the NSC was to advise the president, the preponderance of military membership in the NSC and the importance ascribed to the internal security issue could serve as a constraint on any aberrant behavior by the president. Additionally, Brazil followed the practice traditional to many Latin American countries of having separate ministries for each service, headed by military officers. The head of the military intelligence agency, the chief of the joint general staff, and the head of the president's military household all held cabinet rank as well, further increasing the military presence.

The armed forces also managed to induce a pattern of executive acquiescence to many of their pay and budgetary demands. The armed forces actually did better under Sarney than under the military regime in terms of the defense share of the national budget (see Table 8.1). However, high inflation led to rapid decreases in the buying power of military salaries and helped create uncertainty about military allocations generally. The Sarney government was concerned about fiscal integrity and fighting inflation, but early on the president developed the habit of yielding to military pay demands. Incidents of military dissatisfaction and insubordination were followed by government concessions. Reacting to military unrest in 1986, the government granted increases of up to 105 percent in allowances for officers despite an official freeze on pay.[4] By the end of the next year, the armed forces had gained another of their demands, a salary schedule linked to that of the judiciary.[5]

That did not end military unhappiness over salaries. Another public sector pay freeze the following year led to further trouble. Rumblings of unrest, which included a planned bombing campaign, were widespread. In perhaps the most notable incident, an army captain led an armed invasion of the city hall in Apucarana. Three hours after the incident, President Sarney decreed a 128 percent raise in military pay, which was not followed by

Table 8.1 Military Budget as Percent of Central Government Budget

Country	Year										
	1977	1978	1979	1980	1981	1982	1983	1984	1985	1986	1987
Argentina	18.8	15.5	16.5	16.9	14.8	25.9	14.9[a]	17.2	10.7	8.4	12.0
Brazil	4.0	3.5	3.2	2.8	2.6	3.2	2.8	2.8	3.6[a]	6.1	6.2
Chile	11.6	12.6	12.0	12.1	11.9	12.5	12.7	11.9	11.4	10.9	12.7
Peru	39.3	32.0	24.8	27.0[a]	23.7	30.2	30.0	38.4	42.6	41.2	24.8
Uruguay	9.7	9.7	11.2	13.1	15.4	13.2	12.4	10.9	10.6[a]	10.1	N/A

Source: United States Arms Control and Disarmament Agency
a. Indicates year of transition to civilian rule

comparable raises for other sectors.[6] The captain was ultimately sentenced to eight months imprisonment but was retained on active duty.[7] Junior officers were not the only ones who caused trouble. When the head of the joint chiefs of staff criticized the public-sector wage freeze, he was removed from his post by the military ministers.[8] Again in mid-1989, there was unrest followed by government concessions. After anonymous letters inciting revolt circulated among the officer corps, the administration granted the armed forces pay raises in excess of those granted other federal employees.[9] The military leadership was said to fear an incident like the seizure of the Apucarana city hall the previous year.[10]

The government's budgeting followed a pattern similar to that of military pay. Under Sarney, the presidential cabinet reportedly was issued an explicit order that defense appropriations were to be given privileged treatment in the budget,[11] but by the end of the 1980s, a number of ambitious military programs were not fully funded. Even though the government's requests for 1989 were substantially above the level of the military budget for the previous year, they represented a significant cut over what the services themselves had requested.[12] The 1989 budget necessitated cuts in a number of programs. The navy announced the postponement of plans to construct two new warships, while the air force cut back on expansion of its air traffic control and air defense center.[13] A shortage of funds also threatened the progress of Brazil's nuclear programs.[14] Again in 1990, the Sarney government gave the military precedence. Of the funds set aside for priority investment, the government concentrated 55 percent in defense.[15] Congress balked, and military lobbying became intense. As part of the effort, the Air Ministry claimed that if the Joint Budget Commission cut the ministry's budget, it could lead to the loss of the joint Brazilian-

Italian AMX fighter project, in which Brazil had already invested $700 million.[16]

The Arms Industry. The armed forces had played a key role in cooperating with the private sector to build a national arms industry of global stature. The Brazilian arms industry had been under development since 1964. By the end of the 1980s, the military-industrial complex consisted of 350 medium- to large-sized companies (50 exclusively producing arms), employed an estimated 200,000 workers, and had an estimated value of $12 to $15 billion. Military exports were valued at approximately $1.3 billion in 1984,[17] with arms exports far outperforming those of regional competitors Argentina and Chile (see Table 8.2).

Table 8.2 Defense Industry Exports

Country	Total Arms Exports 1985–87 (1987 US$mil)
Argentina	89
Brazil	1,198
Chile	265

Source: United States Arms Control and Disarmament Agency

Brazil manufactured a wide range of equipment for domestic use and export. Equipment in actual production or under development included: reconnaissance vehicles, medium tanks, armored personnel carriers, field guns, military trainer aircraft with counterinsurgency capability, various other aircraft (a tactical fighter, the AMX, codeveloped with Italy), artillery rockets, air-to-air missiles, air-to-ship missiles, bombs, torpedoes, and antitank rockets.[18] Among the most successful Brazilian export was the Tucano trainer; by 1987, seven countries had taken out orders and options for 556 of the aircraft.[19] Brazil exported to fifty countries in Asia, Africa, and Latin America[20] and, except for South Africa and Iran, showed a willingness to export to any country regardless of ideology.

The Brazilian arms industry entered into production and licensing agreements with numerous countries, among them France, Italy, West Germany, and Israel. Brazil also signed an agreement with the People's Republic of China that included the purchase of Chinese supersonic aircraft, a field in which Brazil has no real entries. The agreement envisioned production of Tucano trainers in China.[21] Brazil has tried to acquire modern technology without political strings on its export or use, to establish a large local role in the manufacturing process where there are joint ventures, and to use, as much as possible, locally manufactured components in complex pieces of equipment. The tendency of the United States to impose export restrictions on licensing agreements rendered cooperation between Brazil and the United States less attractive than arrangements with countries that view military exports in largely economic terms. Indeed, difficulties with the United States led to the development of Brazil's defense industry in the first place.

While the Brazilian arms industry does not challenge the United States, Europe, or the Soviet Union for the leading position on the cutting edge of high technology, its military exports have captured significant sections of the international market because they are often cheaper than those of its competitors and can be maintained in a Third World logistical environment. However, in 1988 and 1989, Brazil's arms sales began to slump for factors noted above. With this downturn and the resulting decline in purchases and funding from the Brazilian military, a number of major arms firms faced serious financial difficulties.

The issue of military-owned state and parastatal corporations in Brazil was not as divisive as it might have been in other countries. Had these enterprises been hugely unsuccessful, as they were in Argentina, they might have become likely targets for privatization or wholesale reorganization. As it was, these corporations were relatively successful and contributed badly needed export earnings to Brazil's balance of payments. Thus, the armed forces could expect political support from private corporate interests with whom they shared a symbiotic relationship.

Civilian Oversight. Under the Sarney government, it was the legislature more than the executive that took the initiative in grappling with military issues. Even here, its oversight did not extend much beyond the budget. Yet considerable potential for a greater legislative role existed.

□ *Selection of the Constituent Assembly*

The process by which the constituent assembly was chosen was itself an issue of great interest to the armed forces and represented their first major victory. There were two principal alternatives available for electing the constitution-drafting body. The first alternative was the establishment of a constituent assembly, separate from the legislature, whose membership could be elected via a potentially more open and less patronage-ridden process than that typical of Brazilian legislative elections. The other alternative was simply to let the new legislature (chosen in November 1986) double as the constituent assembly. The armed forces pressured the dominant Democratic Alliance (AD) to choose the latter course.[22]

This followed a pattern typical of the military's political tactics in the

1970s and 1980s. Stepan describes this tactic as sharpening the separation between political society and civil society and exploiting the resulting weakness.[23] The need to employ this tactic was a rather late development in Brazil. It was not until the 1970s that civil society began to come into its own. Even in the more progressive, populist era of the 1930s, Brazilian politics had been patronage-ridden and corporatist. Social mobilization was limited. Significant change began in the 1970s with the mobilization of neighborhood associations, a grassroots union movement, the political activism of lawyers' and journalists' associations, and the social mobilization sponsored by the Catholic church. These opposition currents arose in the absence of any real party competition, but they pressured the military regime to grant greater political space, which gradually allowed competitive party politics to reemerge.

The new political parties that emerged, however, were rarely new in leadership, ideology, or sometimes even name.[24] In a sense, it was as if politics as usual had begun again after a twenty-year hiatus. This reemergence of old personalities and old organizations provided the military with the opportunity to use old tactics. The armed forces and the state administration could attempt to sway legislators on the basis of narrow personal or organizational self-interest, instead of on the basis of political principle and the interests of major sectors within society. In short, the structure of the constituent assembly was meant to further the containment of the new social forces.

When it convened, the Brazilian Constituent Assembly (1987–1988) had a huge agenda. Members and political activists saw it as a potential solution to many long-standing problems. Thus, the set of issues it faced was wide-ranging and complex and often went beyond organizational issues into areas of policy. This further complicated a deliberative process already beset by many cross-pressures. Military issues were one group among many.

□ The Structure of the Executive

Throughout the 1960s and 1970s, the military's political program had been at heart technocratic. The armed forces tried to establish the autonomy of the state: the ability of technical experts at the highest levels and the supporting bureaucracies beneath them to make and execute policy without partisan, political interference. The technocratic model promised greater autonomy for the armed forces and those sectors most closely associated with the internal security mission. The advent of liberalization and then the transition to democracy necessitated a retreat from the objective of an autonomous, technocratic state. The armed forces, however, wanted to assure that the retreat was a tactical withdrawal and not a strategic rout.

Although opinions wavered, the armed forces generally favored the presidential model over the parliamentary model as the form of government most likely to serve military interests. Public opinion and the constituent assembly followed a different line. At one point, there was a plurality of support within the constituent assembly for a classic parliamentary system. A hybrid system was also suggested that would have placed the military ministers under the direct control of the president and insulated them from legislative control.[25] A poll in eleven state capitals found respondents also favored the parliamentary system over the presidential by a 43 percent to 36 percent margin.[26] Military displeasure and lack of unity among proponents of various parliamentary frameworks, however, led to the retention of a presidential system. Additionally, the armed forces managed to dissuade the assembly from establishing a unified defense ministry.

The new presidential system, however, was not the same as the 1969 model. The assembly stripped the president of a number of prerogatives previously used to dominate the legislature. The new document limited the right of the executive to rule by decree and prohibited the use of special measures to force the president's budget through congress.

☐ *The Length of the President's Term*

The politics surrounding the length of the president's term illustrated the state of civil-military relations in Brazil in a number of ways. It showed the breadth of issues the military considered important to its interest and revealed the dependence of President Sarney upon the support of the armed forces.

When Tancredo Neves and José Sarney (who assumed the presidency because Neves died before inauguration) were elected in November 1984, it was under the provisions of the 1969 constitution (as amended), which provided for indirect election and a six-year term. The electoral system and the six-year term were considered to be illegitimate; the constituent assembly was expected to revise them both.

The issue over Sarney's term seemed moot until he began to indicate that he wanted a full six-year term as provided by the old constitution.[27] The divisiveness of the issue was compounded by the failure of the Cruzado Plan, which had resulted in a lingering cabinet crisis and a persistent fall in the president's popular support. While the Cruzado Plan had attempted to achieve the best of two economic worlds—near zero inflation plus economic expansion—its collapse presaged a return to more orthodox, and in the short term more recessionary, economic policies. This put severe strains on the coalition in congress supporting the government. The dominant party, the Party of the Brazilian Democratic Movement (PMDB), was a polyglot alliance of conservatives, centrists, and leftists; the leftists, at least, could hardly be enthusiastic about a return to economic orthodoxy.

By 1987, a four-year term would be fast running out, thus making 1988 both an election year and a year of economic adjustments. For the military, such a prospect brought into question the stability of the transition and the ability of the government to pursue technically correct economic policies.

Meanwhile, potential presidential candidates and their supporters had an interest in limiting the presidential term, and the unpopularity of the government gave them an opening. Moreover, they could point to the fact that the public favored direct elections as soon as possible.[28]

Such arguments did not wash with the armed forces. They supported Sarney's efforts to prolong his mandate. Unable to obtain the full six years, the president said in May 1987 that he would be willing to settle for five.[29] Even so, he was not able to get the extension of his term without rampant vote buying, which, as *The Economist* put it, turned the assembly into a marketplace where "it is by giving that you shall receive."[30] The decisive intervention came when the military ministers said that a five-year term was "fundamental in order to secure the country's tranquility." This was taken as an implied threat of a military coup.[31] Although military support for the extension was unquestioned, Sarney's minions spread the rumor of a coup should the assembly vote against the wishes of the armed forces.[32] As was typical, the military denied any threat of a coup, the army minister labeling it pure fantasy.[33]

The politics over the length of Sarney's term weakened the president's power base and made him heavily dependent on the armed forces. Before the constituent assembly's vote on the presidential term, for instance, Sarney delivered a speech at the Rio de Janeiro military headquarters praising the armed forces as impeccably cohesive in its defense of the transition while civilian politicians were engaged in a "process of self-destruction which was breaking up [the country's] institutions."[34] Reports also indicated that military urging was behind a tough statement by the president attacking radical minorities in the assembly.[35]

The malaise within the government also worsened the status of the government with the general population. In a São Paulo poll, approximately one-third of the population said they supported a return to military rule.[36] In effect, Sarney wasted nearly a year of his mandate, vitiated his original political base, and made himself dependent on the military for a one-year extension of his term of office.

□ *The Intelligence Services*

Control of the intelligence services stood at the core of the process of consolidating democracy in Brazil. The military intelligence services and the military-controlled National Intelligence Service (SNI), which has had both internal and external security functions, had been key instruments of social control and political repression during the period of military government. For instance, the SNI infiltrated government bureaus, large private firms, labor unions, universities, political parties, and religious sects. During the Figueiredo government, it took over duties from the Federal Police and the Department of Political and Social Order.[37] In addition, a wide variety of acts were subject to the jurisdiction of military courts.

However, by the end of the last military administration, aspects of the intelligence community's activity began to change, especially in the area of public relations. The SNI assumed a position of greater openness to the media, attempting to portray itself as a rather innocuous, information-gathering entity. Although the head of SNI tried to compare the role of his agency to that of journalists,[38] the intelligence agency reportedly vetted the files of potential agrarian reform officials and retained the authority to intervene virtually anywhere. Before the passage of the new constitution, SNI files were not open to those on whom they were kept.[39]

With the accession to power of the civilian administration, however, there may be some hope of at least limited change. The government's draft "law of defense of the democratic state" contained a number of features meant to repeal the Institutional Acts, which, under the military government, permitted severe restrictions on individual rights. The new act would have: denied governmental officials the right to confiscate newspapers; established torture, disappearances, electoral fraud, attacks on party headquarters, unauthorized use of funds in an election, and coups d'état as crimes; and required that crimes of terrorism and participation in separatist movements be tried in federal courts. The law, however, would have legalized wiretapping to "prevent serious harm to the state."[40] The SNI was planning to make its operations conform more to the pattern of the FBI and CIA in the United States and the intelligence services in Britain and West Germany.[41] This involved limiting the number of operatives and removing police functions from the service. Under reorganization, the SNI would not have been able to investigate government corruption. Whether the military, on its own, would actually have made more than cosmetic changes, however, is now a moot point.

Whatever the real intention behind the plans by the armed forces and the executive branch, the constituent assembly preempted the issue by taking the initiative in a number of areas. The new constitution established rights whereby citizens have the legal right of access to information about them in government files, including SNI files. The constitution also prohibited censorship, guaranteed the right of habeas corpus, and guaranteed freedom of association, expression, and privacy, including the inviolability of telephone communications. The document retained the right of the president to declare for thirty days a state of defense or a state of siege to preserve the public order after consulting the National Defense Council and the Council of Ministers. Such declarations would suspend the right of privacy of communications. However, either declaration would require the approval of congress within twenty-four hours, in the absence of which the decree would be immediately suspended.[42] Hence the document liberalized internal security operation much more than the president or intelligence services wanted.

□ *The National Security Council*

Another central institution of the national security state came under challenge by the constituent assembly—the National Security Council. As previously established, the National Security Council was responsible for "the study of problems related to the question of national security, in collaboration with the intelligence agencies . . . and in order to prepare for national mobilization of the armed forces as well as other military operations."[43] In addition, it was empowered to make administrative and economic decisions in areas considered to be, in the council's judgment, of interest to national security. The council was composed of the president, all ministers of state, all members of the high command, and the chief of the president's civilian household.[44]

The new constitution provided for a National Defense Council composed of the vice president; the presidents of the Chamber of Deputies and the senate; the justice, foreign, and planning ministers; and the three service chiefs.[45] The new body is primarily an advisory one and does not have the operational capability of the old National Security Council.

□ *Maintaining Domestic Order*

A key area of dispute over the prerogatives of the military revolved about its right or duty to intervene in the case of political crises. Even before the military constitutions of 1967 and 1969, Brazilian constitutions in 1891, 1934, and 1946 established the military as a permanent, national institution, charged with the task of maintaining law and order and guaranteeing the normal functioning of the three constitutional powers. A second provision made the military obedient to the executive but only within the limits of the law. According to Stepan, these provisions gave the armed forces a de jure check upon the three branches of government.[46] The military was anxious to retain this check.

The initial draft of the constitution, however, restricted the military's mission to external defense. This provoked objections from the service chiefs. The army minister complained that the military was "betrayed by the politicians" and that "an active and vigilant minority is conducting" the work on the draft constitution.[47] The armed forces wanted to maintain the old requirement to defend law and order and were especially concerned about their right to act against strikes affecting essential sectors. Senator Fernando Henrique Cardoso, the PMDB leader in the senate and sympathetic to the left, agreed, in part fearing that state control of state military police could allow the governor of a state (an interested party) to resolve disputed elections.[48] Denying rumors of a coup, the military ministers continued to negotiate with Cardoso.[49] The armed forces were placated by a compromise that allows them to intervene in internal affairs at the request of one of the constitutional powers and makes the state military police (still normally subordinate to state governments) part of the army's auxiliary forces.[50] The armed forces, however, expressed concern that the provision authorizing them to defend the established order by the expressed authorization of one of the established powers might allow the legislative branch to order the armed forces to resist the president, their commander in chief.

□ Other Issues

During the military regime some twelve hundred officers had been cashiered for political reasons;[51] they were not reinstated by the 1979 amnesty. At first, it seemed that the assembly would provide for the reinstatement of those dismissed, but the issue was highly divisive. Army Minister Pires Gonçalves considered the reinstatement proposal a threat to the armed forces and a serious drain on the military budget.[52] Military remonstrances had their effect; the amnesty was softened in the assembly's second draft.[53] In its final vote on the matter, the assembly rejected the amnesty extension altogether.[54] Another issue of some significance was conscription. The military wanted to retain the existing system, while proposals were abroad to abolish the draft. The military's wishes were acceded to. In a related issue, the armed forces wanted to deprive conscripts of the right to vote, claiming politics did not belong in the barracks.[55] The armed forces carried the day again.

The military was also concerned about protecting its nuclear programs, the most controversial part of the defense industry. A number of programs, essentially serving military interests, were in place long before the assembly met. One program involved research on the fuel cycle and the effort to enrich uranium to be used in Brazilian-built reactors (and potentially in atomic weapons). Another was the long-range effort to build a nuclear-powered submarine in Brazil. It does not appear that the new constitution's declaration that Brazil will pursue nuclear programs only for peaceful purposes will have any significant effect on these nuclear programs. The real question revolves not around a statement of principle but around budgets, legislative oversight, and the status of cooperation with Argentina in the nuclear sphere.

□ Results and Prospects

In the area of military affairs, the new constitution provides some basis in principle for asserting civilian control and abolishing the national security state. For example, the armed forces and those seeking to limit the armed forces' role to external defense each received half a loaf. The internal security function was maintained, but the armed forces were prohibited from acting on their own, independent of civilian direction, in containing domestic strife. The real test, however, will come with the passage of enabling legislation—required for many sections of the constitution, including those dealing with the military—and the mundane, day-to-day business of legislative and executive oversight of the military.

It was clear, after the promulgation of the new constitution, that the armed forces were keen to retain as many of their old prerogatives as they could, regardless of the letter or intent of the new charter. One test came immediately—the Volta Redonda steel strike, one of a series of strike actions directed against the government's wage policies, which complicated the government's already foundering economic efforts. Apparently without prior presidential approval, troops were sent to the mill, where they violently expelled the strikers, causing a number of fatalities.[56] This was done in the face of the constitutional guarantee of the right to strike for all workers, even public employees.

Another indication of the armed forces' intentions came with Sarney's efforts to insulate the intelligence services from legislative scrutiny. An executive decree transferred the secretariat of the defunct National Security Council to the National Defense Council, thus preserving the operational capability of the former under a new guise. The government also tried to restrict severely the freedom-of-information provision of the constitution. A decree restructuring the SNI was rushed through before the new constitution was promulgated. Official status was granted to the Departmento de Informática, whose computers store the files of citizens who have been investigated by the SNI. The decree specified that release of information can only be authorized by the head of SNI, a general of ministerial rank. While the constitution provides for the right of citizens to see and correct files, the director of the SNI rejected the claim by legislators, such as Senator Cardoso, that the decree was designed to curtail that right. The SNI chief asserted that the decree was only meant to prevent the release of information that could endanger national security.[57]

What does this presage as far as governmental reform in other countries, or even for Brazil? We ought to note that the constituent assembly took place within a political context that had a number of noteworthy features. Although the transition did not develop as anticipated by the military, the armed forces still possess a good deal of self-confidence and the ability to influence and intimidate the political establishment. While differences of opinion among military sectors were not unknown, the military influence was not dissipated by internal disagreements. The president himself had become increasingly dependent on the military. Not a consensus choice for the office in the first place, his economic failures lost him the initial support he once had. The strongest opposition to the military came from the legislature/constituent assembly, but even there, there was no uniform position among the members in regard to military issues. The strongest party, the PMDB, was, as always, highly factionalized. The assembly as a whole possessed little expertise on military issues, yet more than the president, it was responsible for initiating debate about and elements of doctrinal change into civil-military politics in Brazil. In principle, the new constitution reduced the armed forces' political pretensions, advanced the rule of law, provided for greater oversight, and redefined, in a limited way, the armed forces' role.

The result, as seen in the constitution, was mixed and essentially not divisive: The armed forces retained most of the advantages they sought to preserve. If advocates for civilian control—only moderately strong, not particularly well organized, and distracted by a host of competing issues—could produce some reform, the issue is far from dead. Although victories for civilian control were essentially symbolic, these symbolic victories could yet be converted into real reform.

■ REFORM OF THE STATE IN OTHER COUNTRIES

None of the other four countries we are studying faced the grandiose task of writing a new constitution. Hence, there is no single historical episode on which to focus our attention. We are confronted with countervailing pressures and diverse policy initiatives, which often obscure the underlying challenge of establishing a more efficient, legitimate, and democratic state. Nonetheless, the issue of reform of the state has involved the armed forces in distinctive ways in each of the other four countries.

□ *Argentina*

In Argentina, the grand plans of President Raúl Alfonsín were continually undermined by political and military opposition. Alfonsín was able neither to build the new, natural majority that he envisioned for his Radical Party nor to co-opt armed forces' support for democratic principles. Reforms, grand and small, either died before they could be initiated or received only formal implementation.

While the Radical government was able to reduce the military's share of the national budget, it did so only at a political price. The government's budgetary allocations for the armed forces seemed only to aggravate ongoing disputes over human rights and civilian control. Although the government forced the military's share of GNP below levels it had enjoyed in the early 1970s, it did so at the cost of producing military rancor. Budget reductions depressed military salaries and reduced military readiness to a point where the armed forces were unable to train or equip their personnel. These shortages extended even to such basic items as uniforms and socks.[58] Worst of all, budgetary sanctions did little to enhance military cooperativeness. The path of civil-military relations continued on a downward spiral throughout the Alfonsín administration.

Two grand reformist proposals came to naught. The first, an attempt to amend the constitution to allow the president to serve successive terms, died for lack of support. The same thing happened to the alternate proposal for establishing a parliamentary system. On these issues, the military was more than happy to remain silent.

Initially, the second proposal, a plan to move the national capital, aroused greater interest. Halfway through his term, President Alfonsín announced a project to move the national capital from Buenos Aires to Viedma in Patagonia, over 500 miles to the south. This would have had the effect of shifting the political, and hopefully the economic, weight of the country away from its primary city. It would have matched Chilean efforts to integrate its southern regions with the rest of the country and would have moved the country's center of balance closer to the long-claimed Falkland/Malvinas Islands. The navy supported the idea of the transfer of the capital, while the other services seemed to believe that, though the transfer might be a good idea, the choice of location was questionable from the standpoint of the city's defensibility.[59]

The Viedma project died in the discussion stage for lack of funds and the growing political weakness of Alfonsín and his Radical Party. However, the opening of a naval base at Puerto Deseado, over 1,000 miles south of Buenos Aires, has resulted in the shift of some military power southward.[60]

The Alfonsín government also attempted to rationalize and privatize Argentina's huge state sector, including military industries. Even though the Argentine military sector had done much more poorly than Brazil's, these proposals ran into political and military opposition. Although some restructuring of the defense industry was partially successful, privatization plans and efforts to obtain new foreign partners were never fully realized.

Government-owned shipyards and a number of other companies faced serious financial problems. The major conglomerate producing military equipment for the army, as well as a variety of civilian goods, was in serious difficulty. Probably the most significant failure of Fábricas Nacionales Militares (FM) and its tank-producing subsidiary has been the failure to market the Tanque Argentino Mediano (TAM) internationally. The investment in research and development, the acquisition of foreign technology, and the establishment of a production line has not been cost-effective given the Argentine army's requirement for only a few hundred TAMs. The tank factory has been slated to remain in business but has sought partners for such projects as the manufacture of jeeps and 4x4s.[61]

It was not until 1989 that FM began to find foreign partners. FM and a major Spanish defense company signed an agreement covering technology transfer and production for the home market and export. Reportedly, FM was particularly interested in the manufacture of 5.56-mm assault rifles, the joint development of an antitank missile, and the design and development of multiple-launch rockets with ranges in excess of 18 miles. Argentina also promised to evaluate other Spanish products such as compound propellants. According to the agreement, Spain would consider joint collaboration in the manufacture of infantry weapons, tank artillery, portable weapons components, and mortar and artillery ammunition.[62]

Air force industries have been a little more successful than FM. Projects included the development of a jet-trainer—the Pampa (capable of serving in a ground-attack role as well)—a remotely piloted vehicle, a dual-use (civilian-military) helicopter, and various avionics systems.[63] The air force, however, has not been able to market the Pampa. Like the TAM, the Argentine military's order for one hundred planes would hardly warrant the necessary investment. In sum, military-owned defense industries have been neither sold off nor made productive.

The Alfonsín government attempted to reform the state, but on the whole, its efforts must be rated a failure.

□ Peru

The García government (1985–1990) supported an activist, reformist state. The administration began with a spate of policy initiatives that promised to solve all the country's major problems at once: the foreign debt, the insurgency threat, economic stagnation, human rights violations, and lack of local democracy. García attempted too much. Ultimately, he was forced to backtrack in almost all areas.

Neither García nor his predecessor was able to control military expenditures effectively. As is apparent from Table 8.1, the military's share of the national budget was in the ascent after the transfer of power from the military to the civilian regime in 1980. This pattern was not broken when the García administration took over from Belaúnde. Even during the last half of García's term, for which no firm budget data is available, there were other indications of the president's growing dependence on the armed forces. This dependence was apparently not translated into large budget increases given the desperate condition of the Peruvian economy. Nonetheless, the government undertook a number of initiatives to improve the military budget and pay; deficiencies in both areas were linked to the armed forces' poor performance in confronting the insurgency.[64] García raised military pay, praised the armed forces for their modernization efforts under conditions of budgetary exigency, and took steps to protect the armed forces' budget from the ravages of inflation.[65]

Peruvian plans to use portions of the Amazon basin as a source of mineral wealth and for the settlement of people from overcrowded areas elsewhere, although much touted under the Belaúnde government, have largely come to naught. The scheme had the strong support of the president, but as in the case of Argentina, the government lacked the financial resources to carry it out. Development and control of the border region remained a sensitive issue, however. The García administration signed a number of agreements with Brazil and Colombia that called for development of the border region.[66]

The establishment of regional governments represents a small success, though one with a potential for civil-military conflict. The government has followed a policy of extending emergency zones administered by the military into areas threatened by insurgents. This may bring the armed forces into conflict with leftist politicians who run some local governments.

The first two civilian governments after the transition undertook no initiative in regard to privatization, nor does the country possess much of a defense industry.

All in all, the role of the military within the state grew by default during the latter half of the 1980s. As government initiatives faltered and the insurgents gained new ground, the armed forces became increasingly important and increasingly isolated from effective civilian control.

□ Uruguay

During his term (1985–1990), President Sanguinetti managed to reduce the impact of the military within the state. The size of the military and its budget were trimmed to their pre-1973 levels. However, the consequences of these actions were not entirely positive. Although agitation over the amnesty referendum was by far the major cause of military unrest, pay remained a persistent sore point. The defense minister, General (retired) Hugo Medina, and other senior military spokesmen repeatedly suggested the advisability of salary increases. As in other countries, low pay had an adverse effect on retention and recruitment of officers and NCOs.[67] Eventually, Sanguinetti was able to appoint a civilian defense minister. The administration's record in controlling the military's influence of the state has been modest but positive.

□ Chile

As Chile entered the 1990s, its record on state reform was more of an agenda of future tasks than anything else. In 1990, the military government handed over to the Aylwin administration a streamlined, liberal state by Latin American and Third World standards. Inflation was under control and an independent central bank had been put in place to see that it remained so. Privatization had been a driving goal of the military government for more than a decade, and there were few loss-making state firms remaining to be privatized.

The military government extended national control to the country's vulnerable border regions. Shaped like a snake—2,500 miles on its north-south axis and less than 200 miles east-west with the mass of population in the center of the country—the northern and southern regions are vulnerable militarily and not fully exploited economically. In the far south, the final stretch of an 800-mile-long road was inaugurated in early 1988. The government billed the project as the most important of the century.[68] In 1989, the air force opened a new air base in Punta Arenas near the Strait of

Magellan; the base was built to house sixteen Mirage fighter aircraft.[69] In the north, Inquique was established as a free trade zone in 1975. The zone attracted foreign investors and new immigrants, doubling the population to 135,000 in twelve years.[70] Naval reorganization in 1989 established a new Fourth Naval Zone, headquartered in Inquique, which also was established as a major headquarters in a similar air force reorganization.[71]

The Chilean defense industry is much more modest in scope than its Brazilian and Argentine counterparts; and as was typical of the military government's general policies, defense production has been dominated by the private sector. It produces cluster bombs, runway denial bombs, hand grenades, antipersonnel mines and fuses, aircraft, and artillery for both national use and export.

Unfortunately, along with a balanced budget, a successful (if limited) program of geographic decentralization, and a profit-making defense industry, the military government also handed over a set of roadblocks to democratic consolidation. The first of these was a large defense budget. Table 8.3 shows that Chile (along with Peru) has by far the highest defense burden (measured as a percent of GDP) of the five countries we are examining. Although Chile's expenditures look relatively modest in absolute terms (Table 8.4), this appearance is deceptive. While Argentina's traditional geopolitical rivals were Brazil and Chile, Chile did not have to counterbalance Brazil. Furthermore, Chile lacked Peru's justification of combating an active insurgency. Compounding this problem, before its exit from power, the junta as surrogate legislature of the military government passed a law guaranteeing the military's share of government spending. In its final form, it set a floor for future military budgets at $700 million—the level of military spending in 1988.[72] The support for this preemptive strike on budgetary matters came predominantly from Pinochet loyalists in the army.

Table 8.3 Defense Burden

Country	Defense Expenditure as Percent of GDP (avg. 1986–88)
Argentina	3.4
Brazil	0.7
Chile	7.5
Peru	7.5[a]
Uruguay	2.2

Source: Stockholm International Peace Research Institute
a. 1984–86

Table 8.4 Defense Expenditures

Country	Annual Defense Expenditure 1986–1988 (1986 US$mil)
Argentina	2,695
Brazil	1,906
Chile	1,329
Peru	1,522
Uruguay	146

Source: Stockholm International Peace Research Institute

Other obstacles to democratic consolidation include: a guaranteed term for the army commander and former president (General Pinochet), nonelected members of the senate, and nondemocratic municipal governments.

■ CONCLUSIONS

The evidence of military action in behalf of the complex of issues that deal with state reform generally supports our hypotheses.

Hypothesis 1: The armed forces will vigorously defend their fundamental interest—the armed forces' survival as an institution. The armed forces will defend other interests only to the degree that they are necessary for survival or the maintenance of core interests. In none of the five countries was the survival of the armed forces challenged. In most cases, the armed forces could defend threatened interests by legal means, even though in the case of Chile, the actions were unpopular and open to moral challenge. Thus, the hypothesis was not put to an acid test. The hypothesis is weakly confirmed by the fact that the armed forces in general seemed unwilling to abandon any past privilege or procedure gratuitously.

Hypothesis 2: The more fundamental the interest, the greater the likelihood of the high command's involvement in or tolerance of potentially risky or costly means of resistance. In Brazil, military pressure and influence was orchestrated by the high command, specifically the military ministers. As noted, they did not take great risks and were at pains to formally deny that there was any threat of illegal action. In no other country was there a real possibility that significant state reform would undercut military influence and privileges.

Hypothesis 3: The more uniform the interest across the various sectors of the armed forces, the more likely the success of the armed forces' action in defense of this interest. In Brazil and Chile, the army tended to take a harder line on a variety of issues than did the junior services. This difference did not seem to affect the outcome of controversies except in the case of the Chilean military budget law. No other significant division within the armed forces over state reform issues emerged. The evidence can provide only limited support for this hypothesis.

Hypothesis 4: The lower the prestige of the armed forces and the higher the prestige of the civilian government, the more likely the success of the civilian authorities' efforts to reform the military. In Brazil, where the armed forces' reputation was largely intact after the transfer of power, military influence in the reform process was significant. In Argentina, where the military prestige was lowest, reform of the state did not have the salience either with the armed forces or politicians that it had in Brazil. In Brazil, the armed forces were able to exercise a veto on some but not all issues. In Argentina, no such veto was either exercised or required. The insurgency in Peru also prevented reform of the state from becoming an important issue there. Nor did reform of the state become a central issue in Uruguay. On balance, the only significant test (the Brazilian constituent assembly) provides some support for this hypothesis.

Reform of the state requires astute political judgment on the part of reformers. They often face opposition from diverse political and social sectors and from the armed forces as well. Military resistance to reform of the state is the product of a bureaucratic impulse inherent in any large, complex organization: Changes that undercut established powers and prerogatives will be resisted. Strategies for change can be various. If reformers can rely on intense, widespread public support for dramatic change, they may be able to sweep aside old structures and establish new ones. In the more common case, where public interest in reform flags or reforms are opposed by diverse interests, reformers must use more mundane methods and pursue more limited goals. They must build coalitions carefully and focus on critical issues. In either case, presidential leadership seems to be critical.

■ NOTES

1. In Argentina, for example, the Sindicatura General de Empresas Públicas reported that the joint deficits for state enterprises in the ten years prior to 1986 reached $23.1 billion, just over half the country's external debt. "State Firm Deficits," *Latin American Weekly Report*, September 3, 1987, p. 2.

2. According to unofficial estimates from Peru, the unofficial, black, economy accounts for 61 percent of hours worked, generates 39 percent of GDP, and avoids legal regulations and taxes. Interest rates for the sector are usurious since legal loans require tax registration. As a whole, only 12 percent of Peruvians file tax returns and only 2 percent actually pay income taxes. "The Other Path," *Economist*, December 19, 1987, pp. 62–63.

3. Although estimates are often disputed, they indicate a substantial part of economic activity takes place in the informal sector. For Brazil, the estimates are for 30 percent of GNP in 1986 and up to 50 percent in 1989 (Jorge Zappia and

João Borges, "The Successful 'Informal' Economy," *O Estado de São Paulo*, November 13, 1988, FBIS-LAT-89-004, January 6, 1989, pp. 32–33). For Argentina, the country's Institute for Contemporary Studies estimates the informal sector could account for 60 percent of GNP. Shirley Christian, "Argentina's Dollar-Based Economy," *New York Times*, January 23, 1989, pp. 23, 28.

4. "Pay Rises Help to Subdue Unrest," *Latin American Weekly Report*, October 30, 1986, p. 8.

5. FBIS, "Decree-Law Establishes Military Wage Scale," *O Estado de São Paulo*, December 17, 1987, FBIS-LAT-87-245, December 22, 1987, p. 33.

6. "Sarney Announces Minor Reshuffle," *Latin American Weekly Report*, November 3, 1987, p. 8.

7. "'Undue Criticism' Verdict for Brazilian Captain," *Jane's Defence Weekly*, December 17, 1988, p. 1552.

8. "Camarinha's Sacking Sparks Trouble," *Latin American Weekly Report*, June 7, 1988, p. 5.

9. FBIS, "Sarney Approves Extra Pay Hike for Military," *O Estado de São Paulo*, July 7, 1989, FBIS-LAT-89-131, July 11, 1989, p. 51.

10. FBIS, "Wage Increase Delay Causes Military Unrest," *O Estado de São Paulo*, May 17, 1989, FBIS-LAT-89-096, May 19, 1989, pp. 60–61.

11. "Soldier Lobbyists Fight for Funds," *Latin American Weekly Report*, November 30, 1989, p. 5.

12. "Brazilian Funding Up Despite Heavy Cuts," *Jane's Defence Weekly*, September 10, 1988, p. 495.

13. FBIS, "Military Ministers Concerned Over Budget Cuts," Rio de Janeiro, *O Globo*, December 5, 1988, FBIS-LAT-89-014, January 24, 1989, p. 41.

14. FBIS, "Nuclear Program Threatened," Rio de Janeiro, *O Globo*, July 11, 1989, FBIS-LAT-89-133, July 13, 1989, pp. 48–49.

15. "Soldier Lobbyists Fight for Funds," *Latin American Weekly Report*, November 30, 1989, p. 5.

16. Roberto Godoy, "Budget Cut Curtails AMX," *O Estado de São Paulo*, November 17, 1989, FBIS-LAT-89-242, December 19, 1989, pp. 41–42.

17. Brigagáo, p. 109.

18. João Vitor Strauss and Tania Moneiro, "War Material Complex, Cooperation with Military Viewed," *Folha de São Paulo*, September 16, 1984, JPRS, JPRS-LAM-84-121, November 5, 1984, pp. 4–11; JPRS, "Rio de Janeiro War Industry Increases Production," Rio de Janeiro, *O Globo*, September 8, 1985, JPRS-LAM-85-91, October 30, 1985, pp. 23–24.

19. JPRS, "Arms Sales, Manufactures, Costs, Markets Reported," Rio de Janeiro, *Journal do Brasil*, June 3, 1984, JPRS-LAM-84-78, June 28, 1984, pp. 76–77.

20. "The Week," *Jane's Defence Weekly*, May 30, 1987, p. 1048.

21. "Postscript," *Latin American Regional Reports: Brazil Report*, February 12, 1987, p. 8.

22. Vittorio Bacchetta, "Brazilians Question Makeup of Upcoming Constituent Assembly," *Latinamerica Press*, October 16, 1986, pp. 1–2.

23. Stepan, 1988, p. 6.

24. The exception here, of course, is Luiz Inácio da Silva's PT, which emerged from the new labor movement.

25. "Parliamentarians Gain Lead in Brazil," *Latin American Weekly Report*, October 8, 1987, pp. 6–7.

26. FBIS, "Poll Results on Parliamentary System," *Folha de São Paulo*, October 4, 1987, FBIS-LAT-87-193, October 6, 1987, p. 38.

27. "Planalto Hints at Six-Year Term," *Latin American Weekly Report*, April 28, 1988, p. 8.

28. Several polls showed that by mid- to late 1987 around 80 percent of the public wanted direct elections of a new president as soon as possible. FBIS, "Poll Shows São Paulo Wants Immediate Elections," *Folha de São Paulo*, January 24, 1988, FBIS-LAT-88-018, January 28, 1988, p. 21; FBIS, "Poll Results on Parliamentary System," *O Estado de São Paulo*, October 4, 1987, FBIS-LAT-87-193, October 6, 1987, p. 38.

29. "Postscript," *Latin American Weekly Report*, May 28, 1987, p. 12.

30. "Sarney Will Stay," *Economist*, March 26, 1988, p. 41.

31. Ibid.

32. "Big Majority Vote for Presidentialism," *Latin American Weekly Report*, April 7, 1988, p. 10.

33. "Military Deny Threat of Coup," *Latin American Weekly Report*, April 21, 1988, p. 10.

34. "Nothing but Praise for the Military," *Latin American Weekly Report*, March 31, 1988, p. 8.

35. FBIS, "Military Ministers Urged Sarney Statement," *Folha de São Paulo*, February 27, 1988, FBIS-LAT-88-040, March 1, 1988, p. 36.

36. FBIS, "Polls Show Some Favor Return of Military," *Folha de São Paulo*, November 8, 1987, FBIS-LAT-87-217, November 10, 1987, pp. 17–18.

37. JPRS, "Changes in SNI Role Under Mendes Discussed," *Correiro Brasileinse*, March 24, 1985, JPRS-LAM-85-040, May 8, 1985, pp. 48–49.

38. JPRS, "SNI Chief Octavio Medeiros Discusses Intelligence Service," *Veja*, July 27, 1983, JPRS-LAM-84-206, August 26, 1983, pp. 15–21.

39. JPRS, "Changes in SNI Mission Under New Republic Discussed," *O Estado de São Paulo*, July 28, 1985, JPRS-LAM-85-076, September 9, 1985, pp. 35–37.

40. "National Security Law to Be Replaced," *Latin American Weekly Report*, January 31, 1986, p. 2.

41. FBIS, "National Intelligence Service to Be Reorganized," *Folha de São Paulo*, October 1, 1986, FBIS-LAM-86-192, October 3, 1986, pp. D1–D2.

42. FBIS, "Constituent Assembly on Armed Forces Duties," Brasília, Radio Nacional da Amazonia Network, April 13, 1988, FBIS-LAT-88-072, April 14, 1988, p. 22.

43. Moreira Alves, p. 77.

44. Ibid.

45. "Brazil to Get National Defence Council," *Jane's Defence Weekly*, September 10, 1988, p. 520.

46. Stepan, 1971, pp. 77–78.

47. "Draft Constitution Pleases No One," *Latin American Weekly Report*, September 10, 1987, p. 4.

48. Clovis Rossi, "Military Want Changes in Constitutional Draft," *Folha de São Paulo*, September 6, 1987, FBIS-LAT-87-174, September 9, 1987, p. 9.

49. FBIS, *O Estado de São Paulo*, September 9, 1987, FBIS-LAT-87-176, September 11, 1987, pp. 12–13.

50. *Jane's Defence Weekly*, April 23, 1988, p. 787.

51. Moreira Alves, p. 42.

52. FBIS, Rio de Janeiro, *O Globo*, July 25, 1987, FBIS-LAT-87-144, July 28, 1987, pp. M1–M2.

53. "Parliamentarians Gain Lead in Brazil," *Latin American Weekly Report*, October 8, 1987, pp. 6–7.

54. "Assembly Pleases Military," *Latin American Regional Reports: Brazil Report*, June 7, 1988, p. 3.

55. JPRS, "Role of National Security," *O Estado de São Paulo*, December 2, 1986, JPRS-LAM-87-009, February 10, 1987, pp. 18–19.

56. Julia Michaels, "Brazilians to Vote Under a Cloud of Tension," *Christian Science Monitor*, November 15, 1988, pp. 7–8.

57. "'Dribble' Decrees Anger Congressmen," *Latin American Weekly Report*, October 20, 1988, p. 10.

58. Fraga, pp. 175–176.

59. *Jane's Defence Weekly*, March 21, 1987, p. 475.

60. "Argentina Opens Naval Bases in Patagonia," *Jane's Defence Weekly*, February 4, 1989, p. 166.

61. Joe Schneider, "TAMSE Remains Firmly in Business," *Jane's Defence Weekly*, August 27, 1988, p. 376.

62. Joe Schneider, "Argentina and Spain Sign Up," *Jane's Defence Weekly*, January 21, 1989, p. 110.

63. *International Defense Review*, "The Argentine Air Force Today," 21, no. 9 (September 1988):1099–1100, and "Reviving the Argentine Aircraft Industry," 22, no. 6 (June 1989):853.

64. "Peru's Insurgency Policy Flaws," *Latin American Weekly Report*, May 11, 1989, pp. 6–7.

65. "Senate Is Pressed to Defeat Banking Bill," *Latin American Weekly Report*, August 27, 1987, p. 9; FBIS, "President García's Independence Day Speech," Lima Domestic Service, July 28, 1987, FBIS-LAT-87-156, August 13, 1987, p. R8; "US Advises Peru on Counter-Insurgency," *Latin American Regional Reports: Andean Group Report*, July 28, 1988, pp. 4–5; FBIS, "García Leads Ceremony Creating Armed Forces Fund," Lima, Television Peruana, November 30, 1989, FBIS-LAT-89-230, December 1, 1989, p. 38.

66. *Latin American Regional Reports: Andean Group Report*, July 30, 1987, p. 8; FBIS, "Border Cooperation Agreements Signed with Peru," Bogotá, *El Siglo*, August 25, 1988, FBIS-LAT-88-169, August 31, 1988, p. 27.

67. FBIS, "Military Cuts, Troop Reductions Analyzed," Montevideo, *Busqueda*, January 5–12, 1989, FBIS-LAT-89-015, January 25, 1989, pp. 59–60.

68. "Chilean Road Opening Up Rugged Frontier," *Christian Science Monitor*, March 9, 1988, p. 2; Time Frasca, "Austral Road: Chile Looks to Boost Southern Region," *Latinamerica Press*, August 27, 1987, pp. 6–7.

69. "New Chilean Air Force Base," *Jane's Defence Weekly*, February 4, 1989, p. 166.

70. Tyler Bridges, "Chile Trade Zone Turns Small Town into Booming City," *Christian Science Monitor*, November 24, 1987, p. 12.

71. FBIS, "Fourth Naval Zone Created in North," Santiago, *El Mercurio*, May 18, 1989, FBIS-LAT-89-099, May 24, 1989, p. 35; Adrian English, "Chile Brings Back Air Brigades," *Jane's Defence Weekly*, September 9, 1989, p. 440.

72. "New Military Charter," *Latin American Weekly Report*, January 25, 1990, p. 10.

9∎
Prospects

As Latin America enters the 1990s, civil-military relations in a number of important countries remain in a state of flux. This is not to say that these relations have been or continue to be completely unstructured. Rather, stable patterns have not fully emerged. There are, however, some characteristic patterns and practices that have developed in the 1980s that are likely to set the stage for developments in the immediate future.

In all of the five countries we have examined, the transfer of power to civilian authorities had been completed by early 1990. In most cases, the process of consolidation of the civilian regime had advanced considerably beyond the transition phase. While Chile returned to civilian rule in March 1990, Peru reestablished its civilian government ten years earlier and by mid-1990 had its third elected civilian government. At the same point, Argentina had elected two governments in seven years of civilian rule; Uruguay had elected two governments in five years; and Brazil had had two civilian presidents and one election in a period of six years. On the basis of historical comparisons, this picture appears hopeful. The achievements of Argentina and Peru, the two countries that have shown the most consistent pattern of military coups, stand in sharp contrast with their records through most of this century. Argentina had not seen the transfer of power from an elected civilian president to an elected successor for sixty years. Peru's ten years of civilian government has had few precedents in this century. While the historical record for Uruguay, Chile, and Brazil is not as bleak, it appears that they are reverting to their own, more traditional patterns of civil-military relations, under which the military is less coup-prone.

Yet, the establishment of a regime with an elected government is only one element—albeit an important one—in a pattern of civil-military relations. More mundane matters normally constitute the warp and woof of civil-military relations. At this point, it is worthwhile to review some of these and see how they relate to the two major themes that have underpinned much of the previous discussion: the task of democratic consolidation and the nature of military resistance to civilian initiatives.

■   **A PRELIMINARY BALANCE SHEET**

The task of democratic consolidation is threefold. First, democracy requires that society, not specific elements of the state, possess sovereign power over the state. Second, the state must be organized so that no bureaucratic sector dominates the policymaking process. Third, state bureaucracies, as much as possible, must act as the agents of the state, not as independent executors of policy allied to specific interests within civil society.

□   *The Political Role of the Armed Forces*

One of the major tasks of democratic consolidation is the transformation of the military's role in the political process; the military should not be a privileged corporation juxtaposed to the rest of society. Historically—and certainly during the transition process—the armed forces held just that sort of position; they were open participants in the debate that established overall national policies. Democratic consolidation requires that the scope and nature of their participation be reduced and confined to questions in which the armed forces have a special technical competence. Their participation must be clearly under the control of civilian superiors. Given the history of Latin American civil-military politics, such a transformation is not easy for the armed forces to accept or for civilians to impose.

Military acceptance of a narrow, essentially apolitical role has ranged from a tutelary attitude, manifested in pronouncements by senior Brazilian officers, to the formal acceptance of the authority of elected governments and constitutional norms, more typical of the military establishments in the other countries. This formal acceptance has not been enthusiastic, but it has given governments a certain freedom of action in spheres beyond the military. In general, the armed forces outside of Brazil seem willing to accept or even welcome the civilian government's following a coexistence strategy for reshaping civil-military relations. The armed forces appear in no hurry to assume overall governmental authority or even to assume responsibility for policies beyond the military area.

However, a note of caution needs to be sounded. In Chile and Argentina, this situation may be far from permanent. Pinochet's position as commander in chief of the army coupled with the volatility of the human rights issue has the potential to produce an open confrontation. The potential dispute is underlaid by an interservice debate over the role of the armed forces as guarantors of the constitution. Contrary to the position of Pinochet's defense minister, the air force commander in chief argued that the guarantor role simply means the armed forces could act to guarantee law and order when instructed to do so by the government.[1] As Argentina entered the 1990s, retired officers Mohammed Alí Seineldín and Aldo Rico, the leaders of the *carapintandas* (military rebels), were attempting to construct a civil-military coalition reminiscent of the one that vaulted Juan Perón to power in the

1940s. This movement has not been supported by the high command, and any possibility for its success seems to hinge on the economic collapse of the country and resulting social disorder.

On the other hand, the advent of the Collor administration has produced hopeful signs in Brazil. The new president's military ministers appear more likely than their predecessors to accept a more limited political role for the armed forces.

□ *Oversight and the Rule of Law*

Another mundane but important element in the fabric of civil-military relations is the ability of the civilian element of the executive branch and the legislature to oversee military activities and assure that they conform to national policy and legal norms. The effective exercise of such oversight is a matter of political will and technical knowledge and requires structures adequate to facilitate supervision. The record of civilian control in this area is mixed.

The history of military-imposed amnesties and pacts, and the resistance of the armed forces to civilian action to punish past abuses, show that the ex post facto establishment of the rule of law is difficult, even in the most favorable circumstances. Of the five countries, only the Chilean situation was more or less open at the beginning of the new decade; the serious possibility of human rights prosecutions in the other four countries appears to have vanished. Moreover, much work needs to be done to establish guarantees that would apply in the future. Offenses need to be defined, and the jurisdiction of courts needs to be clarified and corrected. Even in Argentina, where there has been movement in this direction, it has not prevented apparent abuses during the suppression of the Tablada takeover in early 1989[2] nor has it resulted in punishment.

The record on oversight is also less that exemplary. Even governments that have taken initiatives to restructure their defense establishments have lacked the civilian personnel and political support to establish meaningful oversight. This deficiency is virtually universal.

Brazil. Perhaps the country where there has been the most significant improvement in the capacity of the civilian government to oversee military activities has been Brazil, but improvements have been decidedly limited. Historically, there has been a close connection between certain political sectors and the military that far predates the advent of the 1964 military coup. Developments since 1964 have further strengthened this connection. The military's think tank, the Superior War College (ESG), has a substantial number of civilian graduates.[3] In-house and outside military and civilian specialists lecture there. Unfortunately, this cross-pollination may be more of a military vehicle for co-opting civilians than a means of disseminating knowledge of military affairs to civilians in a position to direct the armed forces. Illustrative of this ambiguity was President-Elect Collor de Mello's request for an expert from the ESG to prepare a social and economic plan for his administration.[4]

More hopeful has been the willingness of the constituent assembly to tackle military issues, however gingerly. The 1988 constitution contains provisions prohibiting the manufacture of nuclear weapons and requiring political approval for military involvement in domestic police operations. The University of Campinas has developed a strategic studies center, whose representatives testified before the assembly and congressional committees. Moreover, previously secret programs are beginning to receive legislative scrutiny. Official confirmation of the existence of a test center for nuclear explosives followed state and federal legislative hearings. Up to that time, the armed forces had denied that such facilities existed. Further, Collor fulfilled his promise to abolish the National Intelligence Service (SNI), reducing its staff and placing the new organization under a civilian head.

Argentina. Argentina illustrates a number of points. First, the existence of a single defense ministry, headed by a civilian, does not necessarily make for effective civilian control of the armed forces. Alfonsín's first three ministers were largely ignored by the armed forces. Second, political connections between civilian politicians and military officers may be used to frustrate plans for civilian control. It was not until 1987, over three years into the administration, that the government was able to pass a defense law limiting the mission of the armed forces and providing a structure to assure civilian control. Earlier efforts had been blocked by congressional opponents of the proposed legislation.

The mechanisms provided by this legislation, however, may be defective. The defense council is overly large and includes a welter of officials from the legislative and executive branches.[5] Alfonsín's decision to create an internal security committee by a 1989 decree is testimony to the unwieldy nature of this structure and its inability to provide meaningful supervision for ongoing missions. The Menem administration started the practice of ad hoc consultation between the president and senior service representatives. His first defense minister finally resigned in protest over the habit of the army chief of staff's ignoring the minister and negotiating directly with the president.[6]

The early phases of the Menem government also revealed disturbing developments. Sympathizers with the military rebels had been appointed to posts in the administration and gave Rico, Seineldín, and their followers psychological and possibly financial support.[7]

Peru, Chile, and Uruguay. Developments in the other three countries are even less advanced and uncertain. Peru's President Alan García established a single defense ministry but appointed a military officer to fill the ministerial post. President Sanguinetti in Uruguay appointed a military officer prominent in the transition as his minister of defense, although in 1990, President Lacalle appointed a civilian as his replacement. In Chile, the chief obstacle to civilian control seems to be General Pinochet. While the other three service chiefs were either asked to stay or voluntarily resigned, Pinochet indicated that he intended to serve out his constitutionally guaranteed eight-year term.

□ *The Armed Forces as an Autonomous State Actor*

A variety of factors enable the armed forces to act independently of or contrary to government. Chief among these is the assumption of roles related to the new professionalism. When the military is responsible for an integrated approach to combating insurgency, or when it believes itself responsible for defending the country against other subversive threats, it may have the de facto independence to act as it sees fit. This situation can also arise when the armed forces assume broad authority in remote areas as part of a frontier security mission. These missions, however, may be only contributing causes of such behavior.

A legal restriction on military authority does not of itself ensure military compliance. Despite constitutional guarantees of the right to strike, the Brazilian armed forces suppressed strikes in early 1989. Conversely, even in the case of the more latitudinarian missions, governments with strong popular support seemed to be capable of imposing their authority. During the first period of his government, when his popularity was high, Alan García was able to use a much stronger hand with the armed forces on the human rights issue than during the final period of his administration when his political authority had collapsed. An analogous situation occurred in Brazil, when the armed forces compelled President Sarney to rescind an order calling for the expulsion of gold miners from Indian lands in the Amazon; but four months later, they accepted a similar directive from the new president, Collor de Mello.[8]

■   LEVELS OF INTRANSIGENCE

It is difficult to assess the level of importance the armed forces assign to various interests and the costs they are willing to bear in supporting them, when these interests are handled within a bureaucratic context or involve only normal political activity. However, a better and more easily accessible gauge is illegal activity or activity disruptive of the military's own internal norms. In the 1980s, there was a rash of illegal incidents, although none of them constituted a classic coup d'état. Table 9.1 lists some major types of incidents that have occurred, the country where the incidents have been reported, and the primary motivations behind them. Only in the case of the show of force by the Peruvian air force and the Brazilian actions in strike

Table 9.1 Military Unrest

Type of Incident	Country	Primary Cause
Military rebellion	Argentina	Rights trials
Show of force/small-scale mutiny	Brazil	Military pay/budget
	Peru	Military reorganization
Bombs/bomb threats	Argentina	Rights trials
	Brazil	Pay/budget
Open disrespect	Argentina	Rights trials
Military pronouncements	Argentina	Rights trials
	Brazil	Pay/budget
	Uruguay	Recession of amnesty
	Chile	Military reorganization
Acting beyond authority/failure to act and failure to protect Indians	Brazil	Suppression of strike
	Peru	Counterinsurgency

breaking and failing to act to protect Indian claims in the Amazon can the actions be credibly ascribed to senior officers. Nonetheless, in many cases, a degree of complicity or sympathy has been suspected.

An interesting pattern emerges from the table. Argentina has suffered the most serious incidents of unrest, and generally, these have been associated with the human rights issue. The most serious acts of unrest in Uruguay have been associated with the same issue as well. Pay and budgetary issues appear repeatedly, but incidents associated with them tend to be less serious. The most serious action in Brazil was led by a captain, as has been noted above. This pattern provides partial confirmation of the hypotheses developed in Chapter 3.

Hypothesis 1: The armed forces will vigorously defend their fundamental interest—the armed forces' survival as an institution. The armed forces will defend other interests only to the degree that they are necessary for survival or the maintenance of established practices. The armed forces have defended a variety of interests with a variety of means. The most vigorous means were used during the period of controversy over human rights trials in Argentina.

While protection of military officers from rights prosecution was not an issue of institutional survival, in the minds of the officer corps it came close to being just that. Lesser interests, such as military pay and the military budget, which were not seen as nearly so fundamental, were forwarded largely by legal means. Rarely did members of the military openly break the law to support the armed forces' position on these issues. The armed forces were notably successful in resisting change in policies where civilian passivity was the major requirement for military success. The armed forces, for example, continued to engage in a variety of internal security functions, sometimes in violation of governmental directions.

In addition, the continued prominence of the internal threat in military discussions and pronouncements indicates that interests and views associated with the new professionalism still played a significant role after the transition to civilian government. A generation or more of officers has been educated and has served the early part of their careers in an environment in which the new professionalism was not only taught but applied.

Hypothesis 2: The more fundamental the interest, the greater the likelihood of the high command's involvement in or tolerance of potentially risky or costly means of resistance. Behavior on the human rights issue supports this hypothesis as well. This was virtually the only area in which persistent, widespread behavior destructive of military discipline was tolerated by or beyond the control of the high command. Occasionally, even manifestations expressing solidarity with the high command have been subject to reprimand, as in the case of a public pronouncement by junior officers in Chile.[9] The high command has acted illegally or used methods of questionable propriety to pressure governments or ignore their directives. Such means neither threaten internal discipline nor risk widespread adverse popular reaction. This may be the most important method used by the armed forces to maintain an obtrusive presence within the political system.

Hypothesis 3: The more uniform the interest across the various sectors of the armed forces, the more likely the success of the armed forces' action in defense of this interest. This hypothesis is only partially confirmed. When the interests of the various armed services are clearly divergent (as in the case of establishment of the Peruvian defense ministry), any military resistance to civilian initiatives is likely to be undermined. However, what appears to civilians to be a challenge to only one sector of the armed forces may be perceived by the armed forces to be a serious threat to the institution as a whole. The differences between the armed services and different branches within the same service seem more a matter of nuance than a question of contradictory views. While the split between hard- and soft-liners during the transition shows there are divisions within the officer corps, experience in the 1980s on such issues as human rights provides little evidence that these divisions give civilian policymakers much leverage against the military on a number of sensitive issues. What unites military sectors is more important than what divides them. Their interests may be psychological and not definable simply in functional, careerist terms.

Experience with the rights issue and the persistence of the internal security focus in regional militaries renders suspect the notion that the major division within an officer corps is between advocates of the new professionalism (politically oriented officers) and supporters of traditional Western professionalism (professionalists). A more important split—or a better characterization of the admitted division of opinion—might best be described as fundamentalists versus pragmatists. Fundamentalists are true believers in the national security doctrine and unwilling to compromise with civilian authority except under the most extreme circumstances. They seem to feel a nostalgia for the good old days of the national security states. Except for General Pinochet in Chile, fundamentalists had been removed from most top command posts by the time authority was transferred to civilians. More typically, fundamentalists are junior or middle-grade officers. The pragmatists' Weltanschauung did not necessarily differ from that of the fundamentalists. The pragmatists, however, were more likely to recognize political realities and work with the civilian government to advance the military institution and their own careers. The pragmatists were willing to play the game by the (new) rules; the fundamentalists were not, and they may in the future take more decisive action to bring about the return of the old system.

Hypothesis 4: The lower the prestige of the armed forces and the higher the prestige of the civilian government, the more likely the success of the civilian authorities' efforts to reform the military. This hypothesis is partially confirmed in that politically stronger governments have done better than weaker ones. In no instance, however, has reform been an unqualified success. In Argentina, where the military was thoroughly discredited at the time of the transfer of power, the government was able to make some headway on military reform despite substantial military resistance. Perhaps the government's greatest handicaps during the first part of the Alfonsín administration were financial rather than political. Argentina and the García government in Peru follow a pattern that could become a dangerous trend—popular presidents assume office and undertake sweeping initiatives to reform the armed forces, but well before the end of their terms, their political popularity is so eroded that they are unable or unwilling to maintain the pressure for change. This is especially disturbing because doctrinal reform requires systematic and persistent efforts to reorient the armed forces.

■ PROSPECTS AND CAUTIONS

The 1980s have not closed the book on the issue of military reform. It is still unclear exactly what—or if—settled patterns of civil-military relations will evolve. The trajectory of developments to this point gives rise to a number of expectations.

First, the persistence of economic uncertainty is liable to produce unstable patterns of civil-military relations. Governments that lack the reputation for economic success will be politically weaker than those that have managed to achieve some manner of economic growth and equity. Lack of political support is likely to translate into political weakness vis-à-vis the armed forces. Although an administration begins with public support and initiates plans to further civilian control, it will find it difficult to follow through on its plans. Economic uncertainty also weakens the government in another way; it is difficult to pursue a policy involving military reform without the financial resources to support it. Such a policy is the most likely to garner some military support.

Second, other conditions being equal, the waning of the human rights issue is likely to produce a more-settled pattern of civil-military relations. Governments may be able to direct their attention to other military issues, and the armed forces may feel less skittish toward civilian efforts to change military policy. By mid-1990, the rights issue appeared to be laid to rest in Brazil, Argentina, and Uruguay. In Peru, it had not yet become a serious political issue and did not appear to be on the threshold of doing so. Chile remained the only case where the rights issue retained any likelihood of becoming the basis for a serious political confrontation. Although the legal laying to rest of the rights issue has been on terms dictated by or favorable to the armed forces, widespread popular agitation on the issue may help restrain or prevent further military abuses. Such restraints would be more certain if changes are made in the civil and military code.

Third, in three of the four countries where the civilian regime has seen at least one constitutional change of government during the 1980s, the point of equilibrium for civil-military relations appeared to be a pattern of civil-military coexistence. The new regimes inherited such a pattern; although the armed forces acceded to the reestablishment of civilian governments, they managed to retain significant prerogatives to control military affairs with only nominal civilian direction. Further, the operative definition of military affairs was a broad one. Internal security missions and broad conceptions of frontier security and development remained a reality. Yet, even where they were most influential, the armed forces seemed content to exercise a veto over certain policies rather than wield full authority.

This equilibrium appeared to be stable in the short run. Both civilians and the military have found it difficult to move the system much beyond this equilibrium point. Military reform required the sort of political and financial capital civilian governments often did not have or were unwilling to expend. From the military perspective, the attempt to reestablish a full-blown national security state entailed a number of short-term and long-term risks that would appear to counterbalance any reasonable expectation of institutional benefit for the armed forces. In the short term, an attempted coup might fail, and in the long run, even a regime established by a successful coup might be unable to achieve its major objectives. As the 1990s began, threats or incentives sufficient to induce a coup seemed to be lacking.

Nonetheless, democrats should not take too much comfort in recent experience, which in most cases is less than a decade. Should economic and social crises intensify, coups are entirely possible. The resulting military dictatorships may well learn from the failures of their predecessors of the 1960s–1980s. Repression could be even more intense, and the armed forces might undertake more systematic efforts to remold the political system along antidemocratic lines. A more likely scenario, however, is the gradual loss of de facto power by civilians to the military. The experience of Uruguay in the 1970s could provide a disturbing historical precedent. The risks involved in the formal assumption of power may be too great for the armed forces, but so too may be the temptation to dictate policy to civilians the military views as naive or incompetent.

In short, the effective consolidation of new Latin American democracies will require governments to address a variety of issues of a political, bureaucratic, legal, and—above all—technical nature. In the absence of such efforts, the inertia (and momentum) inherent in the armed forces as a bureaucratic institution may in the long run carry the day.

■ NOTES

1. FBIS, "Matthei Says Military 'Cannot Be Independent,'" Madrid, EFE, December 6, 1989, FBIS-LAT-89-234, December 7, 1989, pp. 32–33.

2. *Latin American Weekly Report*, "Alfonsín's Record Slammed by AI," April 12, 1990, p. 11.

3. Slightly over half of the ESG's 1,276 graduates between 1950 and 1967 were civilians. Stepan, 1971, p. 176.

4. José Paulo da Silva and Roberto Pumar, "Collor Does Not Intend to Dissolve SNI," *O Estado de São Paulo*, November 25, 1989, FBIS-LAT-89-230, December 1, 1989, pp. 25–26.

5. Included are the vice president, the members of the national cabinet, and six representatives of the legislative defense committees.

6. "Defense Minister Quits in Argentine Dispute," *New York Times*, January 25, 1990, p. A4.

7. "And Danger Signs on the Military Front," *Latin American Weekly Report*, January 25, 1990, p. 3.

8. Emily Hughes, "Brazil to Allow Miners to Stay on Yanomami Land," *Times of the Americas*, January 24, 1990, p. 2; James Brooke, "Brazilian Moves to Rescue Tribe," *New York Times*, March 27, 1990, p. 1.

9. "Officers Issue a Second Document," *Latin American Weekly Report*, May 4, 1989, p. 5.

Bibliography

■ BOOKS

Abrahamsson, Bengt. *Military Professionalization and Political Power*. Beverly Hills, California: Sage Publications, 1972.

Americas Watch. *Tolerating Abuses: Violations of Human Rights in Peru*. New York: Americas Watch, 1988.

———. *Human Rights in Peru After President García's First Year*. New York: Americas Watch, 1986.

Amnesty International. *Amnesty International Report 1989*. New York: 1989.

Arendt, Hannah. *The Origins of Totalitarianism*. Cleveland: Meridian Books, 1958.

Argentine National Commission on the Disappeared. *Nunca Más: The Report of the Argentine National Commission on the Disappeared*. New York: Farrar, Straus, Giroux, 1986.

Ballester, Horacio P., et al. *Fuerzas Armadas Argentinas: El Cambio Necesario*. Buenos Aires: Editorial Galerna, 1987.

Boeker, Paul H. *Lost Illusions: Latin America's Struggle for Democracy, as Recounted by Its Leaders*. New York: Markus Wiener Publishing Company, 1990.

Clapham, Christopher, and George Philip, eds. *The Political Dilemmas of Military Regimes*. Totowa, New Jersey: Barnes and Noble, 1985.

Clausewitz, Karl von. *On War*. Baltimore: Penguin Books, 1968.

Comblin, José. *The Church and the National Security State*. Maryknoll, New York: Orbis Books, 1979.

Dahl, Robert. *A Preface to Democratic Theory*. Chicago: University of Chicago Press, 1956.

Debray, Régis. *Revolution in the Revolution?* New York: Grove Press, 1967.

English, Adrian J. *Armed Forces of Latin America*. London: Jane's Publishing Company, 1984.

Feit, Edward. *The Armed Bureaucrats: Military-Administrative Regimes and Political Development*. Boston: Houghton Mifflin, 1973.

Finer, S. E. *The Man on Horseback: The Role of the Military in Politics*. 2d ed. Boulder, Colorado: Westview Press, 1988.

Fraga, Rosendo. *La Custión Militar: 1987–1989*. Buenos Aires: Centro de Estudios Unión para la Nueva Majoría, 1989.

Friedrick, Carl J., and Zbigniew Brzezinski. *Totalitarian Dictatorship and Autocracy*. New York: Praeger, 1965.

Goodman, Louis W., et al., eds. *The Military and Democracy: The Future of Civil-Military Relations in Latin America*. Lexington, Massachusetts: D. C. Heath, 1990.

Gorman, Stephen M., ed. *Post-Revolutionary Peru: The Politics of Transformation*. Boulder, Colorado: Westview Press, 1982.

Guevara, Ernesto (Che). *Guerrilla Warfare*. New York: Monthly Review Press, 1961.

Handelman, Howard, and Thomas G. Sanders, eds. *Military Government and the Movement*

Toward Democracy in South America. Bloomington: Indiana University Press, 1981.

Hayes, Robert A. *The Armed Nation: The Brazilian Corporate Mystique*. Tempe: Arizona State University Center for Latin American Studies, 1989.

Hellman, Ronald C., and Jon Rosenbaum, eds. *Latin America: The Search for a New International Role*. New York: Wiley, 1975.

Huntington, Samuel P. *Political Order in Changing Societies*. New Haven, Connecticut: Yale University Press, 1968.

———. *The Soldier and the State: The Theory and Politics of Civil-Military Relations*. New York: Vantage Books, 1964.

International Bank for Reconstruction and Development. *World Development Report* (various years). New York: Oxford University Press.

———. *World Tables* (various years). Baltimore: Johns Hopkins University Press.

Linz, Juan J. *The Breakdown of Democratic Regimes: Crisis, Breakdown and Reequilibration*. Baltimore: Johns Hopkins University Press, 1978.

Lipset, Seymour M. *Political Man*. Garden City, New York: Doubleday, 1963.

Lopez, George A., and Michael Stohl, eds. *Liberalization and Democratization in Latin America*. New York: Greenwood Press, 1987.

Loveman, Brian, and Thomas M. Davies, Jr., eds. *The Politics of Anti-Politics*. Lincoln: University of Nebraska Press, 1978.

Lowenthal, Abraham F., and J. Samuel Fitch, eds. *Armies and Politics in Latin America*. New York: Holmes and Meyer, 1976.

Luttwak, Edward N. *Strategy: The Logic of War and Peace*. Cambridge, Massachusetts: Harvard University Press, 1987.

Machiavelli, Niccolò. *The Prince*. New York: W. W. Norton, 1977.

———. *Discourses on Livy*. New York: Modern Library, 1950.

Madison, James, Alexander Hamilton, and John Jay. *The Federalist Papers*. New Rochelle, New York: Arlington House, n.d.

Mao Zedong. "Report on an Investigation of the Peasant Movement in Hunan." In *Selected Readings from the Works of Mao Tsetung*. Beijing: Foreign Languages Press, 1971.

Marighella, Carlos. *Manual of the Urban Guerrilla*. Chapel Hill, North Carolina: Documentary Publications, 1985.

Moore, Barrington, Jr. *Social Origins of Dictatorship and Democracy: Lord and Peasant in the Making of the Modern World*. Boston: Beacon Press, 1966.

Moreira Alves, Maria H. *State and Opposition in Military Brazil*. Austin: University of Texas Press, 1988.

Moskos, Charles C., and Frank R. Wood, eds. *The Military: More Than Just a Job?* Washington, D.C.: Pergamon-Brassey's International Defense Publishers, 1988.

Nordlinger, Eric A. *Soldiers in Politics: Military Coups and Governments*. Englewood Cliffs, New Jersey: Prentice-Hall, 1977.

O'Donnell, Guillermo A. *Modernization and Bureaucratic Authoritarianism: Studies in South American Politics*. Berkeley, California: Institute for International Studies, 1973.

O'Donnell, Guillermo, Philippe C. Schmitter, and Laurence Whitehead. *Transitions from Authoritarian Rule: Prospects for Democracy*. Baltimore: Johns Hopkins University Press, 1986.

O'Kane, Rosemary H. T. *The Likelihood of Coups*. Brookfield, Vermont: Gower Book Company, 1987.

Perlmutter, Amos. *The Military and Politics in Modern Times*. New Haven, Connecticut: Yale University Press, 1977.

Philip, George. *The Military in South American Politics*. London: Croom Helm, 1985.

Pike, Fredrick B., and Thomas Stritch, eds. *The New Corporatism: Social and Political Structures in the Iberian World*. Notre Dame, Indiana: University of Notre Dame Press, 1974.

Pinochet, Augusto. *The New Institutional System in Chile*. 1977.

Pion-Berlin, David. *The Ideology of State Terror: Economic Doctrine and Political Repression in Argentina and Peru*. Boulder, Colorado: Lynne Rienner Publishers, 1989a.

Rousseau, Jean-Jacques. *Du Contrat Social*. Paris: Editions Garnier Frères, n.d.

Spector, Leonard S. *Going Nuclear*. Cambridge, Massachusetts: Ballinger Publishing Co., 1987.

Stepan, Alfred. *Rethinking Military Politics: Brazil and the Southern Cone*. Princeton, New Jersey: Princeton University Press, 1988.

———. *The State and Society: Peru in Comparative Perspective*. Princeton, New Jersey: Princeton University Press, 1978.

———. *The Military in Politics: Changing Patterns in Brazil*. Princeton, New Jersey: Princeton University Press, 1971.

———, ed. *Democratizing Brazil*. New York: Oxford University Press, 1989.

Stockholm International Peace Research Institute. *SIPRI Yearbook of World Armaments and Disarmament* (various years). Philadelphia: Taylor and Francis.

Szulc, Tad. *Twilight of the Tyrants*. New York: Henry Holt and Co., 1959.

United Nations. *Resolutions and Decisions Adopted by the General Assembly During the First Part of Its Forty-first Session from 16 September to 19 December 1986*. New York: United Nations, 1987.

United States Arms Control and Disarmament Agency. *World Military Expenditures and Arms Transfers* (various years). Washington, D.C.: US Government Printing Office.

United States Army. *FM 100-20, Low Intensity Conflict*. Washington, D.C.: Department of the Army, 1981.

Valenzuela, J. Samuel, and Arturo Valenzuela, eds. *Military Rule in Chile: Dictatorship and Opposition*. Baltimore: Johns Hopkins University Press, 1986.

Weber, Max. *Theory of Social and Economic Organization*. New York: Macmillan, 1964.

Welch, Claude E., Jr. *No Farewell to Arms? Military Disengagement from Politics in Africa and Latin America*. Boulder, Colorado: Westview Press, 1987.

Welch, Claude E., Jr., and Arthur K. Smith. *Military Role and Rule: Perspectives on Civil-Military Relations*. North Scituate, Massachusetts: Duxbury Press, 1974.

Wesson, Robert, ed. *The Latin American Military Institution*. New York: Praeger, 1986.

Wiarda, Howard J. *Corporatism and National Development in Latin America*. Boulder, Colorado: Westview Press, 1981.

Williams, Edward J., and Freeman J. Wright. *Latin American Politics: A Developmental Approach*. Palo Alto, California: Mayfield Publishing Co., 1975.

■ ARTICLES

Agüero, Felipe. "Democracía en España y Supremacía Civil." *Revista Española de Investigaciones Sociológicas*, no. 44 (October–December 1988).

Brigagáo, Clóvis. "The Brazilian Arms Industry." *Journal of International Affairs* 4, no. 1 (Summer 1986).

Child, Jack. "Antarctica: The South American Geopolitical Literature." *Revista Interamericana de Bibliografia* 39, no. 1 (1989).

———. "Geopolitical Thinking in Latin America." *Latin American Research Review* 14, no. 2 (1979).

Dillon Soares, Gláucio Ary. "Military Authoritarianism and Executive Absolutism in Brazil." *Studies in Comparative International Development* 14, no. 3/4 (Fall/Winter 1979).

Ebel, Roland H. "Cerezo and the Transition to Democracy in Guatemala." Paper presented at the annual meeting of the Southwestern Political Science Association, Little Rock, Arkansas, March 31, 1989.

Favre, Henri. "Pérou: Sentier Lumineux et Horizons Obscurs." *Problèmes d'Amérique Latine*, no. 4 (1984).

Grayson, George W. "Peru's Revolutionary Government." *Current History* 64, no. 2 (February 1973).

Guglialmelli, Juan E. "Argentina-Brasil enfrentamiento o alianza para liberación." *Estrategía*, no. 36 (1975).

Hanson, James, and Jaime de Melo. "The Uruguayan Experience with Liberalization and Stabilization: 1974–1981." *Journal of Interamerican Studies and World Affairs* 25, no. 4 (February 1983).

Huntington, Samuel P., and Jorge I. Dominguez. "Political Development." In *Handbook of Political Science, Macropolitical Theory* (vol. 3). Reading, Massachusetts: Addison-Wesley Publishing Company, 1975.

Kirkpatrick, Jeane. "US Security and Latin America," *Commentary* 71, no. 1 (January 1981).

———. "Dictatorships and Doublestandards." *Commentary* 68, no. 5 (November 1979).

Lane, D. Dennison, and Mark Weisenbloom. "Low-Intensity Conflict: In Search of a Paradigm." *International Defense Review* 23, no. 1 (January 1990).

Linz, Juan J. "Totalitarian and Authoritarian Regimes." In *Handbook of Political Science, Macropolitical Theory* (vol. 3). Menlo Park, California: Addison-Wesley Publishing Company, 1975.

McCann, Frank D., Jr. "Origins of the 'New Professionalism' of the Brazilian Military." *Journal of Interamerican Studies and World Affairs* 21, no. 4 (November 1979).

McClintock, Cynthia. "The Prospects for Democratic Consolidation in a 'Least Likely' Case—Peru." *Comparative Politics* 21, no. 2 (January 1989).

MacDonald, Ronald H. "The Struggle for Normalcy in Uruguay." *Current History* (February 1982).

McKinlay, R. D. "Professionalism, Politicization and Civil-Military Relations." In *The Perceived Role of the Military*, edited by M. R. Van Gils. Rotterdam: Rotterdam University Press, 1971.

Margiotta, Franklin D. "Civilian Control and the Mexican Military: Changing Patterns of Political Influence." In *Civilian Control of the Military: Theory and Cases from Developing Countries*, edited by Claude Welch. Albany, New York: SUNY Press, 1976.

Míguez, Alberto. "Argentina's Defense Impasse." *International Defense Review* 21, no. 12 (December 1988).

Onganía, Juan Carlos. "Texto completo de las palabras pronunciadas por el CJE el 06 Agosto 1964 en West Point." *Revista Militar*, no. 721 (January–June 1989).

Pion-Berlin, David. "Latin American National Security Doctrines: Hard- and Softline Themes." *Armed Forces and Society* 15, no. 3 (Spring 1989b).

Potash, Robert A. "The Impact of Professionalism on the Twentieth Century Argentine Military." Program in Latin American Studies Occasional Papers, 3d ser. Amherst: University of Massachusetts, 1977.

Rapaport, David C. "A Comparative Theory of Military and Political Types." In *Changing Patterns of Military Politics*, edited by Samuel P. Huntington. New York: Free Press of Glencoe, 1962.

Rustow, Dankwart A. "Transition to Democracy: Toward a Dynamic Model." *Comparative Politics* 2 (April 1970).

Saraiva Guerreiro, Ramiro. "Politica Externa do Brasil." *Revista de Escola Superior de Guerra* 2, no. 4 (December 1989).

Slade, Stuart. "How Thais Burnt the Books and Beat the Guerrillas." *International Defense Review*, Editorial Supplement (October 1989).

Smith, Michael L. "Progress in Peru—Maybe." *Washington Post National Weekly Edition*, December 30, 1985.

Zagorski, Paul W. "The Brazilian Military Under the 'New Republic.'" *Review of Latin American Studies* 1, no. 2 (1988).

Index ■

About the Book
and the Author ■

Since the mid-1980s, many countries in Latin America have been struggling to consolidate recent democratic gains. *Democracy vs. National Security* treats one of the key problems in that process: establishing civilian control over the armed forces.

The book focuses on five countries—Argentina, Brazil, Uruguay, Chile, and Peru—that have had similar experiences with military governments and similar transitions to democracy. Avoiding the usual country-by-country approach, Professor Zagorski adopts a directly comparative framework. Chapters on the contemporary Latin American military as an institution and strategies for effecting civilian control are followed by analyses of critical issues in civil-military relations. Each "flashpoint" chapter dissects a key area of conflict between the armed forces and civilian governments and includes a case study illustrating the dynamics of civil-military politics.

A comprehensive overview and analysis, the book provides not only a view of military influence in Latin America but also a basis for evaluating future prospects for democratic consolidation.

PAUL ZAGORSKI is professor of political science at Pittsburg State University, Kansas.